D1546436

# THE JEWS AND GERMANY

TEXTS AND CONTEXTS *Volume 14*

General Editor: SANDER L. GILMAN, *Cornell University*

Editorial Board: DAVID BATHRICK, *Cornell University*

J. EDWARD CHAMBERLIN, *University of Toronto*

MICHAEL FRIED, *The Johns Hopkins University*

ANTON KAES, *University of California, Berkeley*

ROBERT NYE, *University of Oklahoma*

NANCY STEPAN, *Columbia University*

# The Jews & Germany

From the
'Judeo-German Symbiosis'
to the Memory of Auschwitz

•

BY ENZO TRAVERSO
Translated by Daniel Weissbort

•

*(Les Juifs et l'Allemagne: de la
'symbiose judéo-allemande' à
la mémoire d'Auschwitz)*

•

University of Nebraska Press
Lincoln and London

Originally published in French as *Les Juifs et l'Allemagne:
de la 'symbiose judéo-allemande' à la mémoire d'Auschwitz*, copyright © Éditions
La Découverte, Paris 1992. Copyright © 1995 by the University of Nebraska Press. All
rights reserved. Manufactured in the United States of America. The paper in this book
meets the minimum requirements of American National Standard for Information
Sciences – Permanence of Paper for Printed Library Materials, ANSI Z39.48-1984.

Library of Congress Cataloging-in-Publication Data

Traverso, Enzo. [Juifs et l'Allemagne. English]. The Jews and Germany: from the
Judeo-German symbiosis' to the memory of Auschwitz / by Enzo Traverso; translated
by Daniel Weissbort. p. cm. – (Texts and contexts; volume 14) Includes biblio-
graphical references and index. ISBN 0-8032-4426-6. 1. Jews – Germany – Intellectual life. 2. Jews – Cultural assimilation – Germany. 3. Antisemitism – Germany –
History. 4. Holocaust, Jewish (1939-1945) – Influence. 5. Germany – Civilization –
Jewish influences. 6. Germany – Ethnic relations. I. Title. II. Series.

DS135.G33T6413 1995 943'.004924–dc20 94-23294 CIP

The Publisher wishes to thank Stephen Lehmann
for his timely assistance in translating
passages from German
and Yiddish.

# Contents

Translator's Foreword      vii

Chronology      xi

Introduction      xix

PART ONE: EMANCIPATION AT AN IMPASSE

1. The 'Judeo-German Symbiosis': Myth and Reality

*A Long Quarrel*      3

*The Stages of a Negative Dialectic*      9

*Lights and Shades of Assimilation*      13

*The Rise of Anti-Semitism*      18

*Judeity and Germanity*      22

*A Crisis of Identity*      25

*The Turning Point of Weimar*      30

*Judeo-German Symbiosis or Jewish Monologue?*      33

*'We Are Forced to Remain Strangers'*      39

2. The Jew as Pariah

*The* Pariavolk *in German Sociology: Max Weber*      43

*The 'Pride in Being a Pariah': Bernard Lazare*      45

*The 'Hidden Tradition': Hannah Arendt*      48

*The Pariah as* Schlemihl      53

*The Revolt of the Pariah: Hannah Arendt,*
*Zionism, and Socialism*      55

*Judeity and Femininity: Rosa Luxemburg*      59

3. Judeity as *Heimatlosigkeit*: Joseph Roth

*'Hotelpatriot'*      65

*Nostalgia for the* Shtetl      67

*Judaism and the Criticism of Modernity*      72

*'Joseph the Red'*      74

*Exile or the Flight from History*      76

4. The Jew as Parvenu

*A Literary Archetype*                                          81

*From Bleichröder to Wendriner*                                 84

*A Patriotic Jew: Ernst Kantorowicz*                            87

*Pan-Germanism and Zionism: Theodor Herzl*                      88

*An Admirer of 'Nordic Beauty': Walther Rathenau*              93

*A Tragic Epilogue*                                             98

PART TWO: FROM EXTERMINATION TO MEMORY

5. Auschwitz, History, and Historians

*The Jewish Genocide and Others*                               104

*Interpretations of the 'Final Solution'*                      112

*The Aporias of Marxism*                                       123

*Archaism and Modernity*                                       128

6. History and Memory

*The 'Jewish Question' in Germany after Auschwitz*             135

*The GDR or Memory Manipulated*                                136

*Adenauer or the Era of Forgetfulness*                         140

*Disputed Memory*                                              144

*To Free Oneself from 'A Past Which Will Not Pass'?*           146

*An Amnesic Reunification*                                     152

*Sham Memory*                                                  159

Notes                                                          163

Bibliography                                                   187

Index                                                          207

# Translator's Foreword

IN RECOUNTING the tragic history of the so-called Judeo-German symbiosis, the illusory interaction or exchange between German and Jewish cultures, Enzo Traverso persuasively depicts European Jewery in its last great phase. While the pre-Auschwitz world of Judaism is definitively of the past, historical determinants of the modern Jewish 'character,' discernible in key types like the 'pariah' (*Schlemihl*) or the 'parvenu,' are still forces to be reckoned with, particularly on the psychological plane. It takes a lot to catch up with actuality!

In 1935, the year of the Nuremberg Laws, I was born in England into a family of Polish Jews, most of whom had left Poland in the early years of the century, settled in Belgium, in France, and then (my particular branch) in England. My father, as far as I know, had had a traditional upbringing. A Yiddishist, and also a Classical scholar, he combined, I suppose, attachment to the *Haskalah,* the spirit of the Enlightenment, with a Buberist concern for the ancient traditions of Judaism. Thus, he was a Zionist, sympathetic to the movement for the revitalization of Hebrew, but also a staunch proponent of the old vernacular. With little or no schooling, my mother retained a sentimental if ambivalent affection for Poland and the Polish language (she spoke Yiddish, as well) but had continued along the path of assimilation embarked upon by her ambitious and enterprising father. He, my maternal grandfather, left Poland a bearded if not caftan-clad Jew, but he swiftly discarded the more obvious outward indications and much of the way of life of the *Ostjude.* Neither of my parents spoke Yiddish to us children, using the language only as a *lingua franca* when the occasion called for it. Both were supportive of the Zionist movement and of the State of Israel, even though the aggressive secularization of post-Herzl socialistic Zionism might not have appealed to them, at least in the latter part of their lives. It is clear to me that they embodied elements both of the parvenu and pariah, and perhaps that was their destiny. I, of course, like many Jews of

Daniel Weissbort

my generation and type, inherited that mixed and psychologically confusing or frequently contradictory legacy, with its combination of self-hatred, aspirations to assimilation, secularism, and a defiant self-assertion or traditionalism in the face of nonacceptance. In other words, it is impossible not to recognize oneself, to a considerable extent, in Traverso's vivid depiction, for instance, of Joseph Roth, whose life's path is central to the thesis of *Germany and the Jews*. Here is the Wandering Jew of modern times, zigzagging between atheism and religion, revolution and nostalgia for the pre-1914 order, assimilation, and romantic idealization of *Yiddishkeit*.

Translating *Germany and the Jews* for me, then, was something of a journey of self-discovery, like tracing or retracing one's self-portrait, with particular attention to its political, historical, and sociological traits. The coherence of the text, drawing discriminatingly and indeed illuminatingly on the pioneer work of Hannah Arendt, makes this identification possible. And yet, I had not anticipated it, since the locus of this study is Germany, whereas my family was from Eastern Europe. I knew about German assimilationism, about the contemptuous or patronizing attitude of Germanized Jews towards their eastern brethren. In a way, I felt that German Jews, in spite of the fate they ultimately shared with the rest, were not *echt* Jews. I was nationalistically parochial, even though I also imagined myself to be English, taking pride – amid my internationalist socialist reveries – in the fact that even after World War II the British Empire was in principle intact and the map of the world was still largely red!

But then, what is my family name if not German! Memory of my father performing Sholem Aleikhem in Yiddish to a group of admiring friends is still, after forty years, fresh. Besides, my maternal grandfather was able to move from Warsaw to Belgium more easily in World War I exactly because the region was at the time under Germany, German occupation being a great improvement, in his view, on that of Tsarist Russia. My father, in any case, was born in Polish Silesia, in Sosnowice, much of the population of which was German-speaking. Besides, the supranational concept of *Mitteleuropa* was, to a large extent, a Jewish one, even if so many Jews strove to identify with the rising nations of the region.

Gradually, as I read on, I was able to see how the fate of German Jews exemplified that of all Jews as they tried to improve their lot in the modern world, an enterprise which began with much hope and came to such a disastrous and abrupt conclusion. Has not history, in spite of the establishment of the Jewish State, left the Jews stranded, not knowing if they are free at last, or perhaps on the edge – fearful nightmare! – of a truly final cataclysm? Or of a quiet extinction? That is, perhaps Jewery, historically speaking and as an identifiable entity, has been subsumed into something larger. So, what of Israel, drawing as it does on heterogeneous traditions, the nineteenth-century étatism of Herzl's – in inspiration, assimilationist – on colonialist Zionism, so strikingly characterized by Traverso, as well as on the Socialist idealism (also with determinably assimilationist connections) of at least part of the kibbutz movement, and drawing on the traditionalism of the *Ostjuden* as well as on the grotesqueries of the *Nationalverband deutscher Juden*, which wanted to place a corps of young Jewish stormtroopers at the service of the Nazi regime?

Traverso's book is small in size but large in scope. Finally, the questions it addresses are of course broader than those I have touched on by self-indulgently offering my own background. Memory, collective responsibility, and the consequences of ignoring or attempting to repress, transform, normalize, or relativize historical experience are examined in the context of post-War German political and economic developments and finally in the problematical reunification of East and West Germany. Traverso has some harsh but salutary things to say regarding, for instance, the Bitburg meeting between Chancellor Khol and President Reagan. Here one recalls Elie Wiesel's unavailing plea to the President to reconsider his decision!

As regards the translation itself, I draw the reader's attention to the treatment of the two key terms, *Germanité* and *Judéité*, literally *Germanity* and *Judeity*. These were the words finally used, though not without misgivings. French, notoriously from the Anglo-Saxon point of view, deploys abstract terms with abandon! Furthermore, post-War French critical theory added neologistically to this tendency, to the point of elaborating what amounted almost to a new or separate language, which resisted translation, since there was no adequate equivalent in English. The tendency, then, was simply to bring the terms over wholesale, with minimal modifications, into English, taking advantage of shared linguistic roots. *Judeity* and *Germanity*, though readily enough understandable, smack of these neologistic importations. However, in this case, familiarity did not breed contempt. The alternative translation or 'Englishing,' *Jewishness* and *Germanness*, apart from its clumsiness, was too reductive, too suggestive of vulgar stereotyping. The terms *Judeity* and *Germanity* more adequately convey the historical dimension of two cultural traditions of at least equivalent richness, even if the former was helpless in the face of the latter's actual political power.

Finally, in preparing this text for English publication, every effort has been made to identify the original English of citations from English-language texts, or the existing English translations of foreign works, given either in French translation or in the original French. In view of the wealth of such citations, this turned out to be a considerable undertaking, and I am extremely grateful for the help and support of my research assistants at the University of Iowa, especially David Perry.

# Chronology

1778. Translation into German of the Pentateuch by Moses Mendelssohn, one of the principal representatives of the *Haskalah*, the Jewish enlightenment.

1779. Gotthold Ephraim Lessing's *Nathan der Weise* (*Nathan the Wise*): a play pleading the Jewish cause, written by one of the most prominent literary figures of the *Aufklärung*.

1781. Wilhelm von Dohm, *Über die bürgerliche Verbesserung der Juden* (On the civil betterment of the Jews): a pamphlet in favor of emancipation written by a high Prussian official.

1782. Edict of toleration promulgated in Austria by Emperor Joseph II.

1783. Moses Mendelssohn's *Jerusalem:* emancipation manifesto by the most prominent Jewish philosopher of the eighteenth century.

1786. Death of Moses Mendelssohn.

1790–1806. Rahel Levin-Varnhagen's salon in Berlin's Jägerstrasse.

1791. Emancipation of the Jews of France.

1808. Emancipation of the Jews of Westphalia under Napoleon.

1812. Partial emancipation of the Jews of Prussia by Frederick William III.

1818. Ludwig Börne founds the literary critical review *Die Wage,* which is to number Rahel Varnhagen among its contributors.

1819. Germany is swept by anti-Jewish demonstrations, leading at times to pogroms. The *Verein für Kultur und Wissenschaft der Juden* is founded in Berlin by Leopold Zunz and Eduard Gans.

1822. Establishment of the *Zeitschrift für die Wissenschaft des Judentums.*

1823. Michael Beer, *Der Paria* (*The Pariah*): allegorical play dealing with the exclusion of German Jews.

1833. Death of Rahel Levin-Varnhagen. Her correspondence is published the following year in three volumes.

1836. Samson-Raphaël Hirsch, *Nineteen Epistles on Judaism:* most important work of Orthodox Judaism in nineteenth-century Germany. Abraham Geiger founds the *Wissenschaftliche Zeitschrift für jüdische Theologie* (Scientific review of Jewish theology,) a periodical engaged in the movement for the reform of Judaism.

1837. Bertold Auerbach, *Spinoza:* a historical novel by the most popular German Jewish writer of the nineteenth century. Ludwig Philippson founds the *Allgemeine Zeitung des Judentums.*

1840. Heinrich Heine, *Der Rabbi von Bacherach* (*The Rabbi of Bacherach*). During the same decade he also writes his *Hebräisches Melodien* (*Hebraic Melodies*).

1843. Argument between Karl Marx and Bruno Bauer regarding the Jewish question.

1848. Revolutions in Europe. In Cologne, Marx and Engels found the *Neue Reinische Zeitung.*

1849. Laws for the emancipation of the Jews are approved in Austria and Prussia. Their implementation is not to take place until 1867 in the Habsburg Empire and 1869 in Germany.

1850. Richard Wagner, *Judaism in Music.*

1853. Heinrich Graetz, *Geschichte der Juden* (*History of the Jews*): one of the principal works of Jewish historiography in the nineteenth century. The complete edition was to appear posthumously in 1900, in thirteen volumes.

1862. Moses Hess, *Rome und Jerusalem:* a work heralding modern Zionism.

1867. Karl Marx, *Capital.*

1869. Full civil rights granted Prussia's Jews.

1871. Extension of Prussian laws to Germany as a whole. August Röhling, *Der Talmudjude* (The Talmud Jew): anti-Semitic work written by an Austrian Catholic theologian.

1872. Establishment in Berlin of the Hochschule für die Wissenschaft des Judentums (High school for the science of Judaism).

1873. Wilhelm B. Marr, *Der Sieg des Judentums über das Germanenthum* (The victory of Judaism over Germanity): widely read anti-Semitic work, where for the first time the word *anti-Semitism* occurs.

1878. Leopold von Sacher-Masoch, *Judengeschichten* (*Jewish Tales*): stories about Eastern European Jews, showing considerable sympathy for them.

1879. Beginning of the anti-Semitic activities of Adolf Stöcker, pastor at the Prussian court.

# Chronology

1880. Heinrich von Treitschke, *Ein Wort über unser Judenthum* (*A Word about Our Jewry*): collection of articles which had a great impact and marks the official introduction of anti-Semitism into German university circles. Response of the liberal historian Theodor Mommsen. Eugen Dühring, *Die Judenfrage als Frage des Rassencharakters und seiner Schädlichkeit für Existenz, Sitte und Kultur der Völker* (The Jewish question as a problem of race and its detrimental effect with regard to peoples, morality, and culture).

1881. A petition demanding the adoption of anti-Jewish measures receives 225,000 signatures and is presented to Bismarck.

1886. Paul de Lagarde, *Deutsche Schriften* (German writings). This collection of texts, written after 1853, is one of the most significant works of German *Kulturpessimismus*, with a strong anti-Semitic bias.

1890. Karl Kautsky, *Das Judentum*.

1892. Ludwig Jacobowski, *Werther, der Jude* (The Jew Werther): the first novel to engage the problem of Jewish identity in the face of the rise of anti-Semitism.

1893. Sixteen deputees elected on an anti-Semitic platform enter the Reichstag. Founding of the Zentralverein detscher Staatsbürger jüdischen Glaubens (Central Association of German Citizens of Jewish Faith). Oskar Panizza, 'Der operierte Jud' ('The Operated Jew').

1894. Theodor Herzl, *Das neue Ghetto:* play on the Jewish condition after emancipation. Hermann Bahr, *Der Antisemitismus*.

1896. The Dreyfus Affair in France. Theodor Herzl, *Der jüdische Staat* (*The Jewish State*).

1897. First Zionist Congress in Bâle. Establishment of the Zionist weekly *Die Welt* (The world) in Vienna. Jakob Wasserman, *Die Juden von Zirndorf* (The Jews of Zirndorf): a novel on the identity crisis of assimilated Jews. Walter Rathenau writes 'Höre Israel!' ('Listen Israel!') for the magazine *Die Zukunft* (The future). The anti-Semitic leader of the Austrian Christian-Socialists, Karl Lueger, is elected mayor of Vienna.

1898. Karl Kraus, *Eine Krone für Zion* (A crown for Zion), satirical work on Zionism, published a year before the establishment of the magazine *Die Fackel* (The torch) by the Viennese literary critic.

1900. Houston Stewart Chamberlain, *Die Grundlagen des XIX. Jahrhundert* (*The Foundations of the Nineteenth Century*): the principal attempt to systematise modern racist and anti-Semitic theories. Georg Simmel, *Philosophie de l'argent* (*The Philosophy of Money*). Sigmund Freud, *Die Traumdeutung* (*Interpretation of Dreams*).

1901. Theodor Herzl, *Altneuland* (*Old New Land*).

1902. Martin Buber establishes a new Jewish publishing house in Berlin, the Jüdischer Verlag. Hermann Cohen, *Logik der reinen Erkenntnis* (Logic of pure knowledge.)

1903. Otto Weininger, *Geschlecht und charakter* (*Sex and Character*), regarded today as a kind of manifesto of Jewish self-hatred.

1905. Leo Baeck, *Das Wesen des Judentums* (*The Essence of Judaism*): basic theological work of the *Wissenschaft des Judentums* school.

1907. The publisher Theodor Fritsch brings out the anthology of anti-Semitic quotations *Handbuch der Judenfrage* (Manual of the Jewis question) which is very widely circulated. Gustav Landauer, *Die Revolution*.

1908. Arthur Schnitzler, *Der Weg ins Freie* (*The Road into the Open*), a novel on the Jewish condition in Austria.

1909. Moritz Lazarus, *Die Erneuerung des Judentums* (The renewal of Judaism): written in the spirit of liberal Judaism by a philosopher and psychologist of the Science of Judaism school.

1911. Martin Buber, *Drei Reden über das Judentums* (*Three Speeches on Judaism*): a work that marks the rebirth of a messianic and mystical tendency in Central European Judaism. Werner Sombart, *Die Juden und das Wirtschaftsleben* (*The Jews and Modern Capitalism*): a work that responds to Max Weber and attempts to identify the Jews with modern capitalism. Ignaz Zollschan, *Das Rassenproblem unter besonderer Berücksichtigung der theoretischen Grundlagen der jüdischen Rassenfrage* (The racial problem from the particular point of view of the theoretical bases of the question of the Jewish race): Zionist text on racial biology.

1912. Moritz Goldstein, 'Deutsch-jüdische Parnass,' *Kunstwart:* start of a large-scale debate on the consequences of assimilation. Werner Sombart, *Die Zukunft der Juden* (The future of the Jews): brochure in which the author's anti-Semitic tendencies are more openly expressed. Walther Rathenau, *Staat und Judentum* (State and Judaism).

1913. Else Lasker-Schüler, *Hebräische Balladen* (*Hebrew Ballads*).

1914. World War I. Jakob Loewenberg, *Aus Zwei Quellen* (The two wells): autobiographical novel on the dual allegiance of German Jews. Franz Kafka publishes *Der Prozess* (*The Trial*). The Wandervögel youth movement excludes Jews. Karl Kautsky, *Rasse und Judentum* (*Are the Jews a Race?*): the principal German Marxist contribution to the study of the Jewish question before World War I. Magnus Hirschfeld, *Die Homosexualität des Mannes und des Weibes* (Homosexuality in man and woman). Hirschfeld will be persecuted as a Jew and as the main spokesman of the movement for the rights of homosexuals.

1915. Gustav Meyrink, *Der Golem* (*The Golem*): this novel constitutes the most celebrated version of the Golem myth.

1916. Martin Buber founds the cultural and political revue *Der Jude*. Hermann Cohen, *Deutschum und Judentum* (Germanity and Judeity): a philosophical work theorizing the spiritual affinity between Jews and Germans. Max Weber, *Antike Judentum* (*Ancient Judaism*) (which is to become the third volume in his grand work on the sociology of religions).

1917. Franz Pfemfert founds the expressionist revue *Die Aktion*. Eduard Bernstein, *Von den aufgaben der Juden in Weltkrieg* (On the tasks of the Jews in the World War). Lord Arthur James Balfour proposes the establishment of a national home for the Jews in Palestine.

1918. Ernst Bloch, *Geist der Utopie* (The spirit of utopia). Martin Buber, *Mein Weg zum Chassidismus*. Production of Ernst Toller's expressionist play *Die Wandlung* (The transformation). Oswald Spengler, *Untergang des Abendlandes* (*The Decline of the West*), followed by a second volume in 1922.

1919. Spartacist revolt in Berlin; murder of Rosa Luxemburg. Bavarian Soviet Republic, with participation of many prominent Jews. Assassination of Gustav Landauer. Hermann Cohen, *Religion der Vernuft aus den Quellen des Judentums* (*The Purpose and Meaning of Jewish Existence*).

1920. Establishment of NSDAP (National Socialist Workers party) by Hitler in Munich. Max Nordau, *Die Tragödie der Assimilation* (The tragedy of assimilation). Martin Buber, *Ich und Du* (*I and Thou*).

1921. Franz Rosenzweig, *Der Stern der Erlosung* (*The Star of Redemption*). Gustav Landauer, *Der werdende Mensch* (The future of man). Jakob Wassermann, *Mein Weg als Deutscher und Jude* (My journey as a German and a Jew).

1922. Murder of Walther Rathenau, foreign minister of the Weimar Republic. Franz Kafka writes *Das Schloss* (*The Castle*).

1923. Establishment in Frankfurt of the Institute for Social Research, directed by Friedrich Pollock. Möller Van der Bruck, *Das dritte Reich* (The Third Reich), one of the principal works of the 'conservative revolution.' Georg Lukács, *Geschichte und Klassenbewusstsein* (*History and Class Consciousness*). Gershom Scholem publishes his first study of the Cabbala, *Das Buch Bahir.*

1924. Thomas Mann, *Der Zauberberg* (*The Magic Mountain*), where the tragic figure of the Jew Naphta appears.

1925. Adolf Hitler, *Mein Kampf.* Lion Feuchtwanger, *Jud Süss* (*The Jew Süss*). Martin Buber and Franz Rosenzweig begin a new German translation of the Bible. Erich Fromm, *Das jüdische Gesetz. Ein Beitrag zur Soziologie des Diasporajudentums* (The Jewish law: A contribution to the sociology of the Jewish diaspora).

1926. Alfred Döblin, *Reise in Polen* (*Journey to Poland*): a work that highlights the vitality of East European Judaism.

1927. Joseph Roth, *Juden auf Wanderschaft* (Wandering Jews): reportage on the life of eastern Jewish immigrants in the Western metropolises. Ernst Kantorowicz, *Frederick II.* The expressionist poet Alfred Wolfstein publishes his essay 'Jüdisches Wesen und neue Dichtung' (The Jewish Condition and the New Poetry) in the *Tribüne der Kunst und der Zeit.*

1928. Martin Buber, *Die chassidischen Bücher* (The Hassidic books): collection of Hassidic stories and legends.

1929. Arnold Zweig, *Caliban oder Politik der Leidenschaft* (Caliban or the politics of passion): critical study of Jewish assimilation from a Zionist point of view. Karl Mannheim, *Ideologie und Utopie* (*Ideology and Utopia*). Alfred Döblin, *Berlin Alexanderplatz.* Kurt Tucholsky, *Deutschland, Deutschland über Alles!* (work illustrated with photomontages by John Heartfield).

1930. Joseph Roth, *Job:* saga of an East European Jewish family. Theodor Lessing, *Der jüdische Selbsthass* (Jewish self-hatred). Alfred Rosenberg, *Der Mythus des zwangsisten Jahrhunderts* (*The Myth of the Twentieth Century*).

1932. Arnold Schönberg, *Moses und Aaron.* Hannah Arendt begins her biography, *Rahel Varnhagen,* which will be finished in 1939 but is not to appear until after World War II, in 1958. Establishment of the Frankfurt school journal, the *Zeitschrift für Sozialforschung.*

1933. Hitler takes power. First anti-Jewish measures (exclusion from public service and education.) Autos-da-fé of 'Judaized' literary works. Beginning of Jewish emigration. Lion Feuchtwanger, *Der jüdische Krieg* (*Josephus*): first part of his trilogy on Josephus, followed in 1935 by *Die Söhne* and in 1945 by *Der Tag wird kommen.* Theodor Lessing, *Deutschland und seine Juden* (Germany and its Jews). Lessing will be killed shortly after the publication of this work. Arnold Zweig, *Bilanz der deutschen Judenheit* (Balance sheet of German Judaism). Ernst Toller, *Jugend in Deutschland* (*I Was a German*).

1934. Hans Joachim Schoeps, *Wir deutschen Juden* (We German Jews), manifesto of the pan-Germanist Jews. The great reporter Egon Erwin Kisch publishes in Amsterdam his *Geschicthen aus sieben Ghettos* (Stories from the life of seven ghettos).

# Chronology

1935. The Nuremberg Laws, aiming to 'protect German blood' and prevent marriages between Jews and 'Aryans.' First measures of 'Aryanization' of the economy. Hans-Joachim Schoeps, *Geschichte der jüdischen Religionsphilosophie in der Neuzeit* (History of Jewish religious philosophy in modern times). Margarete Susmann, 'Vom geistigen Anteil der Juden im deutschen Raum' (On the spiritual participation of the Jews within the German context). Ismar Elbogen, *Die Geschichte der Juden in Deutschland* (History of the Jews in Germany).

1936. Carl Schmitt presides over a national conference on 'The struggle against the Jewish spirit in German legal studies.'

1937. Max Brod publishes the first biography of Kafka.

1938. *Kristallnacht.* Wave of pogroms throughout Germany and the annexed territories of Austria.

1939. Outbreak of World War II. First Jewish ghettos in Poland. Martin Buber writes 'Das Ende der deutsch-jüdischen Symbiose' (The end of the Judeo-German symbiosis) for a Zionist journal in Palestine. Sigmund Freud, *Moses and Monotheism*.

1940. Walter Benjamin, *Über den Begriff der Geschichte* (*Theses on the Philosophy of History*).

1941. German invasion of the USSR. The activities of the *Einsatzgruppen* begin the Jewish genocide.

1942. The Wannsee Conference discusses the plan for the 'final solution' of the Jewish question (20 January). Gas chambers start functioning in Auschwitz (March). The gassings continue until autumn 1944.

1943. The Warsaw ghetto uprising is crushed.

1945. End of World War II. Six million Jews have been exterminated in the Nazi death camps.

# Introduction

THIS LITTLE BOOK does not claim to be a history of the Jews in Germany or, more generally, in the German-speaking countries of *Mitteleuropa*. Its aim is more modest: to respond to some of the many questions that this history raises. On the cultural level, the contradictions and paradoxes are so extreme that one sometimes wonders why they came to be so little studied.[1] To be sure, the Judeity of Kafka, Benjamin, Buber, as well as of many others, has been the subject of ingenious and absorbing investigations, but the richness of each philosopher's, writer's, or critic's thought, considered in isolation, has too often masked the problems posed by Judeo-German culture as a whole. It is, after all, not hard to see that developments which made German classics of Heinrich Heine, Joseph Roth, or Franz Kafka differ somewhat from those which, quite naturally and directly, did the same for Goethe or Thomas Mann. There is doubtless a certain historical irony in the destiny of so many Jewish intellectuals, neglected or marginalized, persecuted or exiled during their lifetime and now celebrated one after another, filling the shelves of every good library on this planet with their *Gesammelte Schriften*, especially in that unhappy country that did its utmost to obstruct, indeed to destroy their work and to blot it from the memory of humanity.

A historical irony involving both posthumous revenge and a vast misapprehension. Posthumous revenge, in that a very large number, even the overwhelming majority of these Jewish intellectuals and writers, felt profoundly German and regarded their work as belonging to German culture. A misapprehension, because, rightly viewed, they always were excluded from that world which, after having persecuted them for centuries, was momentarily to generate the illusory dream of their possible acceptance (more precisely their assimilation) and ended by expelling and exterminating them. Their contribution to German culture was immense and it is only now that it is being properly evaluated, but it would be false to interpret this abundance in letters, in the arts and the sciences, as the product of the encounter of two traditions or, on the sociological level, as an interaction between Jewish and German intellectuals. Judeo-German culture was certainly engendered by assimilation, the secularization therefore of the Jewish mind and its appropriation of German culture, but it took the form of a *Jewish monologue*. Once they had penetrated the German cultural universe, the Jews nearly always found themselves isolated, without interlocutors to accept them and to dialogue with them, or at the very least, to accept them and dialogue with them as Jews.

A misapprehension, too, because of the problematical nature of the distinction between righting a wrong and 'annexation' pure and simple, a posteriori, without explanation or criticism, of a tradition and of a culture, rejected when they were alive and now insisting on being recognized. That is how the myth of a 'Judeo-German symbiosis' spread, a notion which would have seemed hardly more than a joke at a time when there were Jews in Germany. As against the situation in France where, after the Revolution of 1789, the granting of citizenship made Jews full members of the nation, in Germany civil rights [*Staatsangehörigkeit*] and membership of the nation [*Volksangehörigkeit*] remained distinct (the situation was different in a multinational empire like Austro-Hungary). Thanks to the emancipation, the Jews could be accepted as citizens, but remained excluded from nationality. Assimilation had dissolved the Jewish 'nation' and confessionalized its members within German society, but the former nationality was never replaced by Germanity. Whether consciously or not, assimilated Jews inhabited a no-man's-land. Their monologue drew as much from the scattered remains of a tradition bequeathed to them by centuries of ghetto life, as from contemporary German culture (but they appropriated it so eagerly that they did not even notice how it changed as soon as it fell into their hands). The most striking incarnation of this Jewish monologue was unquestionably the city of Prague, where German-language culture was entirely a Jewish creation. The amazing richness of Judeo-German literature in the Czech capital shows how it had no need of any 'symbiosis' to obtain outstanding results. It might be claimed that *Jewish isolation* was the very condition of this creative richness.

The ups and downs of a culture engendered by the Jewish entry into a world which from the start regarded Jews as undesirable strangers, either *undeutsch* or *Gemeinschaftsfremde,* according to one's choice, brings to mind a prophetic novel of 1922, *Der Stadt ohne Juden (The City Without Jews)* by Hugo Bettauer, gadfly of Viennese conformism and clericalism, who three years later fell victim to an anti-Semite's bullets. He described the cultural decline of the Austrian capital after the expulsion of the Jews was 'democratically' decreed by Parliament. Engulfed suddenly in a dreadful social and spiritual void, the former metropolis had lost all its charm and henceforth resembled a huge country village. No one set foot in the libraries any more, the theaters and concert halls were empty, the lively atmosphere of the cafés was gone, and newspapers were troubled by understaffing. Life as a whole had taken on a provincial aspect; the *Graben* had lost their elegance and could scarcely be distinguished from a Tyrolean fair. The panic-stricken authorities finally acknowledged that the Jewish contribution was indispensable to the city; they appealed to their detested and despised former enemies, whose return was celebrated by the entire population; the nightmare was over. One need hardly add that this happy, if ironical, outcome was not the end of the story, and that Vienna today is a mere shadow of its former self. The prophetic character of Bettauer's novel lies rather in the fact that, without its Jews, Germany today is attempting to fill the spiritual void of a postwar era, as economically prosperous as it is intellectually impoverished, by appropriating and drawing nourishment from their cultural contribution which has at last been discovered and reclaimed.

But one must also acknowledge the factors rendering problematical all attempts to appreciate this complex, many-sided Judeo-German culture. The more one studies it, the richer and more enigmatic it appears. Subject to so many influences, as much on the artistic and literary as on the philosophical and sociological, even political level, this culture was pluralistic, fragmented, like a shattered mirror whose pieces prismatically reflected the contemporary world.

No identification was possible between Jewish nationalism and assimilationism, religion and atheism, Marxism and liberalism, rebellion and worship of order; in other words, between Gustav Landauer and Theodor Herzl, between Joseph Roth and Walther Rathenau, except that all these divisions cut across a world that was regarded as *other* by the German majority. Beyond the fact of Jewish origin – i.e., according to the *Halakah,* the son of a Jewish mother – and of the use of the German language (which, in any case, was not always the mother tongue) it was very hard to say what Judeo-German intellectuals still had in common.

I say *was* advisedly, because today one can easily identify another common characteristic: they all left Germany — at best, by train or boat for French or American exile, at worst, in cattle cars for Auschwitz and Treblinka. Taken as a whole, this last generation of a Jewish intelligentsia born into the German world can be classified as *history's vanquished.*[2]

When one speaks of Jewish-German writers of the beginning of the century, which part of this binomial term should be stressed? It would depend on the particular case, but either way would be reductive. Today, a writer may be celebrated as a classic of German literature, but he will doubtless not have escaped his fate as a Jew. We might also formulate a response like Kafka's, who despised questions of this order, finding them impossible to answer. In a letter to Felice Bauer, he jokingly noted that the *Neue Rundschau* had detected in his art 'something fundamentally German,' whereas for Max Brod his stories were among 'the most Jewish documents of our time.' 'A difficult case,' remarked Kafka, who regarded this disagreement as meaningless and concluded: 'Am I a circus rider on two horses? Alas, I am no rider, but lie prostrate on the ground.'[3] Karl Kraus, for his part, admitted the difficulty he had in distinguishing between Jews and Germans in literature. His strongest inclination was to address men and not nations: 'I really do not know,' he wrote, 'what constitutes Jewish qualities today. . . . I do not know if it is a Jewish quality to find the Book of Job worth reading, or if it is proof of anti-Semitism to throw a book by Schnitzler into a corner of one's room; if one is expressing a Jewish or German sentiment, when one says that the writings of the Jews Else Lasker-Schüler and Peter Altenberg are closer to God and to our language than anything German literature has produced in the last fifty years.'[4]

To understand this cultural enigma, it is therefore preferable to inquire into the status of the Jewish intellectual within German society. We shall attempt to do so by examining two types, central to modern Jewish society — the *pariah* and the *parvenu* — who relate as much to the material conditions of life and the social position of Jewish intellectuals as to their mentality and problematical identity. This is tantamount to saying — I must here acknowledge my debt — that my inquiry owes much to Hannah Arendt, whose reflections on the 'hidden tradition'[5] of Judaism that emerged from the emancipation movement have been at once a source of inspiration and the subject of critical analysis. Quite clearly, one might have tackled this problem from another angle and with other conceptual tools. If I have chosen the Arendtian approach it is because it offers many advantages. From this point of view, certain traditional divisions might appear secondary, even out of date, since the Zionists Martin Buber and Gershom Scholem were no doubt closer to the anarchist Gustav Landauer than to Theodor Herzl or Max Nordau, with whom they had very little in common. The latter, on the other hand, would no doubt have got along better with the Social-Democratic 'revisionists' Eduard Bernstein and Josef Bloch than with the 'Zionist' Franz Kafka. The pariah and the parvenu appear then as two different modes of existence for Judeity in a world that excludes it and with which no synthesis is possible. After stressing the paradoxicality of a country that first experienced the 'perfection of assimilation' and subsequently the 'systematic destruction' of the Jews, Dominique Bourel depicted Germany as the locus of an 'impossible metaphor,' that of the relationship of the Jews to Western civilization.[6]

Another peculiarity of this work lies in devoting an entire chapter to Joseph Roth who, notwithstanding the intrisic value of his work, certainly did not typify the Judeo-German intelligentsia as a whole. What I found fascinating in Roth was his work as a writer and essayist, quite as much as his intellectual and political progress, which covered the entire spectrum: atheism and religion, revolution and nostalgia for a pre-1914 order, assimilation and the romantic ideal of *yiddishkeit*. In this sense, he seemed to me a sort of incarnation of the Wandering Jew of modern times and typical of the pariah Judaism of Central Europe.

To examine the relations between Judeity and Germanity is to evoke a historical landscape which is still close to us and yet has already been utterly destroyed, engulfed, buried under a mountain of debris, vanished — literally — *in smoke.* The longterm endeavor, undertaken by the Germany of today, to assimilate (albeit a posteriori) Germano-Jewish culture, is at the same time a labor of *endless* lamentation, because the loss which gave rise to it is definitive and irreparable. If it is to avoid the appearance of unwarranted and basically obscene annexation, carried out in contempt of the vanquished of history, this work of assimilation is bound to implicate Germany itself again, to question its history, to analyze the breaks in that history, to acknowledge its victims and, above all, to preserve the memory of the past. This is what I have attempted to do in the second part of the book, which analyzes the different historiographical interpretations of the Shoah and which then sets out to uncover the traces left by the Jewish genocide in the collective memory of German society. The reader will no doubt notice a certain discontinuity between the first part of this work, which focuses on the Judeo-German intelligentsia, and the second, where we are no longer dealing with the intellectuals but with the 'Jewish problem' as such. This change of perspective is due to the fact that, if one wishes to take account of the *historical break* represented by the Shoah, one must also take it as given that for National Socialism, the Jews were a negative entity, imbued with a particular racial essence and destined, without exception, to be annihilated. If one wishes to understand the tragedy of Judeo-German culture, one must therefore place it in its historical context, which was that of the destruction of the European Jews. By the same token, today, the rediscovery of this culture raises the question of the relation of Germany to its own past — a past upon which the millenial Jewish presence had left its mark.

\* \* \*

I have drawn on the extremely rich resources of the Bibliothèque de Documentation Internationale Contemporaine (BDIC) of Nanterre and the Germania Judaica department of the Staatsbibliothek of Cologne. A first draft of chapter 5, Auschwitz, History, and Historians, appeared under its French title, 'Auswitch, l'histoire et les historiens,' in *Les Temps modernes*, no. 527 (June 1990), and, in Italian, in *Ventesimo secolo. Rivista di storia contemporanea*, no. 1 (January/April 1991). An initial draft of chapter 3, devoted to Joseph Roth, appeared in the January/March 1992 issue of *Études germaniques*. I wish to thank Alain Brossat, Sonia Combe, Michael Löwy, and Pierre Vidal-Naquet, who offered their criticisms of this work from their different points of view, and to Gilberto Conde, for assistance in preparing the book for publication. Thanks also to Junko and Kumiko, who kept my spirits up during the course of my labors.

# PART ONE

# Emancipation at an Impasse

# The 'Judeo-German Symbiosis':
# Myth and Reality

## A Long Quarrel

THE JEWISH ENTRY into German culture was often understood in terms of symbiosis. Did Central Europe, between the times of Moses Mendelssohn and Adolf Hitler, between the long and agonizing process of emancipation and the rise to power of National Socialism, experience a *Germano-Jewish symbiosis?* How is assimilation to be defined? Modernity's assault on the suspended, frozen world of Judaism? A fusion of Judeity with the German world, based on the abandonment of a past and of a distinct identity, or rather on the encounter and dialogue between two distinct elements? Or, on the other hand, a synthesis engendered by the secularization of the Jewish world, a metamorphosis due to the absorption of Germanic culture by the Jewish tradition?

These questions have given rise to a wide-ranging controversy, which can be approached via an observation taken from one of the richest and most fascinating correspondences of this century. In a letter to his friend Gershom Scholem, written in February 1939, Walter Benjamin criticized the then dominant trend in Jewish studies, presenting Germano-Jewish relations (described by Scholem in his reply as 'an alliance built on deception') in an 'edifying and vindicatory' light.[1] This mystification is in danger of carrying over into the present, fifty years after Auschwitz. Benjamin's and Scholem's observations make it possible for us to avoid the trap of retrospectively idealizing these relations, reminding us of the need, without denying or underestimating their significance, to point out their contradictions.

But first, from where does the notion of *symbiosis* come? The etymology of the term has not yet been finally established, but evidently it was coined in 1879 by the botanist Anton de Bary. As currently used, it signifies 'the durable and mutually beneficial association of two living organisms' (according to the *Petit Robert*). In the natural sciences, this concept is also closely linked to that of *parasitism*. In 1922, the French biologist Maurice Caullery described parasitism as a special form of symbiosis, where 'an organism lives at the expense of another. . . . This association,' he added, 'is of an entirely unilateral nature: it is essential to the parasite, which dies if it is separated from its host, unable to obtain nourishment.'[2] Once social Darwinism had introduced this concept into the humanities, the image of the Jew 'parasite' began to haunt modern anti-Semitic literature. At the end of the nineteenth century, the word *parasitism* was already widely used to describe the economic role of the Jews. Without wishing to enlarge this semantic analysis,[3] it can be said that the history of Judeo-German relations appears to oscillate between two poles: what the Jews tried to paint as a creative, fruitful symbiosis often seemed to the Germans (particularly a substantial section of the intelligentsia) as the intrusion of a foreign element – of a dangerous 'parasite' – into the core of their nation and culture.

Certainly, it would be hard to overestimate the Jewish contribution to German literary culture of the last two centuries, on which Heinrich Heine and Karl Marx, Franz Kafka and Sigmund Freud, Edmund Husserl and Max Horkheimer, Walter Benjamin and Theodor W. Adorno, Ernst Bloch and Georg Lukács, Alfred Döblin and Kurt Tucholsky, Arnold Schönberg and Gustav Mahler, Max Reinhart and Fritz Lang, Siegfried Kracauer and Karl Mannheim, Karl Kraus and Joseph Roth, to name only a few at random, have left an indelible impression. But if these figures belong unquestionably to the cultural history of *Mitteleuropa*, they are, just as decisively and irreducibly, also imbued with a specifically Jewish character. Without doubt there is something ironically paradoxical in the cultural metamorphosis that has transformed into a classic of German literature an archetypal Prague Jew like Kafka, whose connection with the Germanic world was limited to the language and who, except as regards Milena Jesenska (a Czech) spent his entire life in an exclusively Jewish milieu.[4] On the other hand, the central role in contemporary thought that we allot to these German-Jewish figures is a matter of retrospective perception in that it does not always tally with the judgment of their contemporaries: Heine, Marx, and Freud were marginal figures, often opposed, rejected and hated in their own day; as for Kafka and Benjamin, the intellectual influence of their work

4

was quite limited during their lifetimes. Noble representatives of a 'pariah' tradition (according to Max Weber's, Bernard Lazare's, and Hannah Arendt's definition) in most cases they died in exile, only rarely receiving official recognition (in the form, for instance, of university chairs) and their major works often appeared only posthumously. As a result, the concept of a 'Judeo-German symbiosis' seems *problematical* to the highest degree.[5]

The path of Judeity in German culture must be retraced, bearing in mind its effects and the tragic outcome, if we are to define its nature and content. It is worth noting, parenthetically, that the idea of symbiosis has never been employed in tackling the history of the Jews in the United States. Other concepts have served in the study of the Americanization of minorities, such as *melting pot* or, more recently, *cultural pluralism,* which have never involved the notion of the loss of ethnocultural identity on the part of the communities concerned. The second generation of American Jews, which abandoned Yiddish (or German) for English, was not required to deny its own culture in order to merge with the WASP majority. The French case, too, is different. Here, symbiosis – based on the 'moral and physical regeneration' of the Jews (Abbé Grégoire) through their entry into *the* nation – was in effect completed. But in France, despite the persistance of anti-Semitism, assimilation was encouraged by the Revolution of 1789 and approved by the official institutions. At the end of the nineteenth century, the defense of the Jew Dreyfus was evidently identified with the defence of the republic itself,[6] whereas in Germany different state apparatuses – from the army to the university – had already become bastions of the anti-Semitic movement.

In Eastern Europe, on the other hand, anti-Semitism was erecting a powerful barrier to assimilation, which affected only an extremely small and marginal section of the Jewish population. With a few exceptions (mostly Marxist intellectuals like Trotsky or Rosa Luxemburg) the Jews regarded themselves neither as Russian nor Polish but as belonging to a Jewish nation. In the Czarist Empire, the Jewish emergence into the modern world took the form of a revival of *Yiddishkeit,* the golden age of which occurred toward the end of the nineteenth century. It is not overstating the case to assert – contrary to the German Haskalah tradition, generally characterized by a deep contempt for the language of the *Ostjuden* – that the flowering of Yiddish culture in Eastern Europe amounted, in some way, to the continuation under Slavdom of the 'Germano-Jewish symbiosis.'[7] This language, which Heinrich Graetz despised as 'a semibestial jargon' and which gave to twentieth-century literature a Nobel laureate, Isaac Bashevis Singer, saw its birth in the valley of the Rhine around A.D. 1000 and, in spite of numerous Hebraic, Latin, and Slav contributions which enriched it over the centuries, remained essentially a language that was rooted in German. Midway between France (the model for Jewish absorption into the nation) and Eastern Europe (where the Jews remained cultural strangers) the German Reich and Austria were the locus for a spectacularly swift process of assimilation, which nevertheless also exhibited the most harrowingly discordant features.

In a celebrated essay, the great historian of the Cabbala, Gershom Scholem, denied the very existence of a Judeo-German dialogue, which, in his view, 'died at its very start and never took place,' since the Jews were always perceived as foreign elements in the German nation and, in spite of their desire for assimilation, at no time were successful in integrating with it. Once the notion of an identifiable 'Jewish whole' had been abandoned, this being the only possible premise for a dialogue, the encounter of the Jews with German culture, in fact, became a form of self-denial and monologue: 'I deny that there has ever been such a German-Jewish dialogue in any genuine sense whatsoever, i.e., as *a historical phenomenon*. It takes two to have a dialogue, who listen to each other, who are prepared to perceive the other as what he is and represents, and to respond to him. Nothing can be more misleading than to apply such a concept to the discussions between Germans and Jews during the last two hundred years.' As a result, Scholem concluded, when one asks: 'To whom, then, did the Jews speak in that much-talked-about German-Jewish dialogue?' the answer is clear: 'They spoke to themselves, not to say that they outshouted themselves. . . . When they thought they were speaking to the Germans, they were speaking to themselves.'[8]

Scholem had a forerunner. In 1934, Heinrich Mann was portraying the history of German-Jewish relations in terms of a one-sided love affair, forever destined to run into a wall of incomprehension and rejection. 'Thirteen million Jews throughout world,' he wrote in *Der Hass* (Hatred),

> speak a dialect that derives from or is crossed with German. In several countries where no one else understands this language, the Jews preserve their German culture and regard it as a patent of nobility. Any

people other than the Germans, any state other than this one, would benefit greatly from such a fortuitous situation. Germany is unwilling to do so. Those same Jews who carry Germany with them through the world as their second homeland, are deprived in Germany itself of their rights and can hold no public position. What is more, one has the right to murder or ruin them, if in a moment of great good humor one is not satisfied simply with making them pull up grass with their teeth.[9]

The precarious and fundamentally illusory nature of the emancipation was bitterly recognized by the writer Arnold Zweig, who from 1933 was drawing up his *Balance-Sheet of German Judaism:* 'It is certain that henceforth there will be no new place for Jews in the future of German culture [*deutschen Geist*].'[10]

Fifty years later, somewhat less angrily and with several modifications, historiography has reached the same conclusion. Those who have researched the history of the 'Judeo-German dialogue' quickly realized that they were studying the history of a *myth*. No sooner was it engaged than the dialogue was broken off, from the second half of the nineteenth century, when the Jews, assimilated henceforth, remained practically the sole adherents of the *Aufklärung*, as against a German intelligentsia increasingly polarized around the myth of the German *Volk*.[11] Thus, the 'Judeo-German symbiosis' became a cultural phenomenon purely within the Jewish community, unconnected with any social life in common between the two groups that were supposed to comprise it. In fact, the Germans never seriously considered the idea of a cultural synthesis with the Jewish tradition. At best, they accepted the Jews, provided the latter no longer regarded themselves as Jews, provided they had abandoned Judaism.[12]

In the thirties, this problem was seen in a quite different light. In 1935, the year of the Nuremberg Laws, the writer and literary critic Margarete Susmann devoted an article to the 'spiritual contribution' of the Jews in the German context, where she highlighted the Jewish vocation not for 'self-realization [*Selbstverwirklichung*]' but rather for permanent 'cultural symbiosis [*Kultursymbiose*]' with the other peoples encountered in the course of the diasporic wanderings. The Judeo-German dialogue, begun with Yiddish and with Luther's translation of the Bible (in his opinion a testimony to the 'intermingling of the Jewish and German spirit'), and pursued by Mendelssohn, Goethe, and Heine, had been interrupted, at the end of the nineteenth century, as a result of the victory of a perverse Wagnerian spirit of modernity that substituted myth for Reason.[13]

The same despairing note, in the face of the obliteration of the Jewish epic in Germany, is sounded by another great figure, whose life furthermore closely paralleled Scholem's: the philosopher and founder of cultural Zionism, Martin Buber. In 1939, on the eve of the genocide and already fully conscious of the fact that an irreparable breach had been opened up between Judaism and Germany, he was emphasizing the significance and depth of this symbiosis. In Buber's eyes, national socialism was a 'catastrophe' which shattered the 'organic' Judeo-German 'unity [*organische Zusammenhang*]' and created a deep 'schism in the very heart of Germanity.'[14] Apparently this conclusion was shared by Leo Baeck, the former rabbi of Berlin and the last representative of the rationalist and assimilationist trend of the 'science of Judaism [*Wissenschaft des Judentums*].' He regarded Germany as the locus of the third golden age of Judaism, after that of Hellenism, in ancient Greece, and of the Spanish and Portuguese Sepharad from before the Inquisition.[15] These observations seem for the most part like the self-defence of a man who, as a leading Jewish public figure, had been the incarnation for the whole first half of the century of the unshakable faith of his coreligionists in assimilation and the 'civilizing mission' of Germany. But in 1945, under the impact of the genocide which had just taken place, he was forced to acknowledge that a 'historic epoch' had ended. His hopes for 'a meeting between the Jewish and German spirit' had turned out to be an illusion and was gone 'forever.'[16] For those who stubbornly insisted on denying their contradictory nature, Judeo-German relations took on the mythic shape of a lost paradise. Auschwitz, thus, seemed like an abrupt and explosive break in the union of 'Saul and David,' a break which in a few years had transformed 'the loftiest symbiosis' into a 'murderous epilogue.'[17]

Clearly one cannot now study the history of the Jews in German society and culture without taking the genocide into account. Irrespective of its origins – a problematic matter that continues to divide historians – Auschwitz casts a sinister light over the entire course of Judeo-German relations, which are seen in terms of a 'negative symbiosis.'[18] Genocide was not inevitably inscribed in German history. The shadow of Auschwitz covered the landscape after the catastrophe, but it was not visible when it hovered above Weimar Germany. The words of Leo Baeck and Martin Buber no doubt mark the origin of the myth of a 'Judeo-German symbiosis,' but they also show that it was a reality in the eyes, the perceptions, of a very large section of the Jewish population. The idea of a 'Judeo-German dialogue' therefore was not invented a posteriori by historians, but accurately reflected a phenomenon that really existed; namely, the Jewish *illusion* of belonging to Germany. Deeply rooted, this sentiment had a positive effect on the state of mind, the modes of behavior, the expectations of German Judaism up to its destruction. Heinrich Heine, who spent the greater part of his life in France, was being completely candid when he declared that for him Germany was 'what water is for a fish' and that his breast was nothing but 'a repository for German sentiments.'[19]

## The Stages of a Negative Dialectic

Retrospectively, German-Jewish acculturation can be seen as a process covering a period of about 150 years: from Wilhelm von Dohm and Moses Mendelssohn, the two principal proponents of emancipation (respectively a German and a Jew) toward the end of the eighteenth century, up to Hitler's seizure of power (in Austria, until the *Anschluss* of 1938). From a strictly legal point of view, the Jews became German citizens by degree throughout the first half of the last century (a process which was concluded only in 1871) and were then finally deprived of their civil rights in 1935, with the Nuremberg Laws. But the legislation simply reflected the slowness of emancipation — with leaps forward during the Revolution, delays and retreats under the Restoration — and the sudden, savage, and disruptive character of the Nazi regime's anti-Semitism.

In fact, this acculturation had got underway well before the emancipation laws were passed. The Jewish entry into German culture was heralded by the German translation (still keeping the Hebrew letters) of the Pentateuch, in 1778. Its author, Moses Mendelssohn, reinterpreted the Hebrew religion via the philosophy of the Enlightenment and proclaimed the membership of both peoples — Jews and Germans — in the same family of mankind, which should have seemed perfectly obvious to everybody after the Germanization of the Jews.[20] In 1782, Christian Wilhelm von Dohm, a high Prussian government official, published *Über die bürgerliche Verbesserung der Juden* (On the civic betterment of the Jews), which extolled the principle of 'tolerance' and recommended that Jews be granted civil rights to enable them to overcome their 'prejudices' and their 'deficiencies': 'It is possible that a particular defect might be so deeply rooted that it will not disappear entirely until the third or fourth generation. But that is no reason not to begin the reform with the present generation, since without this reform we shall never see a generation that has been corrected.'[21] The anti-Jewish prejudice was, thus, not foreign to the culture of the *Aufklärung* which claimed to be combatting it. Dohm's position presupposed the idea of the equality of men, which did not, in his eyes, signify the equality of the Jews and Germans, but rather the ability of the Jews to Germanize themselves. The entire structure of his argument was based, as Helmut Berding rightly observed, on 'a notion of public, utilitarian education.'[22] His attitude perfectly embodied the wishes of that current of German political opinion that favored emancipation: not the encounter between Judaism and Germany, but the dissolution of the former in the latter. The insistence on the slowness of the process was due to the fact that the 'German-Jewish dialogue,' to the extent that it could exist, concerned at that time only an extremely limited intellectual elite: the acculturation of the Jews in Germany was to take place over a period of several generations.

At the start of the nineteenth century, the most favorable locations for this dialogue were the Jewish salons of Berlin, described by Hannah Arendt as 'a kind of neutral zone,' somewhere between the nobility in decline and the new bourgeois order which was still a long way from being able to take over. Here took place the encounter between two different categories of outsiders: the Jews and the protointellectuals of modern Germany.[23] The rebirth of German national feeling, under Napoleonic rule, again divided those who had shared this experience. In certain respects, the salons of Henriette Herz and Rahel Levin Varnhagen represented the most significant among the rare instances of this Judeo-German osmosis. Recognized, and enjoying a de facto legitimacy as places of social interaction, despite their noninstitutional character, they were frequented by almost all the important German cultural figures of the period: Goethe, Schleiermacher, the brothers Schlegel, Humboldt, Adalbert von Chamisso, Heinrich Kleist, etc. In effect, the salons constituted only a brief interlude, but they marked a fundamental stage in the progress of assimilation and it is symptomatic of their failure that their members, Rahel Levin as much as Henriette Herz, tried to escape their Judeity through conversion.

## The 'Judeo-German Symbiosis'

In 1806, the first German-language Jewish review, *Sulamit*, was founded, preparing the ground for the birth of the Wissenschaft des Judentums in 1819, the year of the last major wave of pogroms in nineteenth-century Germany. Inspired in Berlin by Leopold Zunz and Eduard Gans, two loyal disciples of Mendelssohn and of the Haskalah, this school put forward an interpretation of Judaism that rejected its messianic spiritual sources and limited itself to rationalistic exegesis.[24] Stripped of its mystic dimension, which might evoke the image of the ghetto and identify it with a medieval form of obscurantism, Judaism adapted itself to the modern world and became a 'religion of reason [*Religion der Vernunft*],' according to the definition which the neo-Kantian philosopher Hermann Cohen was to give it almost a century later. In contrast to the old rabbinical schools, Leopold Zunz's school held classes in German and was also patronized by a lay public (including, for the first time, women). Rationalized and denationalized, Judeity was to preserve only its religious character and the Jews were to be transformed into citizens of the 'Mosaic' faith, like German Catholics and Protestants. Judeity and Germanity were to coalesce, since, according to Bertold Auerbach, unquestionably the most celebrated Jewish writer of the nineteenth century, 'the Germanic-national ideal [*deutschnationale*] is at the same time the ideal of humanity.'[25] For Gabriel Reisser, the first Jew elected to a German parliament (the Frankfurt Assembly, in 1848), the Jews were either Germans or 'stateless.' He characterized Germany as the wellspring 'of my feelings and thoughts, the language I speak, the air I breathe.' To deny him his German citizenship was to deprive him of his deepest, most intimate sense of identity.[26]

When, in 1871, Bismarck's Reich completed the process of emancipation, acculturation was no longer the concern only of an intellectual elite but of the entire Jewish community. The foundations had been laid for the establishment of the Central Association of German Citizens of the Israelite Faith [*Zentralverein deutscher Staatsbürger jüdischen Glaubens*]. Created in 1893, the *Zentralverein* swiftly became the main Jewish communal institution, a powerful instrument of assimilation, thanks to an elaborate network of cultural, recreational, and sports associations that comprised about 300,000 people, or more than half the community. Loyalty to the fatherland was inscribed in its statutes and forcefully promoted in all its publications. The slogan of the German nationalists, *Mit Gott für Kaiser und Vaterland*

(With God for emperor and fatherland), was readily adopted by its members. In this same period, the great majority of Austrian Jews were demonstrating their support for the Habsburg Empire, in spite of the attraction exercised by the socialist movement over a significant section of the intelligentsia.

The final milestone in this problematic encounter with the Germanic world was the Weimar Republic, which allowed the Jews to take another stride toward their integration into German society and, at the same time, set the stage for an extraordinary upsurge of anti-Semitism. It would no doubt be an exaggeration to claim, as some historians have done, that without Jews the 'culture of Weimar' would never have existed,[27] but it is clear that they played a prominent part in it. A real 'Judeo-German symbiosis' seemed to manifest itself at that time, though it concerned only a milieu of anticonformist and marginal intellectuals (marginal, in spite of their number and the value and influence of their work).

We have briefly indicated the principal stages in the process of Jewish assimilation, involving an encounter, the initiation of a dialogue and, up to a point, an incipient merging with the German nation. The significance of assimilation within the Jewish community was aptly summed up in a celebrated formula: 'To be men like other men on the outside, and Jews at home.' But one must not forget the limits and contradictions of this process: not only the exceptional slowness of emancipation, but in particular that, to a large extent, it was a consequence of the French Revolution and of its repercussions in Europe under Napoleon rather than the result of an endogenous development. It was not the idea of emancipation that the German *Aufklärung* – from Gotthold Ephraim Lessing to Wihelm von Dohm – had formulated but 'toleration,' as advanced in Lessing's play *Nathan the Wise* in 1779 and as promoted by the edict passed by the Habsburg Emperor Joseph II in 1781; subsequently, the French model prevailed and the integration of the Jews into the nation was conceived and realized as a measure concerning individuals as such rather than the community. The conferment of civil rights was to enable the Jews to discard their distinctive cultural features: in the long run they were supposed to rid themselves of Judeity itself. Gradually worn away, their collective identity was to vanish. Paradoxically, the result was the assimilation of the Jews as individuals and the preservation of Judeity, no longer defined by religion but rather transformed into a 'psychological quality.'[28] In this way, a new figure, that of the *non-Jewish Jew*[29] or the Godless Jew [*gottloser Jude*] arose; namely, one who, according to Freud's definition, 'does not understand the holy tongue, who is estranged from the religion of his fathers (as from all other religions), who cannot participate in the nationalist ideology and yet who has never denied that he belongs to his people, who is conscious of his Jewish distinctiveness and does not want it changed.'[30]

## *Lights and Shades of Assimilation*

Toward the middle of the eighteenth century, the Jewish communities of Central Europe were still much like their medieval precursors: a 'caste,' according to Max Weber, socially, linguistically, and culturally quite separate from the surrounding society. A century later, this picture had changed. They had adopted the German language and broken down the barriers of 'ecological' isolation behind which they had lived for several centuries. Jacob Katz has called the fifty years preceding the emancipation laws a period of 'semineutral social existence,'[31] characterized by the progressive exposure of the ghettos to the influence of the outside world and by the instigation of a dialogue with the gentiles. This transformation had been promoted, in the absolutist states, by the work of the Court Jews [*Hofjuden*], while in civil society the first lay institutions open to Jews, for example the Freemasons, appeared. Gradually the idea of the 'political reformation' of the Jews spread, seen as a necessary step in the general 'progress' of society.

In the Prussian state, where resistance to emancipation was stronger than elsewhere, the Jewish desire to integrate with the German nation even gave rise, for a while, to a wave of conversions. Traces of the desperate efforts of the intellectual elite to escape its Judeity can be found in the words of Rahel Varnhagen: 'The Jew must be extirpated from us, that is the sacred truth.'[32] Several decades later, the same attitude is reiterated in the violent articles — misunderstood in most cases — of Moses Hess and Karl Marx. Hess, regarded today as a pioneer of Zionism, thanks to *Rome and Jerusalem* (1862), where he openly upheld the right of the Jews to a national existence, in 1841 described the modern bourgeois who were beginning to appear in Germany as 'beasts, vampires, Jews and hungry money wolves [*als Raubtiere, als Blutsauger, als Juden, als Geld-wölfe*].' Marx, at this time, saw Judaism as 'objectively based' in 'practical need' and regarded the Jews as prototypes of the 'man of money [*Geldmensch*].'[33] Since the life and works of these two Jewish intellectuals show that they were not anti-Semites, these writings must be put into their historical context, which was that of the first generation of assimilated German Jewish intellectuals, who originated in but were already detached from the Haskalah, impregnated with the philosophy of the Enlightenment (the 'Hegelian Left' of Ludwig Feuerbach) and dedicated to an uncompromising struggle with religion.

The wave of conversions—defined by Heine as the 'entrance ticket to European culture' — assumed relatively significant proportions (approximately 3,500 cases in the Prussian state, between 1812 and 1846, out of a Jewish population of 22,000) but, in general, the Jews integrated into German society without seeking to rid themselves of those features that determined their collective identity. The immediate effect of the laws abolishing the right of residence in the large cities was an intensive process of urbanization: freedom of movement and residency concentrated the Jews instead of dispersing them. At the end of the nineteenth century, out of half a million Jews in Germany, one hundred thousand lived in Berlin and the rest in the most important German cities (particularly Frankfurt, but also Hamburg, Munich, and Stuttgart). Under the Weimar Republic, there were already 175,000 in Berlin; on the eve of World War I, they accounted for almost 10 percent of the population in Vienna, one of the largest European metropolises with its two million inhabitants, and 7 percent of the population of Prague. The preservation of the community manifested itself, among others, in a strong tendency toward endogamy, even more conspicuous if one remembers that most 'mixed' marriages took place between Jews and converted Jews.

Finally, the emancipation considerably improved the living conditions of Jews, but did not eliminate the socioeconomic structure inherited from the period of the ghetto. If in 1780 nine-tenths of the Jews belonged to the poorest strata of the population, a century later the proportion had been completely reversed: the poor constituted no more than a tenth. After spectacular advances, the majority of German Jews boasted henceforth of belonging to the middle classes, even, in the case of a privileged elite, to the upper levels of the bourgeoisie. The Jews participated, on a massive scale, in hitherto prohibited activities (notably the liberal professions) but did not abandon the economic and commercial activities they had engaged in for centuries and which now could be pursued far more freely. In 1895, 56 percent of Jews were active in commerce, a domain that engaged only 10 percent of the German population as a whole.[34] Between 1870 and 1910, two out of every five Viennese Jews were merchants, the others being employees or members of the liberal professions[35] (their role in artistic and intellectual life being especially significant). In 1910, in Germany, they represented approximately 15 percent of the lawyers, 6 percent of the doctors, and eight percent of the writers and journalists, whereas they constituted only 1 percent of the total German population. In Vienna, in this same period, they represented 62 percent of the lawyers, 51 percent of the doctors and dentists, and 70 percent of those engaged in the scientific professions. The Jewish presence was quite substantial in journalism (one result of their exclusion from university teaching). Some of the most important dailies or periodicals like the *Neue Freie Presse* and the *Wiener Tagblatt* in Austria, the *Prager Tagblatt* in Bohemia, the *Frankfurter Zeitung* and the *Berliner Tagblatt* in Germany, were usually described by anti-Semites as the 'Jewish press.' Publishing houses of the first rank like Ullstein, Mosse, or Fischer belonged to Jews. On the whole, emancipated Jews, in Jacob Katz's words, no longer constituted 'a concentrated ecological entity, strictly limited to the economic field and quite isolated socially and culturally,' but remained a 'subgroup' with distinct social and cultural characteristics, far beyond what might be expected of a simple religious minority.[36]

As has already been indicated, a distinguishing feature of this 'subgroup' was its endogamy.[37] Mixed marriages were the exception rather than the rule and the Jews continued to live a life apart. They interacted with non-Jews in their professional lives, but very seldom in private. In his memoirs, Hans Mayer writes that 'without knowing it, in any case without wanting to know it, we lived in a Judeo-German ghetto.'[38] The same view is affirmed in a letter by Franz Rosenzweig who, in 1917, wrote to his parents as follows: 'When you wish to feel German, your choice is limited to those Germans who permit you to exist. These are (1) Germans in the same position as yourself; that is, other Jews, (2) some déclassé individuals and bohemians, (3) some liberally inclined and well-off people, (4) *Die Verjudeten*, (5) your bosom-friends.'[39]

This did not prevent the lifestyle of the German *Mittelstand* from being very widely adopted. In *Berliner Kindheit* (A Berlin childhood), Walter

Benjamin remembers the decorating of the tree on Christmas Eve with far greater pleasure than going to synagogue for the Jewish New Year.[40] And Gershom Scholem, in his autobiography, describes the cultural and psychological climate that prevailed in Berlin's Jewish circles at the beginning of the century, where religious ritual was less and less respected and was often reduced to family celebrations. Not many still fasted on the Day of Atonement, yet they did not dare openly to defy the tradition. Scholem writes ironically how, in the restaurant adjoining the great synagogue of Oranienburgerstrasse, the head waiter invites 'the gentlemen who are fasting' to be seated 'in the back room.' However, he also recalls that baptism was perceived as 'an unprincipled and servile act.' The last page of the newsletter of the Berlin Jewish Community Council, where the names of those who had converted was printed, was often the only one to be read, this being highly disagreeable for those concerned, who felt they had thus been exposed to general opprobrium.[41] Formal allegiance to the community was, thus, for many Jews who had abandoned all religious belief, the telltale sign of a negative otherness from which one could not escape without being stricken by pangs of conscience or accused of cowardice.

Assimilation implied adherence to codes of behavior and a dominant value system. The Jew belonging to the middle levels of society or to the property-owning classes had also to accept the norms of daily life and culture. The entry of the Jews into German society as a process of bourgeoisification [*Verbürgerlichung*] has to be understood in this very broad sense. However, acculturation stubbornly pursued and brought to a triumphant conclusion was not immune to the contradictions mentioned above. The Jews could live *like* but very rarely *with* middle-class Germans; they could become imbued with the values of the host society but strong counterforces prevented them from merging with it; they could recognize themselves there, but were not recognized. At the end of the nineteenth century, the German middle class milieu was composed of clubs, associations, and connections of all sorts, which, though in principle open, in reality were strictly limited to an elite and walled off not only socially but also religiously and culturally. As a result, the *Verbürgerlichung* of the Jews took on the appearance of a 'negative integration.'[42] This contradictory process was evident also in the opposition between education [*Bildung*] and respectability [*Sittlichkeit*]: emancipated Jews had imbibed the former – an education

16

which, at bottom, was nothing but a new form of that *Verbesserung* already propounded by von Dohm – whereas they were still denied the latter.[43]

Gerson Bleichröder seems to typify the contradictions implicit in assimilation. Berlin's most important banker and Bismarck's financial advisor, very close to the Rothschild family and to international financial circles, he achieved a social position utterly unimaginable for a German Jew of his time. In 1872, he was even ennobled and able to add the mark of nobility, *von*, to his name. But Bleichröder's entire career does no more than illustrate the fate of the Jewish parvenu. Although he belonged to the ruling economic elite, he was never accepted into Prussian aristocratic circles, which kept him at a distance and treated him with a measure of contempt. The whole of German high society was imbued with this 'respectability,' drawing on the traditions of the nobility, whereas the sole reason for Bleichröder's respectability was his money. In fact, his mental makeup was still that of a Court Jew: obsessed by his origins and by the negative implications of his otherness, he tried all his life to acquire decorations and official titles, without ever managing to wipe out the memory of his origins.[44] Bleichröder was the paradigmatic embodiment both of the successes and the frustrations of the German Jews of the second half of the nineteenth century. Their minority status, as heirs to a merchant caste, operating within a society that had known considerable economic expansion, but in which commerce had always been seen as disreputable, had a dual effect: on the one hand it encouraged their socioeconomic rise, while, on the other, it helped perpetuate their exclusion.[45]

A typical result of assimilation was the desire to disown Judeity itself. Jews who aspired to integrating entirely with society and to being accepted by a markedly anti-Semitic milieu often succeeded in internalizing and subjecting themselves to the prejudices of which they were the victims. This gave rise to the well-known phenomenon of 'self-hatred,' so widespread among the Jews of Central Europe at the turn of the century (to the point of becoming 'the latest national disease afflicting the Jews,' according to Arthur Schnitzler). Otto Weininger, the young Austrian philosopher, who committed suicide in 1903 after having published a provocative book, *Sex and Character*, in which he theorized on the inferiority of Jews and women, became the symbol of all this, but his was far from being an isolated case. Leaving aside the extreme situations, painstakingly catalogued by Theodor

Lessing in 1930,[46] one easily picks up traces of *jüdischer Selbshass* in many intellectuals, from the composer Hermann Levi, who in his admiration for Richard Wagner was prepared to humiliate himself, to Karl Kraus, who opened the columns of his magazine *Die Fackel* to articles by the racist theorist Houston Stewart Chamberlain, directing his polemical darts at the Jewish 'sharks [*Scheidern*]' who, in his eyes, had transformed Viennese culture into a kind of commercial undertaking, and regarding Judaism as an 'Asian form of barbarism.'[47] On a more general level, this phenomenon reflected a sense of inferiority, frustration, and malaise; in short, a psychological sensibility widespread in the Jewish community. It was deeply rooted in the difficulty experienced by emancipated Jews of living in a society which seemed to them to constitute 'a world of nonacceptance.'[48]

Another form of 'autophobia' could be seen in the rejection by assimilated Jews of their East European immigrant coreligionists, more and more numerous in Germany from the end of the nineteenth century. The opposition between Cravat-Jews and Caftan Jews went far beyond the bourgeoisie-proletariat class conflict: in the eyes of assimilated Jews, the *Ostjuden* inevitably evoked the detestable memory of the ghetto; the Yiddish language sounded in their ears like a barbarous and despicable jargon (the historian Heinrich Graetz even objected to a Yiddish translation of his celebrated *Geschichte der Juden*). In short, the presence of several tens of thousands of Eastern Jews — approximately 10 percent of the Jewish population of Germany at the beginning of the century and around 19 percent under the Weimar Republic[49] — seemed again to call in question their already precarious 'respectability' (in other words, the gains of assimilation) and was perceived as a major obstacle in the path of the 'Judeo-German symbiosis.'

## The Rise of Anti-Semitism

Another critical element was connected with the rise of modern anti-Semitism, which cast a threatening shadow over the Jewish condition. With its racist overtones, hatred of the Jews was transformed not only into an ideologically based intellectual movement, but increasingly into a cultural and psychological bond that subsumed all the social contradictions of a Germany torn apart by intensive industrialization and urbanization. All the reactionary currents — antisocialism, antiliberalism, conservative and romantic anticapitalism, and so on — met in anti-Semitism, which constituted a kind of *negative identity* for different social strata (especially lower middle-class ones) afflicted and destabilized by the abrupt transformation of the country. The emancipatory discourse, thus, gave way to theories which attempted to demonstrate that the Jews did not belong to the Germanic *Volk*.[50]

From the last quarter of the nineteenth century, the opposition between *Judentum* and *Germanentum* had already given rise to a vast anti-Semitic literature, exemplified in the works of many writers. To different degrees, the notion of the basic alienation of the Jews from Germany was shared by Romantic thinkers, representatives of a 'cultural pessimism' that was fundamentally antimodern (Paul de Lagarde, Julius Langbehn, and Eugen Diederichs) by traditional Christian anti-Semites, Catholic as well as Protestant (August Rohling and Adolf Stöcker), by fanatical pan-Germanists and theoreticians of the *völkisch* nationalism (Georg von Schönerer and Houston Stewart Chamberlain), or else, from the beginning of the twentieth century, by the partisans of the 'conservative revolution' (Arthur Möller Van der Bruck, Oswald Spengler, Carl Schmitt). Certainly the 'spiritual' anti-Semitism of Langbehn, an admirer of Spinoza, should not be confused with the frenzy of Houston Stewart Chamberlain about the Jewish *Gegenrasse*, nor should the anti-Semitism of Möller Van der Bruck be put on the same level as that of Alfred Rosenberg, but they were all immersed in a cultural climate whose unifying element was the irreconcilable opposition between 'Aryan' and 'Semite.' Various connections can be made between these different forms of anti-Semitism, as is shown by the case of Wilhelm Stepel, manager of the *Deutsches Volkstum*, proponent of a cultural, nonbiological anti-Semitism, who nevertheless was comfortably accommodated by the Nazi regime.[51] In Germany, anti-Semitism might help build a national identity which the new state still did not have. In the context of the Bismarckian Reich, fragmented and lacking in homogeneity, anti-Semitism might serve as a unifying factor, as against 'Jewish cosmopolitanism.' It might also transform the Jews into scapegoats, so as to divert attention from the social malaise engendered by a rapid and disruptive industrial and economic development that was undermining the traditional order. As Shulamit Volkov stressed, anti-Semitism was taking on the appearance of a 'cultural code.'[52]

Toward the middle of the nineteenth century, a number of writers contributed to the spread of anti-Semitism by inventing stereotypes that em-

bodied all the faults attributed to Jews: dirtiness, laziness, unproductive-
ness, a calculating nature, maliciousness, immorality. The most celebrated
novel of this type, *Soll und Haben* (*Debit and Credit*), written by Gustav
Freytag in 1855, had already reached its thirty-sixth edition by the beginning of the 1880s. The Jew was perceived as the incarnation of all the anti-
national values and anti-Semitism became one of the components of the
prevailing ideology, assembled in the privileged precincts of the universities. The noisiest and most noted spokesman among the anti-Semitic university mandarins was undoubtedly Heinrich von Treitschke. This former
liberal, who in the past had subscribed to the *aufklärisch* ideal of toleration,
in 1880 published an article on the Jewish question, 'Ein Wort über unser Judentum' [A word about our Jewish folk], in which he launched an attack on emancipation.[53] He regarded the Jews as fundamentally alien to a
Christianity-based European civilization, with which they could integrate
only through 'intruding.' 'The Jews are our misfortune [*Die Juden sind unser Unglück*]': this celebrated aphorism by the old professor became the
rallying call of a substantial section of the German intelligentsia.

The liberal point of view, which derived from the *Aufklärung* and supported emancipation, was defended, in a controversy with Treitschke, by
the historian of antiquity, Theodor Mommsen. While recognizing the Jewish right to German citizenship, Mommsen called for the Germanization of
the Jews and urged them to give up their distinctiveness, since Christianity
remained the basis of 'international civilization.' The Jews should try to
conform and stop acting as 'fermenters of cosmopolitanism.'[54] So, they
might be accepted, but only on condition that they renounced their Judeity.
This attitude was to find its epigone in Karl Kautsky, the most important
theorist of German social-democracy and of the Second International, who
drew attention to Jewish participation in the progressive movements of the
period and, at the same time, regarded Judaism as 'one of the last pieces of
debris left over from the feudal Middle Ages.' 'We shall not have completely
emerged from the Middle Ages,' he wrote, 'while Judaism remains with us.
The sooner it disappears, the better it will be for society and for the Jews
themselves.'[55]

It is in this context that the myth of 'Judaization [*Verjudung*]' began to
spread, depicting Jewish assimilation as a threat to German culture. This
notion had first appeared in a work by Richard Wagner on *Judaism in Mu-*

*sic* (1850), in which the composer violently accused the Jews of debasing art so as to turn it into a commercial enterprise. He stressed their inability to understand the 'German soul' and compared Meyerbeer's compositions to a kind of 'jargon' with Yiddish accents.[56] Toward the end of the previous century, the myth of 'Judaization' was widespread; in the anti-Semitic fancy it referred on the one hand to the spectacular rise of emancipated Jews in German society and, on the other, to the spread of the Jewish spirit as it took over German culture so as to dismantle it from within.[57] Anti-Semitic circles invented a new adjective to describe how the German intellectual world had been corrupted: some literature was described as 'yiddified [*vermauschelte Literatur*].'[58] Vienna, which at that time was at its creative apogee and where the entire cultural life – from Austro-Marxism to psychoanalysis – seemed to be dominated by the Jewish spirit, was pointed to as proof of this triumphal march of Judaism toward the conquest and perversion of Western civilization. Karl Lueger, the mayor of the Austrian capital, put the idea forward explicitly:

> In Vienna there are as many Jews as there are grains of sand on the seashore; wherever you go, nothing but Jews; if you go to the theater, nothing but Jews; if you take a walk in the Ringstrasse, nothing but Jews; if you enter the Stadtpark, nothing but Jews; if you go to a concert, nothing but Jews; if you go to a ball, nothing but Jews; if you go to the university, nothing but Jews. We are not shouting *Hep, hep, hep,* but we strongly object to the fact that Christians should all be oppressed and that in the place of the old Christian Austrian Empire a new Kingdom of Palestine should be arising.[59]

For the Germanophile and fanatically Wagnerian English intellectual Houston Stewart Chamberlain, author of *Die Grundlagen des neunzehnten Jahrhunderts* (1899, *The Foundations of the Nineteenth Century*), the corrupting influence of the Jews had already brought about the fall of the Roman Empire and the decline of Great Britain (thanks to Disraeli) and was now threatening to destroy from within the whole of Western civilization, by creating an appalling mixture of races, a *Völkerchaos* that would destroy all spiritual values.[60] In the domain of the social sciences, the notion of *Verjudung* inspired such a work as *The Jews and Economic Life* (1912) by Werner Sombart, which tended to regard modern capitalism as an expression of economic rationalism intrinsically linked to the Jews.[61] In other words, the rise of nationalism (notably in its *völkisch* form) again rendered problematic Judeo-German unity, the basis for which grew more and more fragile and unstable.

## Judeity and Germanity

What was the Jewish response to the rise of anti-Semitism? In general the attitude of the *Zentraverein* was to redouble the declarations of patriotism and loyalty to the state. As for the intellectuals, identification with German culture was almost total, which did not fail to irritate the manic teutono-philes. At a concert in Breslau, in 1863, Wagner realized 'with horror' that the public consisted almost entirely of Jews, an extremely unpleasant experience for him, to be repeated the following day, when he was invited to a dinner in his honor.[62] The founder of the *Goethe Jahrbuch* was a reformed Jew, Ludwig Geiger, as were half of the members of the Goethe Gesellschaft of Berlin at the start of the century.

In 1880, Ludwig Bamberger, a Jewish intellectual of national-liberal leanings and a supporter of Bismarck, responded to Treitschke in an article entitled 'Deutschum und Judentum.' In his view, never, in the entire history of the diaspora, had the Jews been 'so closely' linked with another people as they were with the Germans. They had 'come to adulthood' thanks to the German language and, since 'the language is the spirit,' they had been 'Germanized.'[63] Moritz Lazarus, psychologist and representative of the Wissenschaft des Judentums movement, acknowledged the distinction currently made between 'Germans' and 'Semites,' but specified that the Jews differed from the 'Aryans' only from the point of view of their ethnic origins [*Abstammung*], since in every other respect they belonged entirely to the German nation. Proud of his Jewishness, he wanted to place it 'at the service of the German national spirit.'[64] Eugen Fuchs, a prominent member of the Zentralverein, hoped to bring Judaism 'to life again' in the 'German fatherland,' so as to aid in the creation of 'a more elevated type of human being.' Germanity [*Deutschum*] was his nation and his *Volk*, whereas Judeity for him was a creed and a matter of 'ethnic origins [*Stamm*].' He specified that 'our religion and our *Stamm* do not separate us in a *völkisch* sense from the other Germans.'[65] In an autobiographical work, Eduard Bernstein, one of the principal leaders of the social-democratic movement, stressed the patriotism of his youthful years, just before national unity was achieved: 'I felt completely German, in any case a liberal-democratic German. The national movement of the 1860s for German unity had my total support. Black, red, yellow: the tricolored flag had become my flag.'[66]

The sense of belonging to the nation and to German culture pervaded the Jewish community, cutting across political division. In an essay of 1913, which he was to take up again in his collection *Der werdende Mesch*, Gustav Landauer, the libertarian writer from Munich, acknowledged his double allegiance. Judeity and Germanity were two distinct aspects of a single entity, where there could be neither hierarchy nor preference. He compared them to two brothers who were loved differently but equally by their mother.[67] Even the Zionists seemed unwilling to renounce their Germanity. Franz Oppenheimer, for instance, used almost the same words as Landauer: he was as 'proud' of being German as he was of his Jewish origins and declared himself 'happy to have been born and to have been educated in the country of Kant and Goethe,' to speak their language and to enjoy their culture. 'My Germanity,' he concluded, 'is as dear to me as my Jewish ancestry. . . . I embrace both the Jewish national sentiment and the German.'[68] At first, the Zionists were proud to acknowledge their roots in Western civilization and German culture; the establishment of a Jewish State in Palestine seemed to them a valid objective for the oppressed, persecuted *Ostjuden* of the Czarist Empire, not for the German Jews. Before it became an assertion of ethnocultural, even national, identity, belonging to the Zionist movement often took the form of philanthropic activity within Judaism. While distancing himself from and criticizing assimilationism, Oppenheimer had no difficulty admitting that he was an 'assimilated' Jew and holding his Germanity 'sacred' [*Mein Deutschtum is mir ein Heiligtum*]. In 1910, he established the theoretical basis for his peculiar synthesis of Zionism and Germanity in a much discussed article which appeared in *Die Welt*, one of the publications of the Zionistische Vereinigung für Deutschland (Zionist association for Germany). He made a clear distinction between ethnic fellowship (common to all Jews and crystallized in their *Stammesbewusstsein*) and national and cultural belonging, which on the other hand might vary considerably depending on the different conditions of life in the diaspora. As against the Eastern Jews, endowed with a national tradition and culture, the Jews of Central Europe identified with German tradition and culture.[69]

It should not be forgotten that for Theodor Herzl, founder of political Zionism, Germanity remained in a way the source of any national regeneration of Judaism, as is shown by his wish to make German the language of the future Jewish state of Palestine.[70]

During World War I, almost the entire Jewish community was seized by a patriotic fervor and spared no effort to promote the success of German arms (100,000 Jews were mobilized and 12,000 died in battle). For German Jews the war was a solemn event, a historical opportunity to legitimize their existence in the eyes of society and, thanks to this decisive proof of patriotism, to redeem the privileges of an emancipation won not through struggle but granted by the state. The entire Jewish press, liberal as well as Zionist, competed in a display of loyalty, in harmony with the prevailing chauvinism. 'Our country,' wrote the *Allgemeine Zeitung des Judentums*, the official journal of the Zentraverein, 'faces a major ordeal. . . . We Jews must show that the blood of our ancient heroes survives in us and that we have lived for centuries neither in vain nor as sacrificial lambs. Until the present time, we have been sheltered and protected by our country. Now that the country needs to be protected, it should be able to count on us. To this end, may all-powerful God grant us his blessing and his support.'[71] For the Jews, to defend Germany meant in the first place to defend their *Staatsangehörigkeit*, their rights as full citizens of the state. To this extent, Rabbi Leo Baeck did not regard the war as a struggle for political and military hegemony in Europe, but as an attempt to preserve 'European culture and morality.'[72] Ludwig Frank, Jewish deputy to the Reichstag, who fell at the front in his first battle, was immediately hailed by the *Allgemeine Zeitung des Judentums* as a Jewish martyr and a 'hero of humanity.' Kurt Blumenfeld, out-and-out opponent of assimilationism and representative of the most radical current of German Zionism, declared that 'he who is loyal to the Jewish nation cannot be disloyal to the German fatherland.'[73] Several Zionists who had emigrated to Palestine returned to Germany to volunteer for the imperial army.

It is in these circumstances that the notion of a 'Judeo-German symbiosis' was developed, on the philosophical plane, by Hermann Cohen. Aged seventy-four, the former founder of the Marburg school felt the need to lend his support as a Jew to the German war effort. He lost no time in asserting that, 'contrary to common prejudice,' the emancipation had more solid foundations in Germany than anywhere else and emphasized the crucial role of Judaism in Germany: 'We live in the great German patriotic hope that the union of Judaism and Germanity, toward which the entire history of German Judaism has tended, should at last be celebrated and should stand forth, as a truth of cultural history, in German life and politics as well as in the sentiments of the German people.' Cohen pointed to Hebraic monotheism as one of the ethical sources of German idealism, transmitted by the Jews. Thus, the deep affinity of Jewish messianism for the humanism of the idealist philosophy lay at the basis of the indestructible union linking the Jews and German destiny. His conclusion resounded like an axiom of liberal-democratic culture, defended by the Jewish intelligentsia of the nine-teenth century: 'As Germans, we want to be Jews, and as Jews, Germans.'[74] Hermann Cohen was only expressing – and sanctioning with his moral authority – the prevailing tendency of the Jewish community.

Martin Buber was not the only Jewish philosopher to criticize Cohen's attitude. The young Franz Rosenzweig, who was opposed to the war and to German nationalism, wrote to his parents: 'Cohen's intellectual Germanity is as shaky as your own social Germanity: both are fictions that can be sustained only through feats of acrobatics.'[75]

## A Crisis of Identity

Nevertheless, there were a few voices strongly contesting the notion that Judeo-German relations were so idyllic. The question was first raised by the Zionists. During the winter of 1911–12, *Selbstwehr,* the journal of the Bar Kochba Zionist student circle of Prague, initiated a debate on the role of Jews in literature, enthusiastically accepting contributions from two non-Jews: the Viennese critic Herman Bahr and the economist Werner Sombart, who stressed the need to distinguish between Jewish and German cultural life, in the mutual interest of both peoples. When Sombart restated his views, a few months later, in *Die Zukunft der Juden* (The future of the Jews), the liberal press reacted sharply. According to Sombart, 'it is pre-cisely this mixture of Jewish and German life, which we witnessed in our time, that has contributed so much to the decline of both races.' As a result, his ardent wish 'for the survival of each of them, [was that] this unnatural paring should once and for all be terminated.'[76] He proposed that the Jews be excluded from public service and from the universities, in his view an essential measure if the national purity of the German universities was to be preserved. Criticized by liberal circles, Sombart found himself supported by the anti-Semites and by the Zionists.

In 1912, a young Berlin Jewish writer, Moritz Goldstein, wrote a 'provocative' essay entitled 'Deutsch-jüdischer Parnass' for *Kunstwart*, a literary review (of a somewhat pan-Germanist complexion). He began by remarking that the Jews all regarded themselves as Germans, while the latter saw them as foreigners. However, he had no difficulty in admitting that German culture was to a large extent a Jewish culture: 'Those of pure Germanic extraction,' he wrote, 'may bristle as much as they like (in an entirely Germanic logical manner), claiming to be the trustees of all that is good and attributing to the Jews everything that is bad: they will never be able to get over the fact that German culture is also, to quite a significant extent, a Jewish culture.' He then attacked the Jews who continued to produce works of 'German culture' without realizing that they were addressing a world that rejected them: 'We Jews,' he wrote, 'are managing the spiritual patrimony of a people that allows us neither the right nor the competency to do so.'[77] Goldstein, therefore, called on the Jews to refrain henceforth from submitting to a nation that did not acknowledge their contribution and urged them to develop the specifically Jewish side of their creativity. His conclusions were perceived as proof of his Zionist orientation. Indeed, it was impossible to imagine such observations being made by a liberal or even a socialistically inclined Jew, supporting the most rigorous form of assimilationism. The young writer's article provoked lively reactions and unleashed a huge debate (*Kunstwart* received no fewer than ninety letters). It is interesting to note that Goldstein's views were supported by Ernst Lissauer and Ferdinand Avenarius (the magazine's editor) who, while recognizing the value and significance of Jewish literature, insisted that it was fundamentally foreign to German national culture. The viewpoint of liberal Jews was expressed by Jakob Loewenberg, who vehemently attacked the idea of returning to a kind of 'neo-Hebraic' literature, when German Jews had fought so hard to obtain a freedom of the city in their effective fatherland [*Vaterland*]. 'Here lie our dead,' he wrote, 'and here is our soul-home [*Heimat*]. We are Germans and wish to remain Germans.'[78]

The debate and polemics provoked by the articles in *Kunstwart* lay behind the correspondence between the young Walter Benjamin and the Zionist poet Ludwig Strauss (they were both students at this time). Benjamin's letters are of interest not only in understanding the intellectual path of a central figure in contemporary German culture, but also because they were symptomatic of the changes with regard to identity and the spiritual life taking place among a new generation of Jewish intellectuals. Acknowledging that he had come of age in an assimilated liberal milieu, where Judaism seemed 'distant' from the religious point of view and 'unknown' from a national point of view, he nevertheless laid greater and greater stress on the specifically Jewish aspects of his existence. 'I am a Jew,' he wrote, 'and as a conscious man, I am a conscious Jew.' This did not prevent him from feeling both Jewish and German and from extolling a 'Zionism of the spirit [*Zionismus des Geistes*],' which had nothing in common with the statist, nationalist views of official Zionist circles. Emigration to Palestine was, to his mind, meaningless for German Jews, who were rooted in Europe, where 'in any case, things would go very badly if their intellectual energies were withdrawn.'[79] These words, in which a path distinct from that of Gershom Scholem's could already be observed, mark the beginning of the discovery and recovery of Jewish identity by a section of young intellectuals who, without rejecting assimilation, refused to embrace it in its patriotic form. Contrary to the great majority of Germans 'of the Mosaic faith,' these radicalized young intellectuals (Benjamin, Scholem, Rosenzweig, Bloch, Lukács, and others) were to be pacifists during World War I.

During these same years, Kafka confided to his diary his distress as an assimilated Jew, cut off from his roots, imbued with a culture that did not belong to him and able to express himself only in a language which he did not feel to be his own. In a celebrated passage of a letter to Max Brod, he described the situation of Prague's Jewish writers in terms of a triple impossibility: 'They existed among three impossibilities, which I just happen to call linguistic impossibilities. It is simplest to call them that. But they might also be called something entirely different. These are: The impossibility of not writing, the impossibility of writing German, the impossibility of writing differently. One might add a fourth impossibility, the impossibility of writing.'[80] Kafka was expressing the anguish of assimilation experienced as a permanent rupture; he appeared to be recording the reality and at the same time the impossibility of a German-Jewish symbiosis. Toward the end of his life, in a letter to Milena Jesenska, he declared himself to be that most

'typical' of Western Jews, to whom nothing was given and who had 'to acquire everything, not only the present and the future, but even the past, of
which every man receives his share gratis.'[81]

In Austria, the phenomenom described by Goldstein was perhaps even
more extreme. Here, political life was dominated by two anti-Semitic parties – the Christian-Socialists of Karl Lueger and the pan-Germanists of
Georg von Schönerer – opposed by a strong workers' movement in which a
very large number of Jews participated, starting with the general secretary
of the Socialist party, Victor Adler, the editor of the *Arbeiterzeitung*, Friedrich Austerlitz, and most of the Austro-Marxist theoreticians (Otto Bauer,
Max Adler, and Rudolf Hilferding), while never appearing openly. Cultural life, on the other hand, as Lueger stressed in the passage quoted above,
was strongly affected by the Jewish presence: the press, publishing, literature, the theater, music, and the arts in general (with the exception of
painting) seemed to be Jewish specialties. The Berlin Jewish writer Jakob
Wassermann, in his memoirs, thus described his impression on arriving in
Vienna for the first time, in 1898: 'I soon realized that the whole of public life
was dominated by the Jews. . . . I was amazed to see such a crowd of Jewish physicians, lawyers, clubmen, snobs, dandies, proletarians, actors, journalists, and poets.'[82] According to the writer Stefan Zweig, nine-tenths of
Viennese culture was 'promoted, nourished, or even created by Viennese
Jewry.'[83] One element which gave these cultural circles a typically Jewish
cast was their exclusion from the official institutions. In view of this mass of
intellectuals and artists, it is striking how very few Jews were on the fac-
ulties of universities, not to speak of in the state bureaucracy, the army, or
parliament, where Jews were either exceedingly rare or nonexistent. As has
often been noted, if Germany and Austria never had a Dreyfus affair, it is
mainly because there was no Captain Dreyfus in these countries, since the
Jews were entirely barred from the officer corps.[84]

Two other minor types of reaction to anti-Semitism and to the aporias of
assimilation should be mentioned. The first was expressed in the rejection
of assimilation itself and the discovery of – or nostalgia for – an authentic
Judeity which had been distorted in the *westjüdische Zeit*, the secularized
Jewish world of the West. This was the fascination with, even idealization
of, the cultural universe of the *Ostjudentum* as seen in the works of Franz
Kafka, Martin Buber, or Joseph Roth, who rediscovered in it vestiges of a

common life that had been lost with assimilation and with entry into the modern world. The origins of this turning, on the part of a section of the intelligentsia, to the religious, mystical, and apocalyptical sources of Judaism can be symbolically traced to the appearance, in 1911, of Buber's pamphlet, *Drei Reden über das Judentum* (Three lectures on Judaism). His point of departure was the assertion of the national, not just religious, character of the Jews, who should no longer define their identity in terms of the gentile world but should rediscover the 'primordial' value of Judeity. He urged the young to absorb the universal message of ancient Judaism thoroughly and to reject the persistent self-deceptiveness of the 'diaspora Jew.'[85] The movement provoked by Buber through his writings and above all through his journal, *Der Jude,* extolled a type of 'cultural Zionism [*Kulturzionismus*]' based on the notion of a spiritual renewal of Judeity. Buber's appeal to the communal roots of Judaism made a very strong impression on young people in the midst of an identity crisis, reeling under the impact of the rising anti-Semitism (particularly widespread among students) and rebelling against the father generation (the assimilated Jewish bourgeoisie, attached to the existing order) from which it had inherited only a 'shadow of Judaism,' as Kafka called it in the celebrated letter to his father. But, in spite of everything, assimilation remained the point of departure for this cultural anamnesis, which tried to reappropriate Judaism through the filter of the German language and culture. The case of Nathan Birnbaum, whose rejection of assimilation and whose return to roots took an extreme form, even involving the abandonment of the German language in favor of an exclusively Yiddish literary idiom, was in fact rather exceptional.[86]

The second reaction, a quite different one, consisted in rejecting assimilation in the name of a Jewish nationalism which copied all the traits of the *völkkish* ideology. This was the Zionism of the German supporters of Vladimir Jabotinski, who laid claim to Palestine on behalf of a Jewish nation defined in terms of race and blood. It would probably be an exaggeration to classify as *völkisch* Zionism the thought of the Austrian doctor Ignaz Zollschan, who in 1910 published a sensationalist work on the 'theoretical foundations of the question of Jewish race.' Zollschan would not divide humanity into superior and inferior races, but his definition of Judeity was based on strictly biological criteria and was frankly influenced by the theories of Gobineau and Houston Stewart Chamberlain. His study reached the conclusion that, 'without Zionism,' Jews would inevitably be faced with this alternative: 'Either dissolution of the race or its physical degeneration.'[87]

Without going to such extremes, certain categories of *völkisch* thought were broadly taken up by many Zionist intellectuals, as for instance Buber, who defined the Jews as 'a community of blood . . . the deepest, most potent stratum of our being.'[88] Nevertheless, this language, so surprising today, signified for him an essentially cultural strategy which – contrary to volkism and a certain German kind of Zionism – led inevitably to a reactionary or racist political standpoint (but rather, in the case of Palestine, to a policy of peace and cooperation with the Arab nation). In short, if assimilation remained the dominant ideology, in most cases in the political form of liberalism, it was now affected by new currents which revealed its contradictions: Zionism, universalism, socialist internationalism, cosmopolitanism, the fascination with *Yiddishkeit*. The Jewish culture of Central Europe was henceforth characterized by a very great richness and by a plurality of tendencies.

### The Turning Point of Weimar

The Weimar Republic marked a new stage in the integration of the Jews into German society and, at the same time, set the scene for a very sharp rise in anti-Semitism. With the establishment of new institutions, certain discriminatory practices continued by the Wilhelminian Empire were abandoned. The Jews, who had demonstrated their patriotism during the war, seemed finally to have gained a legitimate place for themselves in the nation. On the other hand, the postwar reality was to put an end to these illusions, since the Jews became scapegoats for all the contradictions and all the problems afflicting a defeated Germany. After the Russian Revolution, the Spartacist revolt in Berlin and the shortlived Bavarian Soviet Republic (in all of which a large number of prominent Jews, from Paul Levi to Rosa Luxemburg, from Kurt Eisner to Gustav Landauer, from Ernst Toller to Eugen Leviné, were represented) the myth of *Verjudung* was replaced by the hunt for 'Judeo-Bolsheviks.' The Jews were held responsible for, and to have profiteered from, the defeat. The institutions established in Weimar were despised as symbols of a Germany transformed into a *'Judenrepublic'* and, in 1923, at the time of the great inflation, the nationalist right launched a violent anti-Semitic campaign against 'parasitic capitalism,' making use of the old stereotypes of the Jew as speculator and monopolist. Anti-Semitism consolidated its base in the parties of the center, the literary circles, and the academic world. It took over the associations of employees, farmers, and above all students (the widescale *Wandervogel* movement excluded Jews from the start of World War I and, in the postwar period, was rapidly Nazi-fied). The Christian Zentrum refrained altogether from denouncing anti-Semitism and the Deutsch-National party excluded Jews from its ranks. In the chaos of the first half of the twenties, the proliferation of paramilitary groups of the extreme right gave anti-Semitism a militant base which it had not possessed before the war.

To form an idea of the climate that prevailed at the end of the war, one need only recall the significant spread of anti-Semitic literature. In 1922, only five years after its appearance, the semipornographic and crudely anti-Semitic novel *Die Sünde wider das Blut* (Sins against the blood) by the na-tionalist writer Artur Dinter, who warned the German population of the monstrous consequences of mixing German and Jewish blood, had sold 200,000 copies and reached about one and a half million readers. Another significant example is the success of the science-fiction novel *Deutsch-land ohne Deutsche* (Germany without Germans), written in 1929 by Hans Heyck. He predicted a state of total decay and dissolution in which his country would find itself by the year 2050, when the 'racial mixture [*Ras-senvermischung*]' would have imposed a ruling caste of 'mongrel despots,' each day devoting themselves to the violation of young white girls, and tra-ditional German values would have been overwhelmed by a *Völkerchaos* of a 'Judeo-oriental' and 'American-negro' character. Fortunately, a last nu-cleus of 2,500 pure Aryans would have taken refuge in the Nordic regions of the Scandinavian countries, establishing there a 'colony of fair-haired peo-ple,' the embryo of a renaissance of the 'Aryan race' destined to reconquer and renew their fallen *Heimat*.[89] These works by Dinter and Heyck are just two examples, among others, of an anti-Semitic literature in full bloom.

The war had plunged Germany into chaos and the Jews were seen as profiting from this national catastrophe. During the entire first half of the twenties, anti-Semitic writers and critics like Theodor Fritsch, Hans Blücher, and Adolf Bartel, forgotten today but very influential in their time, depicted the literary and artistic scene of the new state as being entirely dominated by Jews. The establishment of the republic was described as a

*Secessio judaica*. In 1930, Ernst Jünger called on the Jews to stop dissembling, no longer to pass themselves off as Germans, and openly to acknowledge their Judeity. To pretend to be at the same time Jews and Germans was, in his opinion, sheer 'nonsense [*Wahn*].'[90]

Under the Weimar Republic, the Jewish intelligentsia shifted to the left and the Zionists made significant progress (even if it was only from the thirties that their influence grew substantially, in view of the rise of national socialism), but assimilation remained the principal objective. Rabbi Benno Jacob, one of the deputies of the Zentraverein, declared in 1919 that, since the new German state was neither 'clerical [*Kirchenstaat*]' nor 'racial [*Rassenstaat*],' the Jews could find their place in it as fully paid-up Germans: 'Germanity is to be found in the soul and not in the blood [*Deutschum liegt im Gemüte, nicht in Geblüte*]. . . . We Jews of Germany are and remain Jews by religion, German by nationality.'[91] The philosopher Franz Rosenzweig wrote, in 1923, that Judaism had helped him to become a 'good' and not a 'bad' German.[92] The theme of a 'Judeo-German symbiosis' lay at the heart of Jakob Loewenberg's autobiographical novel *Die Zwei Quellen* (1925): 'The two sources [in question] are Judeity and Germanity. It is from these that I have drawn my feelings and my thought. I have never felt any discord in myself between the Jew and the German. The reason may be tempted to separate them, but feeling — and in this domain that is what counts — rediscovers them as united. If ever I had grounds for pride, it would be the pride of being at the same time Jewish and German.'[93]

For intellectuals of the revolutionary Left, belonging to German culture was anchored in universalistic expectations that rejected the patriotic and nationalist tendencies of the members of the Zentraverein. Ernst Toller, in his autobiography, written in 1933, defined Germany as 'the country where I was raised, the air I breathe, the language I speak, the spirit that has formed me.' At the same time, he regarded himself as a citizen of the world: 'If someone had asked me to whom I belong, I should have replied: a Jewish mother brought me into the world, Germany nourished me, Europe formed me, my home [*Heimat*] is the Earth, the world is my country [*Vaterland*].'[94] For Jewish writers and critics of a nonconformist and pacifist disposition, for leftist Socialists or sympathizers of the Communist party who gathered around the magazine *Die Weltbühne*, assimilation did not imply concurring with a Germany conceived of in patriotic terms, but rather identification with a universal, democratic, progressive culture. What today we call the 'culture of Weimar' was, in reality, despite its richness, its lustre, and its legacy, a minority phenomenon within German society, where all the cultural institutions — starting with the universities — were bastions of conservative thought, entirely under the control of those nostalgic for the Wilheminian Empire or, at best, of *Vernunftrepublikaner*. As Peter Gay put it, the culture of Weimar was a laboratory, bubbling over with innovations, created by a stratum of *outsiders,* which achieved its goal 'in its true home: exile.'[95] It is clear that Jewish intellectuals and artists took their natural place in this 'dance along the edge of the abyss,' which absorbed every new experiment in literature, the theater, music, and the plastic arts. In this sense, the culture of Weimar was the locus for a genuine alliance of Jews and Germans, whose common ground was a rebellion, sometimes against tradition, sometimes against modernity, order, and bourgeois institutions. As in the period of the Jewish salons of Berlin, in the beginning of the nineteenth century, it required the marginalization of an entire section of German cultural life, dislocated and shaken by the war, for this encounter to take place. Soon, the culture of Weimar, as a whole, was to be ejected from Germany.

### Judeo-German Symbiosis or Jewish Monologue?

Judeo-German culture, thus, appeared as a fragmented universe, torn by conflict and divided into a number of distinct constellations. At opposite ends, radically opposed and utterly irreconcilable, were *Jewish orthodoxy* and *atheism.* The former, increasingly of minority appeal after emancipation, survived evidently thanks to the efforts of a minority hostile to the secularization of Jewish religious life and practice. On the theological level, its most important representative was Rabbi Samson-Raphael Hirsch, the author of *The Nineteen Epistles on Judaism* (1836), whose exegetical work was not continued into the twentieth century. Atheists, indifferent, even hostile to their religious and cultural roots, began to appear in the nineteenth century (Karl Marx) and increasingly at the beginning of the following century (Georg Simmel, Georg Lukács, Karl Kraus, Egon Erwin Kisch, Otto Bauer, Victor Adler, Karl Mannheim, Kurt Tucholsky, then Herbert Marcuse, and, at least until World War II, Max Horkheimer and Theodor W. Adorno). Destined to occupy an avant-garde role in culture and proud of their nonconformism, they represented a particularly conspicuous minority, but would no doubt have been unwilling to acknowledge the slightest Jewish element in their *outsider* cultural marginality. Between these two poles was a mass of intellectuals who regarded their German-Jewish *dual identity* as a mission to be accomplished and as a value to be preserved within German or Austrian society. In the field of politics, they could identify, as much with the Left (Heinrich Heine in the last century, then Gustav Landauer, Ernst Toller, Walter Benjamin, Ernst Bloch, Lion Feuchtwanger, Erich Mühsam, Alfred Döblin, Manes Sperber) as with a more conformist, liberal-progressive position (Stefan Zweig, Arthur Schnitzler, Jakob Wassermann) or with those more conservative (Hermann Cohen, Leo Baeck). Attachment to Germany often led to genuine forms of *pan-Germanism:* sometimes, again, indifferent or hostile to Judeity (the young Walther Rathenau, Ernst Kantorowicz, Josef Bloch, Maximilian Harden); sometimes, in its most grotesque and paradoxical versions, basically Jewish (Hans Joachim Schoeps and Max Neumann). The *Zionists,* for their part, were divided between pan-Germanists (Theodor Herzl, Max Nordau, Kurt Blumefeld), Judeo-German 'cultural-Zionists' (Martin Buber), spiritual Zionists who tended to see Judeity and Germanity as opposed (Gershom Scholem), or those who were more inclined toward socialism (Arnold Zweig). For some, Zionism was supposed to promote an internal renaissance of *Deutsch-judentum,* whereas for others this return to the spiritual sources of Judaism could take place only in Palestine.

Beside these main groups, there were also numerous unclassifiable but extremely important figures who were representative in their own way: the rootless 'wandering Jews' (Hannah Arendt, Joseph Roth); Jews who related to Germanity only insofar as they employed the German language (Sigmund Freud); those who saw assimilation as an unavoidable curse (Franz Kafka, Nathan Birnbaum); those for whom Judeity itself was a curse, even a guilty verdict against which there could be no appeal (the young Rahel Levin-Varnhagen, followed somewhat differently by Gerson Bleichröder, and finally Otto Weininger); or again those who might be called the 'Jews of return,' who had reclaimed their Jewish identity essentially because of anti-Semitism (this list must again be headed by Rahel Levin-Varnhagen, who was followed, a century later, by Arnold Schönberg, Hans Mayer, Elias Canetti, Jean Améry, Norbert Elias, Karl Löwith), if not as a result of a genuine cultural, even philosophical process of *dissimilation* (Franz Rosenzweig).[96]

## The 'Judeo-German Symbiosis'

The fact remains that, for the great majority of these intellectuals, the 'Judeo-German symbiosis' was not an end to be realized but a reality. And yet, the overriding need they felt to keep insisting on the fact that they belonged to Germany shows that this identity was not self-evident and posed a problem. Goethe and Thomas Mann belonged unquestionably to German culture, so that the case did not have constantly to be made. As Isaïah Berlin has shown, the ardor with which Jewish intellectuals and artists identified with German tradition was often 'the result of an inadequate sense of kinship, and a desire to have the rift forgotten; since the more insurmountable it was, the greater was the desire to overcome it, or to behave as though it did not exist.'[97] Moritz Goldstein was not mistaken when he compared the complex relations of the Jews with Germany to the sufferings of unrequited love. This one-sided love was to give rise to a golden age of culture that Fredric Grunfeld has compared to the Italian Renaissance,[98] but which took place exclusively within the Jewish world. In other words, this 'symbiosis' was due much more to the appropriation and transformation of the German *Geist* by Jewish culture than to the convergence of two cultural traditions. It would be tempting to see this dialogue as symbolically personified by a few remarkable individuals, as the Berlin German-Israelite Association tried to do in 1879 when it published a *Lessing-Mendelssohn-Gedenkbuch*, in celebration of the hundredth anniversary of the first production of *Nathan the Wise*.[99] Apart from the *Aufklärung*, one might recall the friendship and collaboration of Frederich G. Hegel and Eduard Gans, of Karl Marx and Friedrich Engels, of Walter Benjamin and Bertold Brecht, of Hannah Arendt and Karl Jaspers, of John Heartfield (Helmut Herzfelde) and George Grosz; or again, the German-Jewish 'alliance' which distinguished one of the principal magazines of the Weimar Republic, *Die Weltbühne*, under Karl von Ossietzky's editorship. But, in most cases, the role of Judeity was quite marginal. In the multivolume Marx-Engels correspondence, the Jewish question hardly comes up at all, unless it be in the form of a few nicknames in poor taste applied to Ferdinand Lassalle. As for relations between Benjamin and Brecht, the latter's commentaries on the *Theses on the Philosophy of History* are well known; Benjamin's references to Jewish messianism seemed to Brecht 'a load of mysticism'[100] and utterly incomprehensible. Finally, reflexions on the Jewish question certainly occupy an important place in the Arendt-Jaspers correspondence, but only after World War

II and the shattering effect of Auschwitz. The influence of certain assimilated Jewish intellectuals like Marx or Freud on the culture of their contemporaries was unquestionably very great, thanks mainly to the universality of their message which, in the eyes of most people, eclipsed their Judeity.

Leaving aside a voluminous anti-Semitic literature, German intellectuals never showed any real interest in confronting the Jewish tradition. Among the exceptions which prove the rule, one might mention Max Weber, who carried out some important research into Judaism in connection with his work on the sociology of religion (*Ancient Judaism*), and Thomas Mann, who from 1933 wrote a tetralogy inspired by the biblical figure of Joseph (*Joseph and his Brothers*). While never more than marginal in its influence, a genuine German-Jewish encounter did take place, in the form of a *Judeo-Christian dialogue*, traces of which appear in the correspondence, beginning in Leipzig in 1913 and continuing during the war, between Franz Rosenzweig and the converted Jew Eugen Rosenstock;[101] in the animated discussions that took place in the League of Religious Socialists, between Carl Mennicke, Eduard Heimann, and Paul Tillich; in the magazine *Die Kreatur*, coedited between 1926 and 1930 by Martin Buber and the Christian theologians Joseph Wittig and Viktor von Weizsäcker;[102] finally, in the correspondence between Walter Benjamin and the Swiss Christian Socialist Fritz Lieb.[103] A case apart was that of Nietzsche, who was deeply conscious of the importance of Judaism in the evolution of Western civilization but who, at the same time, could not free himself from the anti-Semitic stereotypes of his period. Thus, in his writings, Jews appear sometimes as bankers with crooked noses, sometimes as people whose mission it was to transmit the values and spirit of ancient Greece to modern Europe.[104]

From the cultural point of view, the 'Judeo-German symbiosis' was in reality a gigantic explosion of Jewish creativity, originating in the encounter between a millenial tradition – a 'hidden tradition,' always marginalized and persecuted – and the German *Geist*. The German language had been the vehicle for this metamorphosis of the secularized Jewish universe. From the sociological point of view, the process of acculturation found its object in a Jewish intelligentsia that at one time discovered in Germany a substitute for its lost historical identity, and at another, the mirage of a new, undiscoverable identity. An intelligentsia that was a 'pariah' in a dual sense: on account of a past that it embodied, and the exclusion from society which it continued to suffer from in ever new forms. This synthesis between Judeity and Germanity seemed doomed to failure, insofar as the Jews were always seen as a foreign body within the nation-state. Rejected by Germany, which they insisted on regarding as their *Vaterland*, they were nevertheless able to find in the German language a *Heimat* with which they might fully identify. Judeity, thus, became one of the components of the cosmopolitan and supra-national spirit of that *Mitteleuropa*, conceived as a unified cultural space that transcended state boundaries, extending from Berlin to Prague, from Vienna to Budapest. A product of the *Aufklärung* and rendered possible by the emancipation, German-Jewish culture was accompanied along the way by the increasingly invasive and threatening shadow of anti-Semitism. Urged to dissolve into the nation, Judeity was obliged constantly to redefine itself, reacting to the surrounding anti-Semitism, only to be utterly annihilated in the end. Where discrimination was put aside and the Jews were fully accepted, as for instance in the socialist movement, it was at the cost of renouncing a specific identity. Since class war admitted no racial or religious distinctions, the Jews could take part in it in exchange for this repudiation.

Nazism shattered the belief that the future of Judeity was tied to that of Germany. Many proponents of assimilationism, such as the president of the Berlin Fine Arts Academy, Max Liebermann, announced that they had finally awoken from the 'dream of assimilation,'[105] but the prevailing attitude was still that of Rabbi Leo Baeck, who reaffirmed his belief that his place was in Germany: 'As long as there is a single Jew, I shall stay with him.' In 1933, the Jews who were leaving were mainly leftist intellectuals and militant Socialists or Communists. The specifically Jewish emigration increased in 1935, following the Nuremberg Laws, and reached a substantial size in 1938, after *Kristallnacht* and the Austrian *Anschluss*. Often, Jews left in the hope of returning as soon as the situation returned to normal. Hitler seemed to them an unfortunate, but finally ephemeral, footnote to German history.

German-Jewish culture was, thus, preserved, outside Germany, by exiled Jewish intellectuals. While their works were burned in National Socialist autos-da-fé, they did their utmost to publish magazines in emigration. For the leaders of the Frankfurt school, in American exile, the publication of a German-language magazine was regarded as a sort of duty, a pledge of faith in a tradition that had been destroyed, testifying to their will to resist the perversion of German culture by nazism.[106] Toward the end of 1936, Walter Benjamin published a small book in Zurich, *Deutsche Menschen*, which he had conceived of as 'an ark' to save the humanistic tradition and German culture from the Nazi flood.[107] In 1944, Elias Canetti insisted on his own need to write in German so as to preserve the memory of a shattered community and culture, as well as to repay an intellectual debt to the world, now defunct, that had formed him. 'The language of my intellect,' he wrote, 'will remain German — because I am Jewish. Whatever remains of the land which has been laid waste in every way — I wish to preserve it in me as a Jew. *Their* destiny too is mine; but I bring along a universal human legacy. I want to give back to their language what I owe it. I want to contribute to their having something that others can be grateful for.'[108] The history of Judeo-German culture ended in exile, where some of its greatest works were produced: Norbert Elias published *Über den Prozess der Zivilisation* in Bâle, in 1939; Walter Benjamin wrote his *Theses on the Philosophy of History* in Paris, in 1940; Ernst Bloch drafted *The Principle of Hope* in New York, during World War II; Max Horkheimer and Theodor W. Adorno published *The Dialectic of Reason* in 1947, while they were still in the United States, and so on. In the postwar period, various thinkers who had emerged in the pre-1933 German-speaking intelligentsia came to maturity. Outside this context, it would be hard to appreciate the sociological works of Hannah Arendt, Norbert Elias, Erich Fromm, Lucien Goldmann, and Siegfried Kracauer; the philosophical reflections of Ernst Bloch, Leo Löwenthal, Herbert Marcuse, and other representatives of the Frankfurt school; the historical works of George L. Mosse, Peter Gay, or Jacob Katz; the literary oeuvre of Elias Canetti, Paul Celan, and Manès Sperber; the psychoanalysis of Bruno Bettelheim or even the quite unique intellectual path followed by a historian of the Cabbala like Gershom Scholem.

In 1838, Heinrich Heine was stressing the 'elective affinity [*Wahlverwandschaft*]' linking two 'ethical nations' like the Jews and the Germans, whose union would have created a new cultural universe in Europe. Germany was to transform itself into a sort of 'fatherland of literature [*des heiligen Wortes*], the mother country of prophecy and the citadel of pure spirit.'[109] A century later, this cultural universe had become a reality but had already come to the end of its fragile existence in a Central Europe fallen under Hitler's domination. The finality of the rupture caused by national socialism is crudely revealed in the words of Carl Schmitt, the theorist of the totalitarian state who saw the alliance between the Jews and liberalism as the cause of Germany's decline, 'we need to liberate the German spirit from all Jewish falsifications, falsifications of the concept of spirit.'[110] From March 1933, a large announcement was hung up in the German universities declaring that henceforth any work by a Jewish author published in German would carry the words: 'translation from the Hebrew.'[111] The Nuremberg Laws marked the end of the 'Judeo-German symbiosis.' That the Jews were alien to the 'Aryan race' was embodied in utterly unambiguous legislation, aiming to maximize the definition of *Jude*. This legislation was not limited to distinguishing Germans from 'non-Aryans,' but also took into account all forms of crossbreeding as represented by 'half Jews [*Mischlinge*]' of the first and second degree, through the strictest regulation of marriage between the different categories. The literary critic Jean Améry (Hans Mayer) 'discovered' his Judeity when he read an article on the Nuremberg Laws in a newspaper in a Viennese café, in 1935, and realized that these laws might apply to him as well. Up till then he had never considered himself to be Jewish, but for the Nazi state, which was universally recognized as the legitimate representative of the German people, he was none other than 'a Jew,' 'formally' and 'beyond doubt.'[112] In 1938, Ludwig Wittgenstein, whose parents had given up Judaism and who received no religious education, wrote to John Maynard Keynes that, since the Austrian *Anschluss*, the laws of the Third Reich had 'transformed [him] into a German Jew.'[113]

### 'We Are Forced to Remain Strangers'

In 1839, the writer Oskar Panizza, one of most acute and irreverent of Wilhelminian German critics, published a satirical story entitled *Der operierte Jud* (The Operated Jew), a kind of fable on assimilation. In it he narrated the story of Itzig Faitel Stern, an East European Jew of irredeemably 'Semitic' appearance who spoke German with a strong Yiddish accent, and who decided to have himself operated on so as to acquire a more 'Aryan' look, thereby gaining respectability and achieving success in German society, his chosen milieu. The operation seemed to have been a success and Itzig, who now looked like a true 'Aryan,' after much effort gained access to the privileged lifestyle of the German elite, while his charm enabled him to win the heart of Othilia, a girl of solid German stock. Unfortunately, on the day of their wedding Itzig allowed himself to be carried away by his success. He overindulged and, in a drunken stupor, fell at the feet of his hosts, in particular of the illustrious surgeon who had operated on him. The transformation had been illusory; he was no more than an 'Asiatic figure in a dress coat, a simple piece of deceitful human flesh, Itzig Faitel Stern.' In this humorous portrait of a self-hating Jew who wanted so much to be transformed into a German that he allowed himself to be operated on, Panizza was expressing total skepticism with regard to assimilation, which seemed to him to be sheer illusion. Several years later, at the start of the Weimar Republic, the philosopher Salomo Friedländer, under the pseudonym Mynona (i.e., anonymous), wrote a parodic reply entitled *Der operierte Goj*, in which the noble Baron von Reschok, whose appearance could not have been more 'Aryan,' scion of a Prussian family with a strong anti-Semitic tradition, fell in love with a Jewish girl, became a 'rabid' Zionist, and settled down in Jerusalem, changing his name to that of Moische Koscher (*Reschok* backwards). The historian Jack Ziper has emphasized the paradigmatic nature of these two stories in which, as in a mirror, were reflected the complex and contradictory relations between Jews and Germans, based more on these transformative kinds of operation than on straightforward, honest collaboration.[114] This conclusion is certainly born out, provided one adds that the transformation undergone by an Itzig Feitel Stern was a far more frequent occurrence than that of a Baron von Reschok/Moishe Koscher, a figure whose very unlikeliness made him even more irresistibly comic.

The disappearance of the ghettos, the granting of civil rights to Jews, their entry into society, and their adoption of the German language gave rise to a German-Jewish culture, which, however, was never the result of a genuine symbiosis. Instead of inaugurating a dialogue between Jews and Germans, assimilation led immediately to a *Jewish monologue,* which took place in the Germanic world, was expressed in the German language, and was nourished by the German cultural legacy, but which, in fact, was carried on in a void. True symbiosis presupposed a pluralistic society, capable of acknowledging the Jewish *tradition* as well as Jewish *otherness*. The *Aufklärung* and emancipation, however, had prepared Germany only to assimilate the Jews, not to welcome their tradition and incorporate their culture, in all its specificity. The Jews, thus, remained *outsiders* in the Germanic world. The rise of anti-Semitism crystallized Jewish otherness, surrounding it with negative connotations. *Gemeinschaftsfremde,* they were a negative pole with the help of which German national identity could define itself. In Germany, as in Italy, as distinct from in France, emancipation had not followed, but rather coincided with, the process of national unification. The result, however, was different: if in Italy, as Momigliano and Gramsci had noted, assimilation was almost complete, so that the Jews became Italians on the same terms as the Sardis, Lombards, or Venetians,[115] in Germany the formation of a national consciousness tended to set Judeity and Germanity in opposition as representing antithetical and incompatible values.

The clearest evaluation of the failure and impossibility of a 'Judeo-German symbiosis' was made by Franz Rosenzweig, who in a few words summarized a century of Judeity in German culture: 'It is impossible for us to remain strangers,' he wrote,

detached from the intellectual and spiritual life of those peoples who permit us to share in it, detached also in our innermost being from what we are trying to contribute, by way of compensation for having been permitted to take part in it. What we receive, as Jews we have no right to receive; what we accomplish, we ought not to as Jews. And yet, unity of spirit compels us to establish what are of necessity specific relations between our Judaism and that which we receive or achieve; and even if our actions were submitted to the judgment of the peoples, even if they felt obliged to tell us whether they accepted or rejected them, their jurisdiction would extend no further; we are the sole judges of any attempt to understand the world on the basis of Judaism itself.[116]

# CHAPTER TWO

# The Jew as Pariah

*The* Pariavolk *in German Sociology: Max Weber*

THE DEFINITION of the Jews as a 'pariah people' crops up in nineteenth-century sociology and economics, especially in Germany where the concept became typical of the liberal outlook.[1] In 1823, the Berlin theaters were staging a play by the scenographer Michael Beer entitled *Der Paria*, in which the sufferings of Jews in a society that persistently denied them full civil rights was evoked through the allegory of a Hindu, Gandhi, excluded by the caste system. He addressed God in these terms: 'Why is your eternal hatred directed against this unfortunate race that gave birth to me?' Goethe saw in Beer's play a symbol for 'the degraded, oppressed and despised strata of humanity,' which made his hero supremely 'human and poetic.'[2] For Heinrich Heine, inspired by Beer's work, the pariah was the very image of the 'oppressed' and the voice of 'suffering humanity, whose soul utters a shout that reaches our very hearts.'[3] Appearing regularly in the works of numerous writers, this figure was systematized and theorized by three thinkers during the first half of this century: Max Weber, Bernard Lazare, and Hannah Arendt. If for the former its significance is largely economic, for the other two it embodies the existential condition of the Jew in the modern world.

Max Weber's first reference to the Jews as a 'pariah people' (*Pariavolk*) can be found in his 1904–05 studies on *The Protestant Ethic and the Spirit of Capitalism*. He regarded them as representatives of an 'adventurist capitalism' or rather of a '*Paria-Kapitalismus,*' unproductive and tending toward speculation, bereft of the rationalistic Puritan *ethos* that was capable of adapting itself to modern industrial production.[4] In successive works, like *Ancient Judaism* (1917) and *Economy and Society* (1920), the concept of pariah was applied to the diasporic condition of the Jews in antiquity and in the Middle Ages. According to the Heidelberg sociologist, they differed from Indian pariahs, forming a caste in a society that had no caste system. Weber wrote: 'Sociologically speaking, the Jews were a pariah people, which means, as we know from India, that they were a guest people [*Gast-volk*] who were ritually separated, formally or *de facto*, from their social surroundings.'[5]

In *Economy and Society*, he listed a series of traits that distinguished the Jewish pariahs: (a) they did not possess citizenship and remained everywhere foreigners (which marked them off radically from Christians involved in pawnbroking, as for instance the Lombards or the Cadurciens); (b) they lived in the interstices between the nations, without ever being concentrated in a single territory; (c) their separation vis-à-vis other peoples was 'ritualistic' in nature, since it was not imposed on them but voluntarily adopted for religious reasons; (d) they were not peasants and formed essentially urban communities; (e) they practiced a 'double morality,' one within the community and the other governing their relations with the outside world, which allowed them to act as intermediaries between different social classes and economic bodies (they could thus administer the finances of several states, etc.) while continuing to preserve their group identity; (f) they displayed a very strong tendency toward endogamy. All these elements made of the Jews a kind of economic 'caste' identified with a religion; in short, a 'pariah people' leading a life strictly apart within the Christian societies. According to Weber, Jewish traditionalism as embodied in the Talmud was basically reluctant to accept any kind of economic innovation and was partly responsible for cornering the Jews in a premodern economic situation. However, he modified this position when he drew attention to a highly significant contribution of Judaism to the rational economic outlook of the West: its hostility with regard to magic. This seemed to him the Jewish religion's sole contribution to modern capitalism.[6] The 'pariah people' described by Weber related therefore to the period preceding emancipation, but, as he made it clear, the emancipated Jews retained certain 'negative privileges' of the pariah peoples; namely, exclusion from a whole series of professions, officialdom, the army, as well as German academia, which he himself regretted with regard to some of his students.[7]

Another element that distinguished pariah Judaism from its Hindu counterpart was the messianism that impelled the Jews to rebel against existing injustices. In contrast to the Indian pariah, who accepts his condition of exclusion as a natural and immutable law, to such an extent that his major characteristic is submissiveness in the expectation of redemption through metempsychosis, the Jew is always haunted by the hope of messianic deliverance that will put an end to his earthly sufferings and reestablish an elemental harmony in which he will once again find dignity and justice.

In the context of German sociology, Georg Simmel preferred the notion of 'foreigner [*Fremde*]' to that of 'pariah' as a way of explaining the exclusion of Jews and their marginality. To the rootlessness, mobility, and predisposition to commercial activities that characterized their economic situation, he added certain basic psychological traits, such as lack of prejudice, considerable open-mindedness, extreme vulnerability due to their precarious social status, etc. In his opinion, Jews classically exemplified the *foreigner* in European history.[8] As we shall see, these latter characteristics are at the heart of successive definitions of the pariah.

Several decades later, the concept was to be taken up again, from a radically different point of view, by Hannah Arendt: it was to be applied now to the condition of the Jews in the modern world, after emancipation. Furthermore, in Hannah Arendt's thought, the concept of pariah seemed to lose its economic significance and to gain essentially political and spiritual connotations. While recognizing the Weberian origin of the idea of the pariah in the social sciences, she stressed the importance of the legacy of Bernard Lazare, who had developed his own vision of the pariah Jew at the turn of the century (in all probability, quite independently of the contemporary elaborations of German sociology).

### The 'Pride in Being a Pariah': Bernard Lazare

The description of the Jews as a pariah people can already be found in *L'antisémitisme, son histoire et ses causes,* written by Bernard Lazare in 1893. Here, the concept of pariah did not yet occupy a central place: the word simply served to emphasize the oppressive conditions suffered by Jews. It is nevertheless interesting to note that Bernard Lazare was inclined to associate the pariah with a revolutionary tradition. All his work – he was later to claim that it did not, in fact, represent his last word on the subject, since he was still affected by traces of a native anti-Semitism of which he was only just beginning to rid himself – revolved around the division of Judaism into two distinct and different branches: on the one hand, that of illuminati, initiated by the theophanies and continuing through the 'mystical musings of the Cabbala' up to Spinoza; on the other, a positivist and rationalist current, crystallized into dogma by rabbinical law and in the final analysis manifesting itself in commerce, greed, the mercantile spirit, and the urge to acquire wealth. The latter lay at the root of the stereotype of the Jewish 'man of money,' usurer and capitalist. Contrary to Weber, who regarded the Talmud as a collection of obscurantist and irrational doctrines, Lazare concluded that the calculating spirit of the Jewish people was not rooted in the Hebrew religion but was rather a consequence of the Protestant Reformation.[9] However, the pariah tradition seemed to him quite assimilable with the first current of Judaism, since it belonged not to the 'Jews of money' but to the excluded and persecuted. According to Lazare, the isolation brought about by the religious exclusivism of the Jews enabled them to survive 'up to modern times, as a race of pariahs, persecuted, often martyred.'[10] But the pariah was still seen as the traditional Jew, unemancipated and living in his ghetto. In modern times, after he had freed himself from the reactionary and conservative ideological yoke of rabbinical orthodoxy, the Jew ceased to be a pariah and became a revolutionary. 'The emancipated Jew,' he wrote, 'being no longer bound by the faith of his ancestors, and owning no ties with the old forms of a society in the midst of which he had lived as outcast, has become in modern nations a veritable breeder of revolutions.'[11] The pariah, thus, prepared the ground for the revolutionary, though the two did not merge: the former gave way to the latter.

In *Le fumier de Job* (Job's manure), a work that remained uncompleted and that was published posthumously in 1928, Bernard Lazare's thought underwent a profound transformation. The pariah now symbolized the Jewish condition in history, before and after emancipation. Reversing the negative image of the Jew cultivated by the anti-Semites, Lazare no longer saw the pariah just as one of history's vanquished, but also as the bearer of a 'hidden' tradition, sustained by pride and the nobility of the persecuted. 'The pride in being a pariah,' he wrote, 'and particularly the pariah that the Jew is, from whom the master of the world is made. What pleasure it is to create something noble out of his disgrace, something regal from his debasement. You, Schlomo, pitiful brother toiling away in Brody, in your stinking cellar, did you know that you ruled the universe? Did you know it was your hidden will, your well hidden will, that moved the secret springs of empire, your very own will, wretched Schlomo, you who eat but four times a week?'[12]

Alongside the pariah, emancipation created a new figure in Judeity: the *parvenu*, one who, under the illusion that he might be admitted into the ranks of the ruling classes, rejects his identity, his tradition, and his history. He was to renounce pride and the pariah's spirit of revolt, only to suffer the humiliation and contempt that the well-to-do reserve for those who are not of their kind. The parvenu condition was that of Jews who had rejected their people, yet without becoming Christians; having lost what might have united them as human beings, they now lived separate lives, 'egotists incapable of solidarity.' A product of assimilation, the parvenu Jew found it painful 'to be reminded of his origins'; he was 'ashamed' but tragically for him could not escape 'his race, no matter what vile deed he commited to make the Christian riff-raff forget it.'[13] In 1897, in an article, Lazare deployed all of his caustic humor to sketch a portrait of the parvenu Jew: 'Rich Jews lick the hand that strikes them, they prostrate themselves before those who trample on them, they kneel before those who insult them. . . . They are the ones who stand in the way of all efforts of self-defence; their degradation, their cowardice is such that it invites the justified disgust of their enemies, that it has sickened the entire Jewish soul.'[14]

The Jews, therefore, were not to renounce their identity but to accept with dignity their pariah condition. In other words, they were to become 'conscious pariahs' and to fight for their freedom. This attitude brought Bernard Lazare closer to Zionism and to what he called 'Jewish nationalism.' But his conception of Zionism was poles apart from the political movement created by Theodor Herzl, to which he belonged for a very short time. He soon realized that the differences separating them were radical ones. In his view, Zionism should not be a colonial enterprise aiming at the establishment of a state but rather the means of conferring national dignity on a persecuted people. It was not a matter of making the Jewish people appear 'respectable,' with its own state, vis-à-vis the European powers, but of assembling and urging the pariah Jews to rebel against the bourgeois order that excluded and despised them. The letter in which he dissociated himself from Theodor Herzl is famous: 'You are of the bourgeoisie of ideas, the bourgeoisie of feeling, the bourgeoisie of thought, the bourgeoisie of social concepts. As such, you are trying to guide a people, our people, which is composed of the poor, the downtrodden, the proletarians.'[15]

It is remarkable that the author of this eulogy of the pariah had begun his career as a critic and journalist by defending the French *israelite* against the Ashkenazi 'Jew,' to the extent of opposing the immigration of *Ostjuden* into France.[16] Three factors doubtless account for this intellectual and political metamorphosis. First the Dreyfus Affair, Bernard Lazare being the Captain's primary champion, which made him aware of the Jewish lot and the traps of emancipation. As he was to write during the trial, Captain Dreyfus for him became 'the symbol of the Jew' and, 'from one day to the next,' he himself felt he had become 'a pariah.'[17] At the same time, the Dreyfus Affair made him aware of the strength of anti-Semitism and of its reactionary nature. If in his work of 1893, which appeared just before the Dreyfus Affair exploded, anti-Jewish prejudice seemed to him an essentially ideological and literary phenomenon, he now understood the full destructive potential of anti-Semitism as a mass social and political movement. Finally, his involvement in the defence of the captain who was being persecuted by French justice brought him into touch with a world hitherto unknown to him: that of the Jewish proletariat of Eastern Europe, composed of immigrants who were often politically conscious, socialists or even anarchists. This encounter showed him the possibility of a Jewish identity that was different from that of the French Jews, who in his view were soon to embody the archetype of the parvenu.[18] It is on account of these three crucial experiences that Bernard Lazare placed the notion of pariah at the center of his thought.

## The 'Hidden Tradition': Hannah Arendt

Hannah Arendt first encountered the pariah type in Rahel Varnhagen, the young romantic intellectual who enlivened the Jewish salons of Berlin at the beginning of the nineteenth century and about whom she wrote a remarkable biography in 1933 (reworked during the thirties and unpublished until 1958). However, it was her introduction to the works of Bernard Lazare, notably *Fumier de Job*, during her French exile between 1933 and 1941, that enabled her to develop her thought on pariah Judaism. She refined this concept in a series of writings during the 1940s, published in German as well as English in several New York magazines. The situation Arendt found herself in during this period certainly had an effect on her thought. And it is no accident that it was an exiled Jewish intellectual who uncovered in France of the 1930s the stimulating work of Bernard Lazare, a writer already totally forgotten after World War I and the moving homage paid to him by Charles

Péguy in *Notre jeunesse* (Our youth).[19] Hannah Arendt had been an émigré
since 1933, and soon she was to be stateless, too. Living in Paris in an anti-
Fascist émigré milieu (Bertolt Brecht, Arnold Zweig, and Walter Benjamin
were among her friends) she underwent the tragic experiences that the first
half of the century was to reserve for this generation of German Jews: not
only the hard condition of exile but also, after the start of World War II, a
double persecution. She was first interned at Gurs, in a French camp for
German nationals, who were regarded as potential enemies (in reality, like
the others, this camp swiftly filled with anti-Fascist exiles, very often Jews).
After the French defeat, she had to face Nazi persecution and the collabora-
tionism of the Vichy regime.

When she arrived in New York, in May 1941, she began to write for
a number of political and cultural magazines, with the object of helping
to instigate Jewish resistance to nazism. Her position was very clear from
1933: 'When one is attacked as a Jew, one must defend oneself as a Jew. Not
as a German, not as a world-citizen, not as an upholder of the Rights of
Man.'[20] A humanistic and universalistic attitude ought not to hide the Jewish dimension of the sufferings inflicted by nazism on its victims, since it
was precisely their Judeity that accounted for the persecution they suffered.
At a conference on Theodor Lessing, held in Germany after the war, Arendt
was to make a highly revealing observation. With regard to the celebrated
passage in *Nathan the Wise*, in which the protagonist, when summoned
with the words 'Come here, Jew,' replies, 'I am a man,' Hannah Arendt
declared that this behavior seemed to her a flight from reality and that,
throughout the period of anti-Semitic persecution, she herself could only
have responded to the question 'Who are you?' quite simply with: 'A Jew.'[21]

Just as they wanted at all costs to appear as true Germans, during the
Wilheminian Empire and the Weimar Republic, the Jews in exile tried desperately to turn France or the United States into their new country. They
struggled to suppress their accent when speaking French, yet at the beginning of the war they were interned as '*boches*'; in occupied France, they remained in the camps as Jews. In 1943, Hannah Arendt described the tragic
situation of the Jewish exiles in a moving article entitled *We Refugees*, in
which she summoned up an entire generation of German Jews: 'The story
of our struggle has finally become known. We lost our home, which means
the familiarity of daily life. We lost our occupation, which means the confi-

dence that we are of some use in this world. We lost our language, which means the naturalness of reactions, the simplicity of gesture, the unaffected expression of feelings. We left our relatives in the Polish ghettos and our best friends have been killed in concentration camps, and that means the rupture of our private lives.'[22] It was this situation which helped her to formulate her idea of the 'Jew as pariah,' an image which, during World War II, was close to the concrete reality, that of the Nazi persecution, rather than a literary metaphor or sociological abstraction.

Hannah Arendt reevaluated the dichotomy, already explored by Bernard Lazare, between pariah and parvenu. In her view, modern Jewish history was dominated by the opposition between two traditions: on the one hand, that of the wealthy Jews – a line that went from the *Hofjuden* to the Rothschild family – who had succeeded in a material sense and had achieved an illusory 'respectability' by submitting to the prevailing social norms (those of a nation-state which emancipated the Jews because it could not accept Jewish otherness); on the other, that of an underground, muted, 'hidden tradition,' represented by those who did not wish to sell their souls and who had not agreed to play the part of parvenu, even if it meant finding themselves again in the position of pariahs. According to Arendt, this tradition was upheld by different and apparently heterogeneous figures like Heinrich Heine, Rahel Varnhagen, Schalom Aleichem, Bernard Lazare, Franz Kafka, Rosa Luxemburg, and Charlie Chaplin.[23] The pariah Jew was defined simultaneously by the conditions of a hostile environment and by subjective qualities, engendered and developed in reaction to this same outside hostility. The starting point was inevitably the exclusion and marginality of the Jews, a condition that the *Aufklärung* and assimilation served only to highlight, but which perpetuated, under new forms, a secular past of segregation. The pariah's rootlessness was also characterized by Hannah Arendt as a state of 'worldlessness [*Weltfremdheit*],' or denial of the existence of the universe, forcing the pariah to create his own on the basis of values other than those prevailing in society.[24] But what distinguished the pariah above all was his lack of rights, his statelessness and his outlaw status which made him the scapegoat and preferred victim in all the crises that affected a society organized according to nation-state principles. The essentially political character of the Arendtian concept of pariah, which seems at times to define the condition of Jewish exiles during the 1930s and 1940s ('statelessness'), should be stressed.

Beside these determining external factors, the pariah also displayed a number of subjective qualities that contributed to the richness and nobility of his character. If Max Weber spoke of the 'negative privileges' of the pariah, for Arendt his condition implied also 'privileges' of an eminently intellectual and spiritual nature which were far from negative. In a letter to Karl Jaspers on the subject of the Rahel Varnhagen biography, she listed the 'qualities of the pariah': 'an extraordinary awareness of injustices; great generosity and a lack of prejudice,' as well as great respect for matters of the intellect.[25] At the conference on Lessing, mentioned above, she spoke of a 'humanity' and of a 'fraternity,' qualities belonging to the 'humiliated and injured,' indeed to a community of 'pariahs' excluded from society. She explained, too, the fascination and sympathy with them frequently felt by the great minds of our age, since it was the pariahs, in the midst of a world torn apart by violence and hatred, who preserved 'warmth' and human feelings. This 'warmth,' she wrote, 'which is the pariah's substitute for light, exerts a great fascination upon all those who are so ashamed of the world as it is that they would like to take refuge in invisibility.'[26]

Elsewhere, she attributed other qualities to the pariahs, such as a carefreeness, humor, disinterested intelligence, independent judgment — the *Selbstdenken* that she insisted on during the famous controversy with Gershom Scholem over the Eichmann trial[27] — and even the tendency to utopianism. In all probability, it is no accident that the outstanding representative of utopian thought, in German culture between the wars, was a marginalized Jewish exile: Ernst Bloch. In the United States, where he was neither given a grant nor offered employment by any institution, he began his search for the utopian prefigurations of a free and egalitarian social order, in a solitary work of genius, *The Principle of Hope,* written between 1938 and 1947.

According to Arendt, the pariah's sensitivity exposed him in particular to the afflictions stemming from another eminently human emotion: shame. In 1943, she began her review of Stefan Zweig's memoires, *Die Welt von Gestern* (World of yesterday), by narrating a dream that Rahel Varnhagen had recorded in her journal. With her friends Bettina von Arnim and Caroline von Humboldt, Rahel was meditating on the painful experiences of life. A great sense of fellowship united the three women when they recalled the sufferings caused by deception in love, unfaithfulness, sickness, and so many of the other pains of this world. Arendt concluded her narration of the dream thus: 'Finally Rahel asked: have you known shame? Scarcely had she uttered these words, than silence fell; her two friends turned away from her, thinking that she had been overcome or that she was demented. Rahel realized then that she alone had known shame and that her heart would never be relieved of this burden.'[28] Rahel's shame reflected the impossibility of escaping from Judeity and, at the same time, of living with it, as a fact of nature. It was the emotion that resulted from a double impossibility: the impossibility of being accepted in the normal way by an environment that was impregnated with anti-Semitism and the impossibility of living within Judaism as a totality. It was also the shame of the victim before his executioner, the oppressed before the oppressor, or that simply of belonging to the human race that Arendt expressed, in 1945, in an article on the Jewish genocide.[29] It was, one might add, the shame that overwhelmed Josef K., the hero of *The Trial,* when the death sentence was carried out.

Seen in terms of 'a category of public life,' the pariah's shame resulted from his exclusion, his inability to cast a reassuring shadow like any other respectable person with a place in society; or from his being a shadowless being in a world where all were reduced to shadows. If, for the businessman in pursuit of wealth and success, shame is poverty and, for the writer who dreams of fame, shame is anonymity, Jewish intellectuals in exile experienced both types of humiliation, the more painfully in that in the past they had often been able to live by the pen and had enjoyed a certain notoriety. Their shame was transformed into the pride of the pariah when they accepted their new condition, at the same time remaining themselves. Many celebrated writers and essayists who, in 1933, had seen their works burned in the Nazi *autos-da-fé* were obliged now to adapt themselves to financially straitened circumstances and anonymity. With the exception of a few exiles who were hospitably received – Thomas Mann and Bertolt Brecht were reasonably well off in Hollywood; a man of science like Albert Einstein and the sociologists of the Frankfurt school resumed their work in American universities – the great majority of émigrés were reduced practically to destitution. Walter Benjamin wrote his *Theses on the Philosophy of History* in a poorly heated room he had rented in Paris; Ernst Bloch was able to write *Das Prinzip Hoffnung (The Principle of Hope)* in the United States, thanks to his wife Karola (a student of Walter Gropius), who had got a job as a waitress in a restaurant; Heinrich Mann, a literary celebrity during the Weimar Republic, drew a small sum in unemployment benefits, in Los Angeles, and lived in fear of its coming to an end; Alfred Döblin wrote to a friend that he no longer belonged to the elite of famous writers, but to another category: 'Those who live in filth.'[30]

As a stateless and rootless individual, the pariah was a person without ties, whose perspective on the world was huge, not narrowly national. In 1946, Hannah Arendt rewrote a poem of Rilke — 'Lucky is he who has a country [*Wohl dem, der eine Heimat hat*]' — reversing the sense and transforming it into a eulogy of the pariah: 'Lucky is he that has no home; he sees it still in his dreams.'[31] It must be stressed that for Hannah Arendt, to be a pariah implied a conscious choice. The reality of anti-Semitism united all Jews in a single destiny, but it was not enough to have been excluded and persecuted to become a pariah: it was necessary also to rebel against this situation. She wrote that 'the decision to remain socially a pariah—even if in the form of the rebel — was more or less left to the personal choice of the individual.'[32] For the great majority of Jews, who found themselves in a no-man's-land, the hostile reality they were faced with seemed absurd and incomprehensible. The average Jew, who was neither a parvenu nor a rebel, was haunted by a feeling of otherness, by an 'innate foreignness' which made the reality he was faced with an enigma. This otherness turned him into an outsider in spite of himself; someone with no place in this society and who, once the latter entered a critical phase, was unable to merge with the amorphous, atomized mass upon which the totalitarian regimes were based. From the moment 'an alliance' was forged 'between mob and capital,'[33] his fate was sealed.

## *The Pariah as* Schlemihl

The dichotomy between pariah and parvenu also occurs in Hannah Arendt's writings, in another form: that of the division between *schlemihl* and *schnorrer*. Already in her biography of Rahel Varnhagen, the latter appeared as a '*shlemihl:* not rich, not beautiful, and Jewish.'[34] The *schlemihl* — a figure that she saw personified not only in Varnhagen but also in Heinrich Heine and Charlie Chaplin — possessed all the qualities of the pariah, except that he was not yet conscious of the need to rebel and tried to handle reality drawing on the inexhaustible resources of his insouciance, humanity, and fatalism. As against that, the *schnorrer* possessed all the faults of the parvenu. 'Once he adopts the role of *schnorrer*,' wrote Arendt, 'he is nothing worth, not because he is poor and begs, but because he begs from those whom he ought to fight, and because he appraises his poverty by the standards of those who have caused it. Once he adopts the role of *schnorrer*, the pariah becomes automatically one of the props which hold up a social order from which he is himself excluded.'[35] If he had not already become a rebel, the *schlemihl* refused to conform to the values of a society that rejected him. His flight from reality was an illusion and accounted for all the comical aspects of his behavior, which was fundamentally alien to the norms imposed by the powers that be. He was an outsider, but he preserved his dignity as a marginal individual, as well as his own culture. The *schnorrer* wanted at all costs to be accepted by the society, in which he could live only if he was prepared to endure the contempt and hatred of others. He lost all his pride, broke with the tradition of his people but, at the same time, was unable to get himself accepted by non-Jews. According to Hannah Arendt, the figure of the *schnorrer* was first adopted not only by the Jewish bourgeosie but also by the assimilated intellectuals, stubbornly intent on asserting their respectability as German *Staatsbürger*. Nothing was more humiliating and distressing, she felt, than the vision of a Jewish intellectual flaunting his doctor's degree but routinely perceived as a Herr Schnorrer.[36]

The allegorical figure of the *schlemihl* was made famous by Adalbert von Chamisso's novel *Peter Schlemihls wundersame Geschichte* (1814, The wonderful history of Peter Schlemihl), whose hero exchanges his shadow for eternal wealth but then finds himself excluded from the world, where everyone possesses this indispensable extension of the self and he who cannot project his own reassuring shadow seems despicable. If Chamisso has introduced the image of the *Schlemihl* into German literature, its origins are unquestionably Jewish (he seems to have learned the word from Rahel Varnhagen)[37] and it is to be found in the works of a large number of Yiddish writers, from Mendele Mocher Sforim to Schalom Aleichem, without forgetting, more recently, Isaac Bashevis Singer.[38] Controversy surrounds the actual derivation of the term *schlemihl*. According to some philologists it comes from the Yiddish adjective, *schlimazl*, which is an amalgamation of the German word *Schlimm*, 'bad,' and the Hebrew word *mazl*, 'luck'; according to other sources, it is simply a deformation of the Hebrew word *shelû-nu-el,* 'he who is worthless.' In Yiddish literature, the *schlemihl* is, thus, an unfortunate, a perpetual loser, a victim of fate who keeps coming a cropper on account of his naïveté. A simple, comical figure, both ironical and melancholic, he is nevertheless no plain unfortunate but, on the contrary, is filled with a wisdom that transcends the limited rationality of this world, neither whose order nor hierarchies he accepts. Imbued with spiritual values, the *schlemihl* is unable to adapt to a society dominated by purely material ones. As a result, he remains marginal, an object of ridicule and contempt.

Hannah Arendt seems almost to be contrasting the innocence and irony of the *schlemihl* with 'the hopeless sadness of the assimilationists.'[39] However, she was not taking into account certain characteristics that distinguished the traditional Yiddish *schlemihl* from the Western Jewish pariah. It is not so much that the *schlemihl*, instead of rebelling against reality, tries to fend it off with laughter and a carefree attitude, as that his identity is one the pariah no longer possesses. If, as Ruth R. Wisse has shown in an illuminating study, the *schlemihl* 'represents the triumph of identity over adverse circumstances,'[40] the pariah's identity as explained by Hannah Arendt has been utterly transformed as a result of assimilation. In the world of the *Shtetl,* the figure of the *schlemihl* is not radically opposed to that of the *schnorrer,* who is a beggar but not a parvenu.[41] The *schlemihl* is deeply rooted in the world in which he lives, whereas the pariah has to be assertive about his culture and tradition in a continual battle with the prevailing conformism and is in constant danger of turning into a parvenu. Finally, the *schlemihl* is sustained by faith, he lives in a world where order still exists and where there is a Law to make sense of life, whereas the pariah has to sustain himself spiritually and build a future for himself in a secularized world. In a word, the *schlemihl* is a hero of *yiddishkeit,* whereas the pariah belongs to what Kafka called *westjüdische Zeit.*

### The Revolt of the Pariah: Hannah Arendt, Zionism, and Socialism

What forms did the pariah's revolt take? This question inevitably brings one back to Hannah Arendt's relationship with Zionism. Generally she is regarded as being a Zionist with critical reservations. In fact, between 1933 and 1939, she worked for agencies connected with the Zionist movement: first a society that handled the emigration of Jewish children to Palestine and subsequently an agency assisting Jewish refugees. However, she always kept at a distance from the mainstream of the Zionist movement, not hiding the fact that she preferred Bernard Lazare to Theodor Herzl. The Zionism she supported had nothing to do with Herzl's statist and colonialist obsessions, but concerned itself above all with the autoemancipation of the Jewish people. In her view, there were two forms of Zionism: on the one hand, the pariahs' struggle for freedom; on the other, the movement of the *schnorrers*, who begged concessions from the great powers. She did not share Herzl's belief that anti-Semitism was 'the natural response, constant and universal, of all peoples to the sheer fact of Jewish existence'[42] and hoped to realize Zionist ambitions through pressure exerted by certain 'influential individuals.' 'Zionism,' she wrote, 'has never been a really popular movement. It is true that it has spoken and acted in the name of the Jewish people, but, all things considered, it has never concerned itself with whether the masses followed it or not. From Herzl's dealings with ministers of Czarist Russia or the German Empire, up to the memorable letter that an English lord, Lord Balfour, wrote to another English lord, Lord Rothschild, the subject of which was the fate of the Jewish people, the Zionist leaders have been able, without much support from the Jewish people, to work out deals on behalf of this people with statesmen who, themselves, were acting for their own peoples and not as their representatives.'[43]

In contrast, Hannah Arendt wanted to turn Zionism into a mass movement capable of mobilizing the oppressed and persecuted Jews of the whole of Europe. They were to mobilize themselves not as Frenchmen or Americans, nor just as democrats or anti-Fascists, but principally as Jews, because it was their Judeity which made victims of them. In her view, it was only in this way that they would be able to recover their dignity. In 1942, in the pages of *Aufbau*, a New York journal directed at German émigrés, Hannah Arendt carried on a vigorous campaign for the creation of a 'Jewish army' which was to take part in the war against nazism. The object of this, as she explained very clearly, was to 'change the law of extermination and the law of flight through the law of combat.'[44] Her position was quite distinct from that of Jabotinsky's revisionists, who she described as 'Jewish fascists' (they too supported an independent Jewish army), for Hannah Arendt came out at the same time in support of a dialogue and of Jewish-Arab collaboration in Palestine. It is interesting to note that, in her writings on Zionism after 1948, it was no longer the Jews but the Palestinians who were called pariahs.[45]

For Max Weber, the definition of the Jews as pariahs was a scientific category that attempted to embrace their socioeconomic role in the Europe of antiquity and the Middle Ages. Bernard Lazare and Hannah Arendt have added to this concept a cultural, psychological, one might almost say spiritual, dimension, which has greatly enhanced it. Their theory contains none of Weber's scientific *Wertfreiheit*, but implies a deep involvement, even a moral connection with its subject. It was as a pariah that Hannah Arendt, in exile in Paris, wrote a biography of Rahel Varnhagen and, shortly after her arrival in New York, a long article entitled 'We Refugees.' That said, the concepts of the pariah developed by Bernard Lazare and Hannah Arendt are quite close, even if they do not entirely coincide. If for the French anarchist, the Eastern European proletarian Jewish immigrants were fully paid-up members of the great family of modern pariahs, the German philosopher seemed to restrict the notion to the political sphere. For Hannah Arendt, pariahs comprised the vast mass of those without rights and without countries who wandered endlessly about Europe during the first half of the twentieth century, not economic *luftmenshn* [airheads; intellectuals]. This distinction became more and more tenuous and absurd as Europe moved toward World War II: in Auschwitz Jews were exterminated en masse, without regard to class or citizenship. Nevertheless, the highly political nature of the Arendtian definition of pariah is worth stressing, as it reflected a pervasive tendency to underestimate the social dimension of historical processes. This aspect of her work was more noticeable in certain books written after the war, as for instance her essay *On Revolution* (1963), where the latter, defined as 'the cause of freedom versus tyranny,' was hardly perceived as freedom from social oppression, too.[46] As she explicitly stated, the task of revolution was to bring freedom and not happiness (as dreamed of by the Jacobins who, in her view, drove the French Revolution into the impasse of the Terror). Those who had been excluded had to be made 'visible,' so that they could enter the political arena, guaranteed participation in public life – a participation moreover based on rights and not on needs.[47] In her opinion, the exclusion of the masses from public life and their atomization were among the principal characteristics of the totalitarian regimes, which no longer tolerated pariahs.

This primacy of politics over the social and economic spheres – a vision no doubt inherited, as Martin Jay shows, from the German *Existenzphilosophie* tradition[48] – led Hannah Arendt to underestimate a typical phenomenom of the twentieth century; namely, the alliance of pariah Judaism and the working-class socialist movement. How can one explain the Jewish presence – impressive both quantitatively and qualitatively – in all the revolutionary movements that shook Central and Eastern Europe during the first half of the century, without seeing in them an expression both of the pariah's revolt and his [or her] rejection of the parvenu option? It was precisely the qualities of the pariah defined by Hannah Arendt – 'an extraordinary awareness of injustices; great generosity and a lack of prejudice' – that accounted for the attachment of a large number of Jewish intellectuals to socialism, where they could overcome their 'worldlessness' and their exclusion as well as give to their social rebellion an organic shape. A product, as she liked to emphasize, of 'the German philosophical tradition' and entirely absorbed, during her years of French and American exile, in Zionist activities, Hannah Arendt never perceived either the importance of the relationship between Judeity and socialism (in spite of her marriage to the Marxist philosopher Günther Anders and later to Heinrich Blücher, a former Bukharinite Communist) or its wide-ranging implications. She appeared to be dealing with the phenomenon much later, when she discovered the figure of Rosa Luxemburg, but this did not lead to an appreciation of the commitment to socialist and revolutionary aims as a major aspect of pariah Judaism. To give only one example, one might quote Manès Sperber, who pointed to 'solidarity' with the 'victims of injustice' as one of the sources of his Judeity. His way of being Jewish was inseparable from his socialism and, instead of resulting in 'unconditional' allegiance to the Jewish people, implied a critical attitude to everything that seemed to him 'unjust, opportunistic, unworthy and inauthentic' in the life of his people.[49] The paths of several generations of socialist Jews – from Marx, exiled in London, to the numerous revolutionaries of Czarist Russia who emigrated to Germany or Austria – come fully under the heading of pariah Judaism. The pariah / parvenu dichotomy is evident in the autobiography of Leo Trotsky, when he describes the unease he felt in Vienna, with regard to the leaders of Austrian social democracy, most of whom were Jewish intellectuals, deeply skeptical of any notion of a Russian revolution and insisting on being respectfully addressed as 'comrade doctor.'[50]

Other examples could be given of the consequences of this notion, in Arendt's work, of the 'primacy of politics.'[51] As for Arendt herself, she jettisoned the status of pariah in 1951, when she obtained U.S. citizenship, after the great success of her work on *The Origins of Totalitarianism*, and embarked on a brilliant university career. There was perhaps an element of *schlemihlitude* in the fate of this book, which though widely read had the misfortune of being almost always misunderstood. Although debatable, her analysis of Stalinism never resorted to crude anti-Communist clichés and even contained a radical criticism of imperialism; nevertheless, in the climate of the fifties, it swiftly became 'a bible of the cold war.'[52] Around this same time, a new generation of pariahs appeared in America, that of the victims (often Jews) of McCarthyism.

## Judeity and Femininity: Rosa Luxemburg

It is interesting to note that, from the nineteenth century, the concept of pariah was used (notably by Flora Tristan and George Sand) to define not only the Jewish condition but also the status of women.[53] In spite of their different origins, religious in the first case and sexual in the latter, these two forms of otherness lead to the same social condition of exclusion and discrimination. Jewish emancipation and the emancipation of women are homologous in certain respects. It is true that in the latter case, civil rights took longer to attain, but resistance and the prejudices encountered were often analogous to those encountered by the Jews. For women it was the family that constituted a ghetto and home: emancipation and entry into public life were perceived, just as with the Jewish emancipation, as typical manifestations of modernity, breaking up and overturning the hierarchical order (national, religious, and sexual) of traditional society. Just as emancipation for the Jews translated itself into the appropriation of a non-Jewish culture and assimilation into a non-Jewish environment, emancipation of women was often conceived of in terms of adaptation to the values and behavioral codes of a society dominated by men. Furthermore, from the end of the nineteenth century, anti-Semitism and antifeminism once again came to resemble one another in the tendency to *biologize* Jewish and female differences.[54] Thus, the latter was regarded as the expression of an inferiority, the theoretical argument for which drew on the conceptual arsenal of sociobiology.

In the context of his self-destructive interpretation, internalizing cultural anti-Semitic stereotypes, Otto Weininger, in his own way, had already seized on this 'elective affinity' between Jew and woman.[55] When Hannah Arendt discovered the figure of Rahel Varnhagen, at the beginning of the thirties, the image of the pariah, in her eyes, was nothing but a paradigm of Judeity. While it entered into her pariah sensibility, Rahel's femininity was not an essential constituent. After the feminist wave of the sixties, on the other hand, Arendt seemed to highlight the 'feminist' dimension of the pariah condition and emphasized the profound affinity between femininity and Judeity. The occasion for building a bridge between these two forms of cultural and sexual otherness and social exclusion was the appearance of a biography of Rosa Luxemburg, written by the British historian John Paul Nettl.[56] This work rescued from obscurity the mythical figure of a martyr of the Spartacist Revolt, while at the same time revealing the depth and richness of Rosa's thought. It brought us her writings on the accumulation of capital, mass strikes, and workers' spontaneity; on her controversy with Eduard Bernstein and her criticism of the Russian Revolution; but it also presented a picture of a bluntly militant individual, utterly devoted to the revolutionary cause and indifferent to the 'petty details' of her existence: those of being a woman (not only in a society, but also in a workers' movement dominated by men), who furthermore was Jewish (in a world — Poland and Germany at the turn of the century — saturated with anti-Semitism) and even a cripple (she had been lame since childhood). Hannah Arendt's approach was different. Her interpretation of Rosa Luxemburg's life can be summed up in one sentence: 'She was an outsider, not only because she was and remained a Polish Jew in a country she disliked, and a party she came soon to despise, but also because she was a woman.'[57] To put it in more general terms, the contradictions in Rosa Luxemburg's life were clearly manifested in three regards: the clandestine nature of her relationship with Leo Jogiches, her indifference to the movement for the emancipation of women, and, finally, in the suppression of her Judeity.

Her relationship with Leo Jogiches revealed a permanent split between the frustrated desire to live the 'normal' life of a married woman and her profound aspirations to social, intellectual, and political independence which could not be gainsaid and which inevitably led to marginalization. Rosa and Leo met in Switzerland, in exile, and from there directed the Social

Democratic movement of the kingdom of Poland and Lithuania (SDKPiL), an underground revolutionary organization which opposed the Czarist regime. They became lovers in 1891, in Zurich, but their love relationship was never known to more than a few close friends. Over the years – their liaison was to last until 1907 – they were careful not to disclose in public the nature of their ties, in spite of Rosa's protestations against the 'hypocrisy' of this pretense. To avoid family conflict, Rosa even invented a fictitious marriage with Jogiches. Born into a rich Jewish family from Lithuania, the latter financed the publications of the SDKPiL as well as those of Rosa, who sent him a detailed list of all her expenses. Relocating in Berlin – Rosa in 1897, Leo a little later – they continued to live separately. Leo's room, at his companion's home, passed as a guest room. Not only did Rosa's unconsummated marriage to Gustav Lübeck (with the object of obtaining German citizenship) not meet with Leo's disapproval, he took care of all the details. They had reached a precise division of labor: Rosa was the public figure who wrote for the press and intervened in SPD congresses; Leo worked behind the scenes, never appearing either in print or in public. A remarkable organizer, he kept in the background. He wanted to control Rosa, to direct her activity and almost to dictate how she used her time, but Rosa became increasingly independent. The more aware she became of her own capacity and was publicly recognized for her propagandist work, the more Leo felt everything was ending for him. Rosa no longer needed him and he suffered long periods of inactivity and isolation. Rosa's letters to her lover reveal her longing for a quiet and 'respectable' life at his side, which would give her far greater satisfaction than her intellectual celebrity and success as a political leader. Sometimes she was overwhelmed by the desire for children, which she would try to alleviate by taking in animals: 'Without children, home is empty and stupid, and I feel so alone! It seems to me that a child would bring me back to life. Meanwhile, I should like at least to have a dog or a cat.'[58]

Tragic fate was to join Rosa and Leo in death, too. They were murdered in 1919, a few weeks after one another, by the *Freikorps*, which was charged with crushing the Spartacist Revolt.

Rosa's attitude with regard to the question of women is somewhat surprising. According to Hannah Arendt: 'Her distaste for the women's emancipation movement, to which all other women of her generation and political convictions were irresistibly drawn, was significant; in the face of suffragette equality, she might have been tempted to reply, *vive la petite différence.*'[59] A friend of Clara Zetkin, who was the moving spirit in the Socialist women's movement, Rosa never displayed the slightest interest in the question of sexual oppression and always remained skeptical as regards the possibilities of a movement for the liberation of women. She rejected, with indignation even, the proposal that she devote herself to the women's movement, a task which seemed to her marginal and without significance.

In 1902, Rosa wrote an article for the Polish newspaper *Gazeta Ludowa* entitled 'Ladies and Women,' in which feminism was stigmatized as a leisure activity for middle-class women who, 'weary of their doll's role or of being cooks for their husbands, are looking to action as a way of filling their empty heads and empty lives.'[60] This form of feminism she contrasted with the attitude of proletarian women, who were not fighting for their 'personal interests' but for the liberation of their class, without sexual distinction. The idea of an autonomous movement of women seemed to her a petite-bourgeoisie deviation. She could scarcely have been more blind in this respect. Certainly, this attitude was by no means a minority one in the workers' movement of that time, but neither should it be forgotten that other militant women had already expressed positions that were far more advanced (for example Alexandra Kollontaï). It seems even more nonsensical and contradictory when one remembers that Rosa was the only woman in the ruling group of the SPD. In 1909, at the time of the debate about a general strike and the strategy to win power, she was the only one among the German Marxists who dared challenge the authority of Karl Kautsky, the 'pope' of the Second International.

It has, therefore, to be admitted that if her political biography made Rosa the very model of the emancipated woman, her ideas were far from being feminist. How is this contradiction to be explained? According to Hannah Arendt, there was a secret, unconscious, feminist side to Rosa Luxemburg, but, at the same time, the stubborn insistence on affirming her 'little difference' could find outlet only through social emancipation — in the workers' movement, journalism, politics — where there was no place for women. Christel Neusüss is no doubt correct when he writes that Rosa's entire life bears witness 'to a nonpatriarchal mode of thinking and experience' and that the criticism she levelled 'at her male comrades was a criticism of the patriarchal elements in their ways of thinking.'[61] The suppression of her femininity – in her relations with Leo Jogiches as much as in the workers' movement – was, thus, the price she paid for asserting her independence and her *specificity* in the face of male dominance.

Even more ambiguous and contradictory was Rosa's relationship to Judeity. Her actual name was Luksenburg, which she changed to Luxemburg, probably so as to make it less Jewish. She was born in Zamosc, a Polish town which possessed quite a considerable Jewish community. Her father, a well-to-do merchant, was a first generation, Polish-speaking, 'assimilated' Jew. Her mother was an orthodox Jewess, who counted seventeen generations of rabbis among her ancestors. In his biography of Rosa, Paul Frölich writes that 'the Luxemburg household was replete with Polish and German culture,'[62] but no doubt the reality was different. The father, taken up with his business, showed no particular interest in culture and the mother, for her part, had nothing of the assimilated intellectual Jewess in her makeup. Her funeral ceremonies, in 1897, followed the strictest traditional practices, with her brothers all day long intoning the prayer for the dead and, finally, chanting the *kaddish*.

Rosa wished for nothing better than to leave this world behind her. The ostentatious contempt for Jewish culture that she displayed throughout her life revealed a complex and ambiguous relationship with her family and her origins. In her eyes, everything relating to Judaism testified to an obscurantist set of beliefs which had to be cleared out of the way. Here, according to Tadeus Radwanski, is what she had to say about Yiddish literature: 'Literature in jargon! Who do we think we're kidding? And especially Peretz, that daft fellow, who has the cheek to insult Heine with his translation of the beautiful German language into this Old-Swabian dialect corrupted with a sprinkling of Hebrew words and distorted vernacular Polish.'[63]

The contrast between this contempt for the Jewish tradition and her exaltation of Polish virtues is striking. In 1898, after a propaganda tour of Silesia, she wrote the following to Leo Jogiches: 'How delightful – fields of wheat, meadows, forests . . . the Polish language and Polish peasants . . . a little barefoot cowherd and our magnificent fir trees. It is true, the peasants are hungry and dirty, but what a handsome race!'[64] One is almost tempted to see in this Polish version of *völkisch* romanticism, a typical form of Jewish anti-Semitism.

Her attitude to Germanity was more complex. For instance, she admired the nationalist and anti-Semitic composer Richard Wagner, but was at the same time disgusted by the German public's enthusiasm for Beethoven. One should remember that in Germany, in spite of her naturalization and her literary success, Rosa Luxemburg continued to be regarded as a Polish Jew and that in Poland she was detested by the entire anti-Semitic press.

According to Hannah Arendt, Rosa's suppression of her Judeity was, paradoxically, a typical manifestation of pariah Judaism which could never appreciate the significance of linguistic barriers and was perpetually searching for a 'home,' identifiable with no particular 'country.' At the same time, Rosa's career confirmed yet again what she had already written about Rahel Levin-Varnhagen, that 'one does not escape one's Judeity.' For Hannah Arendt, Rosa's anti-nationalism—her criticism of Polish demands for independence – was undeniably linked with the condition of being a Jewess.[65]

In a famous letter to her friend Mathilde Wurm, written from the Wronke prison in February 1917, Rosa declared that there was no 'special corner' in her heart for the ghetto, adding: 'I feel at home in the huge world everywhere that there are clouds, birds, and tears.'[66] In another letter, she was urging her friend, sorely tried by the horrors of the war, 'to remain a human being. That's the essential thing, really. And it means: to be firm, lucid, and cheerful, yes cheerful in spite of all and everything, because moaning is for the weak. To remain a human being is to cast one's entire life joyfully 'into the great scales of fate,' if necessary, but at the same time to be glad for each sunny day, each beautiful cloud. . . . The world is so beautiful in spite of the horrors and it would be more beautiful still if there were no cads and cowards on earth.'[67] Here in a few words, all to be found in her correspondence with Rahel Levin-Varnhagen, is further testimony to the pariah's humanity, carefreeness, and warmth, in the face of worldly violence and injustice.

# CHAPTER THREE

# Judeity as *Heimatlosigkeit:*
# Joseph Roth

*'Hotelpatriot'*

THE INTELLECTUAL and political career of the writer Joseph Roth, with all its contradictions, seems to mirror the condition and fate of Central European pariah Judaism. From the Galician *Shtetl* to Habsburg Vienna, from Berlin to Paris, this outsider crossed and recrossed interwar Europe. Sharing the fate of many other German-speaking Jewish intellectuals of his generation, Roth died in exile. On 27 May 1939, a few months before the start of World War II, he succumbed to drink, in Paris. He had just finished one of his best stories, *The Legend of the Holy Drinker,* which he managed to write, in moments of lucidity, seated at a table in the Café Tournon. His funeral at the Thiais Cemetery was an odd affair and its tragicomic outcome revealed, once again, the ambiguity of the man. When the Austrian monarchists, who were there with an official delegation, laid a wreath in the colors of the Empire and signed by Otto de Habsbourg, the leftist exiles, among whom could be seen the Communists Egon Erwin Kisch and Bruno Frei, noisily displayed their opposition. This altercation had hardly died down before another broke out: it was the turn of Joseph Gottfarstein, who protested against a Catholic priest blessing the coffin, when he wished to recite the *kaddish.*[1]

In fact, no one ever knew whether Roth had actually converted to Catholicism, as he claimed toward the end of the thirties. The fact remains that he liked to present himself in the contradictory guise of a 'papist' Jew and 'libertarian' monarchist. *Heimatlos* and a nonconformist intellectual, paradoxicality was his middle name. Already in 1926, in a letter to Bernard von Brentano, he called himself 'A Frenchman of the East, a humanist, a rationalist with religion, a Catholic with a Jewish brain, a true revolutionary.'[2] Of only one thing can we be sure — that he was Jewish, and it was primarily as a Jewish journalist and writer that he was known during his lifetime. On the other hand, his socialist involvement during the twenties, like his monarchist attachments, in the following decades, reflected a quite personal and specific path, that of a thinker who refused to submit to any orthodoxy and to be constrained to any particular form of militant activism. Basically, his politics as they evolved – passing from the extreme Left to the extreme Right (in the form of a monarchically inclined anti-Fascism) – projected a romantic, anticapitalist vision, nourished by a radical critique of Western progress and modernity. His socialism and monarchism bore their own particular stamp and did not have much in common with official Marxism and Bolshevism, or the reactionary ideology of exiled royalist circles.

Joseph Roth was the archetypal incarnation of the rootless Jewish intellectual; in other words, he seemed to exemplify Karl Mannheim's theory of 'free-floating intellectuals [*freischwebende Intelligenz*].' In his case, this formula would have to be taken literally: except for a very brief period, in 1922, after his marriage to Friedricke Reichler (Friedl) when he lived in Berlin in an ordinary apartment, Roth lived his entire life in hotel rooms. When he described himself as *Hotelbürger* or *Hotelpatriot*,[3] he was not referring to a haphazard way of life but to deliberate choice. From the luxury hotels that he could afford when he worked as a special correspondent of the *Frankfürter Zeitung* to the much more modest boardinghouses which were the setting of his exile, these premises left him convinced at least of one thing: that he was living provisionally and that existence was a perpetual odyssey. This refusal to own an apartment reflected as much his attraction to luxury and to an aristocratic way of life as his rejection of any kind of middle-class respectability and stability. He invested the heroes of his novels with his own character: Gabriel Dan, in *Hotel Savoy*, returns to his hotel room 'as to a long lost home.'[4] Roth's correspondence offers some explanations regarding his lifestyle. As against hotels, true 'windows opening on the world . . . a house is a definitive thing, like a crypt,' he said to his Hungarian friend Géza von Cziffra.[5] In another letter to his editor, Gustav Kiepenheuer, he claimed for himself the status of *Heimatlos:* 'Apart from the fact that I am and feel at home only in myself, I have no country [*Heimat*]. There where things are not going well for me is my country [*Vaterland*]. I feel well only

abroad [*Gut geht es mir nur in der Fremde*].'⁶ A difficult childhood – marked
by the absence of a father who, before his birth, left the family home in the
course of a business trip – is doubtless another factor behind his almost
'congenital' rootlessness.

## Nostalgia for the Shtetl

His insistence on passing through the world as a stranger, making a virtue
out of marginality, casting an *other* look on the society of his time, reflected
his origins. A German-speaking Galician Jew, Roth was born in 1894, on
the borders of the Habsburg Empire, in Brody, which had already succes-
sively been one of the capitals of *Hassidism* and of the *Haskalah*. He was a
pure product of the Eastern European *Shtetl* and, at the same time, of Judeo-
German culture. Deeply attached to the cultural universe of the *Ostjudentum*, he regarded it as his mission to defend its values and set himself up
as a stern critic of assimilation. However, his weapons – journalism and
literature – were drawn from the arsenal of Germanophone culture. Like the
majority of Galician Jewish intellectuals of his generation, he was a product
of an Austrian *Bildung* which in any case he acknowledged quite openly:
in a letter to Stefan Zweig dated March 1933, he accepted the legacy of
the emancipation when he wrote that 'our ancestors are Goethe, Lessing,
Herder, quite as much as Abraham, Isaac, and Jacob.'⁷

What distinguishes Roth is his dual allegiance to German and to Eastern
European Jewish culture. However, for a young intellectual, educated at the
universities of Lemberg and Vienna, who had become a writer in Berlin, to
return to the *Shtetl*, employing Yiddish as his means of literary expression,
was almost impossible. In most cases, the discovery of the sources of East
European Judaism took the form of a fascination with this 'exotic' and almost unknown world.⁸ For Roth, on the other hand, flight from the *Shtetl*
and criticism of assimilation led to a cosmopolitan and supranational orientation. It was his deep attachment to the values of this *ostjüdisch* universe,
where the idea of a nation was unknown, that made Roth a citizen of the
world, conscious and proud of his *Heimatlosigkeit* (his 'stateless' condition).

His position was, indeed, exceptional. German – the language of the
Jewish intellectuals of Galicia, and indispensable if any impact was to be

made socially within the bounds of the Habsburg Empire – was his mother tongue, but Austro-Germans saw him as a Galician Jew, while Polish nobles or landowners and Ukrainian peasants regarded him as a German Jew. It might be added that, as a German-speaking Jew, Roth was in a way a stranger in the eyes of the Galician Jews themselves, for the great majority of whom Yiddish remained their mother tongue. A product at once of the *Shtetl* and of assimilation, he belonged to these two cultures without being able really to identify with either. This dual cultural allegiance is of course discernible in other writers with the same background, as for instance Alfred Döblin or Manès Sperber, but with Roth it was much more marked. A sociosemiotic analysis of his work – and especially of a novel like *Job* – reveals the German language used as a 'mimetic tool,' helping to convey a universe of values that have remained Jewish.[9] In this sense, Roth's German could be described as a 'borrowed language' used, as he explained, to describe a non-Jewish reality [*gojischen Realität*], whereas Yiddish embodied in his view the life of a 'community of destiny [*Schicksalsgemeinschaft*],'[10] that of the Eastern European Jewish nation.

The cultural no-man's-land that is characteristic of Roth brings to mind Kafka. German-speaking Habsburg Jews, they shared the same negative vision of assimilation as a loss of roots, as against the authenticity of *Shtetl* life. Thanks to his encounter with the Yiddish theater – we could almost call it a revelation – Kafka discovered the world of the East European Jew, in which being a Jew was as natural as breathing and eating. The East European Jew possessed a culture, a memory, and identified with a past; he did not suffer from an agonizing sense of alienation, from himself and from his roots, which, according to Kafka, characterized *westjüdische Zeit*.[11] The world did not appear to him as unintelligibly chaotic, but as resting on solid foundations; as an organic whole. In short, the Jews of the East, in his view, represented the dreamed of *Gemeinschaft* as against those of the West, assimilated, rootless, memoryless, and traditionless. Watching the Russo-Jewish immigrants passing through Prague where they awaited their American visas, Kafka was suddenly seized by the desire to take the place of a 'little Eastern Jew' who, in the midst of his family and surrounded by his own people, seemed the very embodiment of happiness.[12] The same criticism of assimilation and the same valorization, even idealization, of *yiddishkeit* may be found in Roth (especially in a work like *Juden auf Wan-*

68

*derschaft* (Wandering Jews). However, for Roth, as opposed to Kafka, the *Shtetl* did not represent a mythical place, a dream world, but the concrete reality of his childhood and early adolescent years. In a number of his novels, he gave us a detailed description of life in the *Shtetlakh* of Eastern Europe, clustered around the station, synagogue, marketplace, and with their procession of Chagallesque figures: artisans, workers, *cheder* and *yeshiva* teachers, rabbis, *luftmenschn* of all sorts, and in particular small traders. In *The Radetzky March,* he painted a very lively portrait of the Jewish pedlars:

> In these parts the tradesmen made their living far more by hazard than by design, more by the unpredictable grace of God than by any commercial reckonings in advance. Every trader was ready at any moment to seize on whatever floating merchandise heaven might throw in his way, or even to invent his goods if God had provided him with none. The livelihood of these traders was indeed a mystery. They displayed no shopfronts. . . . Forever shifting, ever on the road, with glib tongues and clear, quick brains, they might have had possession of half the world if they had had any notion of their world. But they had none. They lived remote from it, wedged between East and West, cramped between day and night, themselves a species of living ghosts, spawned by the night and haunting the day.[13]

These Jews of the East, whose blood was more Slav than German, still formed an organic community, a collectivity which, while it might not be classified as national, embodied authentic values. Roth was quite aware of their difficulties and was careful not to idealize the conditions of their life naively. As he recalled in *Juden auf Wanderschaft* (1927), they lived 'on dirty streets, in dilapidated houses,' despised by the Christians and persecuted by the authorities. They were taught 'in dark *cheders*. From their earliest childhood, they were inured to the painful absence of hope in Jewish prayer, they learned to contend doughtily with a God who punishes more than he loves, who condemns all pleasure as sinful.'[14] But for those who lived according to the Torah, God did not confine himself to condemning and punishing, since he was also their source of delight. Returning to Galicia in 1926, Roth was fascinated by the dances of the *Hassidim,* for whom the encounter with God was as sensual as the act of love. They held hands, danced in a circle, broke the circle to clap hands, stretched their heads to the right, then to the left, seized the scrolls of the Torah, twirled them, like young girls, pressed them to their breast, kissed them, and wept with joy. There was an erotic pleasure in this dance. I was deeply moved that a people was offering God its sensual enjoyment, that it turned this Book, containing the strictest laws, into the beloved, and that it could not distinguish between carnal desire and intellectual enjoyment, combining the two.[15]

In the West, these values had disappeared and the Jews were once again cut off from their history. Assimilation was utterly and finally condemned. Jews with cravats despised their Eastern brothers in their caftans. They feared the presence of *ostjüdisch* immigrants, who compromised their recently acquired and still precarious respectability and recalled their highly unaristocratic origins in the ghetto. Sometimes, they tried to avoid this accursed association by converting to Christianity but, as Roth ironically pointed out, that was not much use, since 'the parents of the happily assimilated one could not be avoided' and sooner or later he found himself face to face with some family member who would give the parvenu's game away through his 'very appearance.'[16] In *Juden and Wanderschaft* (1927, *Flight without End*), Roth sarcastically described the Jews of a German town who, claiming to have settled on the banks of the Rhine in Roman times, before the Germans, asked the local university association to introduce a *numerus clausus* for immigrant Jews.[17]

Roth well knew the psychology of the assimilated Western Jew: it had been his own for a brief period, after his arrival in Vienna, on the eve of World War I. As his biographer David Bronsen informs us, he dropped Moses from among his given names, tried to eliminate his Galician accent and adopted the aristocratic habit of wearing a monocle. It is easy to hypothesize that these pretentions related to the well known phenomenon of *jüdische Selbsthass* [Jewish self-hatred], particularly widespread in Vienna at the turn of the century.[18] Discovering the marginal condition of the immigrant Jews of Lepoldstadt, and in particular anti-Semitism – which at that time took a popular demagogic form with the Catholic mayor of Vienna Karl Lueger, and the pan-Germanist, Georg von Schönerer, and was very different in character to the premodern and 'eastern' anti-Semitism of Galicia – Roth at first rejected Judeity. But soon, due especially to the impact of the war and the disintegration, along with that of the Habsburg Empire, of the traditional structure of society, he overcame this assimilationist syndrome, of which not a trace remained in his novels. Once integration with the West was no longer a victory to be achieved and became instead a condition of life, Roth renewed his links with the world of his origins.

If, for Kafka, *westjüdische Zeit* represented a state of permanent disjunction and of profound existential agony, Roth saw the Western Jews simply as 'parvenus.' Cut off from their tradition and their spiritual reality, they no longer wished to be called Jews but 'citizens of the Mosaic [*mosaïsch*] faith,' dressed in frock coats, did away with their long beards, and went to synagogues that resembled Protestant churches. Proud of their 'Western culture,' they had a deep contempt for their coreligionists of the East, any one of whom possessed 'a greater sense of the human and of the divine than all the preachers and theological schools of Western Europe.'[19] Roth's sole hope was that the *Ostjuden* might find the strength to resist assimilation, as the flight from the *Shtetl* signified nothing but loss of values and decay. In *Job* (1930), Roth described the emigration to America as an inexorable process of decomposition for the traditional Jewish world. The family of Mendel Singer, a poor, God-fearing *melamed* [schoolmaster], 'an entirely commonplace Jew,' did not survive its encounter with the 'fatal country [*todlisches Vaterland*]' that was the New World and was shattered by it: his sons were carried off by the war: one was killed in battle, the other vanished; his daughter went mad after having 'sinned' with *goyim*, and his wife, with whom his relations had become mechanical and passionless, died of the pain all these misfortunes caused her.[20]

Assimilation had to be rejected also in its Zionist form, that of a movement aiming to Westernize the Jews by setting them in a national context. The colonization of Palestine seemed to him a kind of 'Jewish crusade' of which the Arabs were quite right to be wary. Zionism brought them 'electricity, fountain pens, engineers, machine guns, banal philosophies and all the clobber England provides us with'; in short, it brought a Western civilization that violated their culture.[21] To accomplish this, the Zionists had to betray the most authentic tradition and values of Judaism. As Wolfgang Müller-Funk wrote, for Roth, Zionism, the notion of a Jewish country, was nothing other than an expression of disloyalty to, repudiation of the 'Jewish tradition of *Heimatlosigkeit*, a legacy of the wandering Jew.'[22]

## Judaism and the Criticism of Modernity

Rejection of assimilation and of Zionism reflected the critical romantic attitude to modernity that was widespread in Germany at the turn of the century. Inaugurated by Roth in the early twenties, this trend was to develop and grow more radical over the following decades, to the point of regarding the entire tradition of rationalist thought as the source of a false order leading directly to the dictatorships of our period. Criticism of the technological ugliness and coldness of industrial society – which is reminiscent of certain passages in Ernst Bloch's *Geist der Utopie* (1918–23) – is a salient feature of Roth's writings from 1920, the year he settled in Berlin to work as a journalist on the *Börsen-Kurier*. Unlike Walter Benjamin and Franz Hessel, he was not charmed by the German capital at the beginning of the century. He hated this inhospitable, soulless city, obsessed with commerce, money, and industrial production; attacked the 'yoke of industrial culture,' the 'satanic currents of the period,' and the 'locomotive of technical progress'; condemned his times in which 'the machine subdued the spirit [*Die Maschine den Geist unterjochte*]' and man found himself 'submitting to the materiality of the present.'[23] In 1924, he described the Berlin quarter of Gleisdreieck as a symbol of this industrial hell. This 'steel mask, this vast temple of technology open to the skies' will soon have replaced the common idea of 'landscape,' which usually evokes forests and meadows. In a spirit of romantic resignation, he concluded that 'the world of the future will be a gigantic Gleisdreieck.'[24] While participating in the activities of the Expressionist movement – especially Group 1925 – he declared his admiration for a work like *The Decline of the West* (1920) by the Prussian reactionary Oswald Spengler.[25]

In almost all his Berlin writings of the early Weimar Republic, there was one central theme: urban and industrial modernity as the locus of alienation and loss of human values. Roth's enemy was *Zivilisation,* which for him, as for Max Weber, took the shape of a mechanized, quantified, rationalized, bureaucratized, and 'disillusioned' world. He described the birth of the skyscrapers which, with the rattle of typewriters and the ringing of telephones, shattered the mystery and romantic aura of the clouds; attacked 'readers of no quality,' who no longer tried to communicate with authors but restricted themselves to 'buying words'; looked at the lines before the ticket counters, a new phenomenon relating to the reification of social relations in the modern city; noticed the spread of jazz, a music 'without melody' which in his opinion expressed the chaos and 'brutish' nature of metropolitan life; finally stressed the growing number of 'nameless dead' who each day were discovered in the poor districts of Berlin.[26] Uncompromisingly, he described the Prussians as 'defenders of the chemical and industrial hell of this world.' But, he felt, they simply embodied a general tendency of the period. What characterized bourgeois society was precisely the 'transformation of all values into stocks and shares [*Umwertung aller Werte in - Börsenwerte*].'[27]

In *Der Antichrist* (1934), his first published work in exile, written under the impact of the National Socialist rise to power, as well as the influence of Max Picard, author of *Das Menschengesicht* (The human face) (1930), Roth reformulated his criticism of modernity from a mystical and theological point of view. Arriving silently and without any apocalyptical display, the anti-Christ was henceforth thoroughly to permeate the modern world. Lost in a cold, rationalized, technologized reality, and surrounded by objects that had no meaning and were without content, twentieth-century Western man had been reduced to a shadow. Modernity was a kind of 'Hades on earth, home of dead men who had become shadows.'[28] If the realm of shadows in antiquity belonged to the dead, in contemporary society it described the condition of the living. The allegorical expression of this alienation was the cinema: 'The Hades of modern man is Hollywood.' Haunted by shadows (the actors or men understudied by their own shadows), the cinema seemed to him the perfect type of art for an alienated, aberrant society.

One of the sources Roth drew on for this analysis was no doubt *The Mass Ornament* (1927), in which Siegfrid Kracauer had already analyzed the cinema and photography as the artistic forms par excellence of our time, representing the 'illusory externality' of a world in total 'historical decline' and characterized by progress that amounted to a 'descent into hell.'[29] We know, too, that Roth was much affected by a work like *Brave New World* by Aldous Huxley, who was one of the first (after Zamyatin and before Orwell) to represent the negative utopia of an entirely alienated world, subject to a totalitarian order.[30]

In *Der Antichrist*, Roth's romantic sensibility began to take on a religious dimension. It was not just a matter of condemning modernity through the metaphoric image of the anti-Christ but, more generally, of perceiving a divine essence in all human values. Certain passages of this book brought to mind the young Walter Benjamin's theory of language. The latter, who like Roth had written for the *Frankfurter Zeitung* during the Weimar period, spoke in biblical terms of an original 'adamic language' in which words did not designate the different objects of reality, but rather were expressive of the name of God. For Roth, however, 'Adam, originator of humanity, embodied the primordial principle of all languages, all races, all peoples, all colors of skin.' God epitomized in his own image all the physical and cultural differences distinguishing humanity: 'If we offend the Jew's nose, the Negro's lips, the Mongol's eyes or the white man's paleness, we are offending also the nose, lips, eyes, and color of God.'[31]

### 'Joseph the Red'

Although it underlay the Rothian *Kulturpessimismus,* this religious dimension was not explicit in his writings of the twenties. After the war and the collapse of the Habsburg Empire, Roth's criticism of modernity began to draw on another powerful spiritual force: the revolution. During the war, he had been a pacifist and antimilitarist. In the revolutionary circumstances of 1918–23, he saw the Russian Revolution as a testing ground for the regeneration of the West in decline. He described himself as a socialist and revolutionary and wrote for the leftist press – his first novel, *The Spider's Web* (*Das Spinnennetz*), had appeared in 1923 in the *Arbeiterzeitung,* the newspaper of the Austrian Socialist Party – where he signed his articles with the pseudonym, *Joseph the Red* (Der rote Joseph). It was this radical political stance that accounted for his break with the *Börsen-Kurier,* the conservative daily for which he had worked since his arrival in Berlin, and for his collaboration with the Social Democratic *Vorwärts* (subsequently he became a prestigious contributor to the *Frankfurter Zeitung,* unquestionably the most important liberal German daily of the Weimar period). In 1924, he hailed the release of Ernst Toller, who had just completed a five-year prison sentence for his leading role in the Bavarian Revolution, describing him as a 'martyr of the proletariat.'[32]

In 1926, Roth went to Russia to write a series of reports for the *Frankfurter Zeitung.* He remained there for a period of about six months, between June and December, during which time he observed Soviet reality from close up and radically modified his view of the revolution. In a letter to Bernard von Brentano, written just before his departure for Moscow, he confessed how impatient he was to see what bolshevism had achieved: the Russian Revolution seemed to him an event of the first importance, not only and not essentially on account of its socioeconomic and political consequences, but mainly because of its 'cultural, spiritual, religious, and metaphysical' dimension.[33] In *The Silent Prophet*, the novel Roth wrote on his return and did not wish to publish during his lifetime, Friedrich Kargan, the hero, vaguely modeled on Léon Trotsky, was waiting for a class war to break out against the bourgeoisie and its notion of 'progress.' He described himself as 'stateless' — one who wanted to wage war to build a world in which he would at last feel at home.[34] In *Flight without End*, this messianic vision of the revolution as a purificatory apocalypse is expressed through the allegorical image of fire: 'The great ocean has no bounds; and a great fire — there must somewhere be a great fire like this, as great, as boundless as the ocean, perhaps inside the earth, perhaps in the skies — a great fire has no bounds. The Revolution is like that. It has no body, its body is the flames if it is fire, or the flood if it is water. We ourselves are only drops in the water or sparks in the fire, without it we are nothing.'[35]

The reality turned out to be quite different. His encounter with the Russia of 1926, still trying to heal wounds left by the civil war and already infected by the germs of bureaucratization, was extremely disappointing. Walter Benjamin, who met him in December and had a long conversation with him, was to write in his *Moscow Diary* that Roth had arrived in Russia parading his Bolshevist convictions and that he left it a monarchist.[36] This journey certainly constituted a turning point in Roth's life, since it put an end to his revolutionary hopes. However, just as he had been a Bolshevik *sui generis*, he did not become a blinkered anti-Communist. His articles painted a vivid picture of the country of the soviets, where the fires of the October Revolution had not yet entirely died out. He described admiringly the social achievements of the Bolshevik state, acknowledging its fierce determination to build a new world. Basically, Roth's profound disillusionment was caused not so much by the process of bureaucratization and the descent into authoritarianism in the USSR at the dawn of the Stalinist era, as by its 'occidentalism.' He had perfectly grasped the nature of the changes which were taking place in Soviet society, where revolutionary fervor had been replaced by 'the silent, blinkered terror of the bureaucracy.'[37] But what was leading the revolution hopelessly astray, was the concentration of all its released energies on a vast modernization drive. Incapable of renovating humanity as such, the Soviet regime limited itself to Westernizing a backward Russia, by directing the revolution along 'a road that led directly to New York.' He had looked for a great spiritual event in the revolution and now he was forced to admit his blindness. 'From a material, political, and social point of view,' he wrote, 'it was a true revolution. From an intellectual, ethical, and spiritual point of view, it represented no more than a huge quantitative advance.'[38] For him, Russian Bolshevism appeared only as 'a form of European bourgeois civilization' which seemed almost to have charged Marxism with 'the task of blazing the trail for it in Russia.'[39] During the following years, the total victory of Stalinism, forced collectivization of the countryside and the start of the five-year plans, only reinforced Roth's skepticism with regard to the Soviet experiment.

In short, after this journey to Russia, his romantic vision was no longer socialist and revolutionary in orientation but, as we shall see below, became increasingly conservative.[40] He ceased to regard the working class as historically destined to bring about the reconstruction of the world on a new social and spiritual basis. In 1929, he wrote to his friend Ephraïm Frisch that 'even the proletariat is in the process of dissolving.'[41] This disappointment coincides as well with the mental illness (diagnosed as schizophrenia) of his wife, which no doubt further deepened his pessimism.

### Exile or the Flight from History

On 30 January 1933, the very day Hitler seized power in Germany, Roth left Berlin to settle in Paris, where, in exile, he was to spend his last years. While continuing to pursue his literary endeavors, he began to write for the German émigré press and even for several French magazines. His scathing articles, devoted to the denunciation of nazism, vividly and movingly reflect the intellectual atmosphere of the world of the German anti-Fascist emigration of the thirties.

With Hitler, the anti-Christ was showing its worst face. The path taken by the West had led finally to a radical antihumanism, embodied in totalitarian dictatorship. This immense catastrophe enabled Roth now to understand and highlight the spiritual contribution of the Jews, since German culture had been created and consumed by them: 'Only the Jews . . . took an interest in books, the theater, the museums, music. . . . Magazines and newspapers were published, bought, and read by Jews.'[42] For the most part, writers of non-Jewish origin extolled a *Heimatliteratur* that described German landscapes and country life, whereas Jewish writers had grasped and entered the very soul of modern urban civilization, with its cafés and its factories, its wealth and its poverty. 'For foreigners, there was only "Germany," whose literary interpreters were, for the most part, Jewish writers.'[43] Referring to the autos-da-fé where the Nazis had just burned 'degenerate' literature (including his own works), he concluded: 'We have celebrated Germany, the real Germany! That is why, today, we are burned by Germany.'[44]

In February 1934, the Austrian workers' movement was crushed by Dolfuss's army. Roth opposed this and strongly condemned Austro-Fascism, but all he could do was serve as a witness and display his moral outrage. Confronted by an endless stream of catastrophes, increasingly his pessimism took the form of a 'flight from history' and a falling back on the mythic.[45] He began to express monarchist and conservative convictions, as well as his belief in a Christianity obedient to Rome. The utterly individual nature of his attachment to monarchism, never taken very seriously in German exile circles and which Arthur Koestler regarded as the 'Don Quixotery' of an eccentric,[46] needs to be emphasized.

When, at the end of World War I, the Austrian Empire fell, Roth had expressed no sense of nostalgia. Between 1918 and 1920, he had even written articles against 'the parasites of the Habsburg monarchy.'[47] In 1927, with a mixture of irony and compassion, he described the tragedy of the exiled Czarist nobility, with its princes living in Paris in rented rooms and its countesses working as waitresses in fashionable Russian restaurants. They seemed to him 'ruins who did not appreciate their catastrophe.'[48] Several years later, his perspective on the Austrian past had entirely altered.

He was not, for that matter, the only one, during the thirties, to idealize the Austrian Empire as an oasis of happiness and humanism before the catastrophe which was to overwhelm Europe. Other Austrian Jewish intellectuals like Franz Werfel, Stefan Zweig, and Hermann Broch shared with Roth a mythical vision of the former Habsburg monarchy.[49] No doubt with a certain dose of self-irony, he had acquired the habit of appending to his name the anachronistic title of 'lieutenant in the imperial and royal army [*kaiserlich und königlich*].'[50] A Jew and *heimatlos,* the author of *The Radetzky March* projected onto the multinational empire of Franz-Josef, in which the mingling of Slav, Jewish, and German cultures had not yet given way to the outburst of chauvinistic hysteria, his aspiration toward a cosmopolitan and open fatherland. Already in 1932, in a letter to the literary critic Otto Forst de Battaglia, he described the war and the end of the Austro-Hungarian monarchy, the 'only homeland' which he could be said ever to have possessed, as 'the most significant experience' of his life. He cherished the memory of his *Heimat* as 'a relic' to be piously preserved.[51] In his story 'Die Büste des Kaisers' (The bust of the emperor) (1934), Habsburg Austria seemed to him like 'a country, the true one, that is the only possible one for men without a country.'[52]

As Claudio Magris has clearly shown, Roth identified the Habsburg monarch with a spiritual *Heimat* which had nothing in common with the imperialistic and authoritarian German *Vaterland.*[53] In 1938, he accused the Germans of having been responsible for the fall of the former empire, which died 'of this Teutonic *Nibelungen* fidelity.' The real Austria ought not to be looked for at the center of this vast empire, but rather at its edges, because it was 'the Slovenes, the Poles and Galicians from Ruthenia, the kaftan-clad Jews from Boryslaw, the horse traders of the Bacska, the Moslems from Sarajevo, the chestnut roasters from Mostar who sing our national anthem,' not the Austro-Germans of Vienna.[54] Contrasting Habsburg universality with German nationalism, he was convinced that the restoration of the monarchy was the only viable alternative to totalitarianism. This explains his contributing to certain journals, supporting the legitimist Habsburg cause, as well as his pathetic journey to Vienna, in February 1938, on the eve of the *Anschluss,* to try to persuade the chancellor to carry out a monarchist coup d'état. But, in truth, at no time did he regard the plan to reestablish the former empire as realistic. His deep nostalgia for the lost harmony and grandeur of the Austrian past took the form of an essentially resigned romanticism. What he was celebrating in *The Radetzky March* was not the splendor of the Austro-Hungarian monarchy, but rather its inexorable decline.

In his last novel from 1938, *The Emperor's Tomb,* Roth also explained the nature of his 'conversion' to Christianity. In his opinion, the Roman Catholic church remained 'in this decadent world the only provider and defender of form.' It embodied the old values in the midst of catastrophe and moral decay. A last shelter in a world in the grip of violence and confusion, it preserved what remained of a classical culture that was being lost. In fact, it was even coming to the acknowledgment of sin, since it no longer regarded those who did not sin as faultless human beings, but declared them to be either 'blessed or sainted.'[55] In the novel, he put these words into the mouth of Count Chojnicki, who belonged to the Slav nobility and was naturally loyal to the Austrian monarchy, the inevitable fall of which he was fatalistically awaiting.

A key to understanding the religious dimension of Roth's thought is perhaps provided by the testimony of Gustav Regler, a Catholic turned Marxist, who entered into a problematical dialogue with the exiled writer during the thirties. Roth accused him of endangering the 'hierarchy of the world' with his 'Red barbarism' and read him passages from *Christentum oder Europa*, by the Romantic, Novalis, stressing that 'true anarchy is the element that gives rise to religion.'[56] This detail nevertheless illuminates the significant continuity between the world vision of 'Joseph the Red' and that of the writer 'catholique.'

Roth's Christianity remained rooted in his Jewishness, as 'the Jews are the earthly matrix of Jesus Christ' and 'whoever is Christian values the Jews.'[57] The former anticlerical writer of the twenties who held priests responsible for the dreadful carnage of World War I (along with the Junker nobility and capital)[58] had become a Catholic, but was unwilling to abandon the metaphysical sensibility of the Hassidic rabbis. His view of the Catholic hierarchy and the Vatican, which would not openly oppose nazism, was highly critical. Roth's religious position did not translate into a political or militant engagement, but represented rather an aspect of the myth he had taken refuge in after having been disappointed by the Russian Revolution and horrified by Nazi Germany. For him, the Church remained the sole force that might still oppose the advance of the anti-Christ, which threatened to eliminate all traces of God on earth. The inner strength of Judaism had been destroyed by assimilation, and the Jews were no longer capable of resisting. In 1933, he regarded them as a people in dissolution. Since they had abandoned their 'spiritual homeland [ *geistigen Heimat*]' and lost their inner cohesion, they could no longer endure — as distinct from their ancestors – the sufferings and persecutions of the present: 'Have they studied the Talmud? Do they wear phylacteries? No, all that is over,' he wrote to Stefan Zweig.[59]

He felt defeated and was overwhelmed by pessimism. There was no alternative to Fascism, that pure product of modernity which punished men for wishing to create a Godless world, apart from a totally anachronistic religious and political attitude which had much more to do with bearing witness than with resistance. Only literature enabled him to preserve the illusion of having abandoned reality and fled history. So, he searched for places where time was suspended and seemed to have escaped the madness of the modern world: the Capuchin crypt in Vienna, where the Habsburg tombs were situated, the bridges over the Seine in Paris, inhabited by tramps like Andreas, hero of *The Legend of the Holy Drinker,* or again the Siberian steppes discovered by Franz Tunda in *Flight without End.*[60] Alcohol had become another fleeting escape from the decadence of a world which, as he wrote again to Stefan Zweig, had been transformed into 'the antechamber of hell.'[61] Many of his friends were, moreover, convinced that his alcoholism was in fact a kind of 'secret suicide,' more or less conscious.

According to Magris, Roth saw history as 'the story of those who had been defeated; historical representation as the allegory of a painful mystery, depicting it as a *via crucis.*'[62] He was not the only one, among the German exiles in France, to characterize history as a terrifying procession of conquerors and an endless chain of oppression for the defeated. But, as against the hell Benjamin describes in his 'Theses on the Philosophy of History' [in *Illuminations*], in Roth's hell redemption was no longer a possibility.

# CHAPTER FOUR

# The Jew as Parvenu

## A Literary Archetype

SIDE BY SIDE with the 'hidden tradition' of pariah Judaism there was another one, undoubtedly shared by a large number of Central European Jews during the first half of the century; that of the *parvenus* (but for whom there would have been no pariahs). As a general rule, they belonged to the upper and middle bourgeoisie, hoped to blend with the German or Austrian middle ranks, turned their conformism into a sort of intellectual habit and a moral duty, and were particularly reluctant to abandon the reassuring anonymity which was the sole guarantee of a doubtless precarious respectability, but also was too valuable to put at risk. In most cases, the Jewish parvenu was an 'unconscious parvenu.' This figure has frequently been depicted in literature, where it seemed that whenever an author drew the portrait of a Jew an attempt was made to set him in his sociocultural context. Here are a few random examples.

First, the upper middle-class individual, the one least tormented by problems of identity, who accepted the given state of affairs as a fact of nature and had no difficulty situating himself in it. Such was Monsieur Fischel, director of Lloyds Bank, described by Robert Musil in *The Man without Qualities*. His 'philosophical' reflections were limited to a few commonplaces drawn from the prevailing positivist ideology and were never permitted to take up more than ten minutes a day: 'He liked to contemplate the rational foundations of human life and believed in its intellectual lucrativeness, which he imagined as something like the well-constructed order of a large banking concern; and he duly noted with approval whatever he read in the newspapers about new progress.'[1]

Then came the Jew who had had to struggle to acquire his status of parvenu, which he proclaimed with pride. Recalling the social and psychological milieu in which he had been raised, that of a middle-class Jewish Stuttgart family at the time of Weimar, Fred Uhlman writes that Germany was his country and his fatherland. 'Foremost we were Swabians, then Germans and then Jews. . . . We were not poor "Pollacken" who had been persecuted by the czar.' For him, to be of 'Jewish origins' meant going to synagogue once a year with his mother, on Yom Kippur. His father missed no opportunity to parade his Germanity. He was a respected doctor, his picture had been published in the *Stuttgarter Zeitung*, and on his forty-fifth birthday he had received a visit from the mayor at the head of a delegation of leading citizens. He had fought in the imperial army during World War I, a fact about which he was extremely proud. An Iron Cross First Class and his officer's sword hung over his bed, next to a painting of Goethe's house at Weimar. He did not fear Hitler, because he knew perfectly well that nazism was only a 'temporary illness,' bound to disappear once the economic situation improved. 'Do you really believe,' he thought, 'the compatriots of Goethe and Schiller, Kant and Beethoven will fall for this rubbish?'[2]

Finally, there was the parvenu already assailed by self-hatred, obsessed, oppressed by his Judeity and haunted by the desire to escape the curse of his origins. This was the most distressing figure, shabby and tormented. Oskar, one of the Jewish characters in Arthur Schnitzler's novel *Der Weg ins Freie* was determined, cost what it may, to live the life of an aristocratic Viennese and never frequent Jewish circles. He no longer wished to work for a Jew, because this made him ridiculous in the eyes of his friends, and he hoped to find an editorial position with the *Christische Anzeigen*. When his father used Yiddish expressions at table, he would have fits of hysterics which might soon have led to a final break with his family.[3]

Kafka, a large part of whose literary production could be read as an allegory of the impossibility of assimilation, painted in *The Trial* a caricatural portrait of a Jewish parvenu in the person of the merchant Block, a 'wretched' figure, repulsive and pathetic, who had lost all his dignity and was entirely dependent on the authorities (personified in this novel, among others, by the lawyer Huld, who held in his hands the keys to Block's salvation). 'He was not a client,' writes Kafka, 'he was the lawyer's dog. If the lawyer had ordered him to crawl under the bed as if into a kennel and to bark there, he would have done it willingly.'[4]

The figure of the parvenu represents a certain approach to Judeity and constitutes, along with that of the pariah, one of the two poles of Jewish life produced by assimilation and now having to cope with the modern world. Parvenus were doubtless very numerous within the 'Judeo-Geman economic élite,' which was formed during the first half of the nineteenth century and whose golden age occurred under the Wilhelminian Empire. It was a social class made up of leading citizens, bankers, financiers, and a few influential industrialists, whose history has been thoroughly studied by Werner Mosse.[5] The Jewish parvenu was, in the first place, the product of the social metamorphosis Central European Judaism underwent in the course of the nineteenth century. The parallel advance of cultural assimilation and socioeconomic integration – in other words, the transformation, in the heyday of capitalism, of traditional merchants into a modern bourgeois class – irresistibly impelled the Jews to adopt a conformist attitude, respectful of the existing order. The figure of the parvenu might almost be accorded the status of a sociological category. Pariahs certainly were to be found more frequently among the generation that came of age during World War I – a generation confronted with a highly destabilized bourgeois order and which rebelled against the conformism of the father generation, an assimilated, liberal, and patriotic Jewish bourgeoisie, created by those who had been described as *Kaiserjuden*. If the pariahs were Jews without a country and without roots, the parvenus clung desperately to their new country or to their illusion of finally belonging to one. Actually, the parvenu manifested only the ambiguities of assimilation. He personified the syndrome denounced by Arnold Zweig in *Caliban* and by Woody Allen in *Zelig* as a typical trait of the emancipated Jew: loss of identity, a constant dissimulation into 'every modern social type,' and especially his identification with those 'peoples thirsting for power.'[6]

Certain elements that foreshadowed the parvenu could already be detected in Moses Mendelssohn and the tradition of the *Haskalah*, which in modernizing and secularizing Jewish culture involved also a conscious attachment to the ideological models prevailing in the Germanic world. To be sure, Mendelssohn was deeply attached to the Jewish religion and would not have accepted von Dohm's formula, 'Allow them to stop being Jews,' but his vision of Judaism as a rational faith adapted to the principles of the *Aufklärung* opened the way to a complete identification of Judeity with Germanity. As we have seen, this was the very conclusion drawn a century later by his leading disciple: Hermann Cohen. The fierceness of Mendelssohn's struggle to impose the German language on his coreligionists and his deep contempt for Yiddish, the language of the ghetto and of shame, unworthy of a civilized people, testified to a desire for assimilation conceived also as a break with the tradition and as an acceptance of the prevailing cultural paradigms.[7]

The parvenu was an ambiguous, contradictory figure, hard to define precisely. We can attempt a portrait, listing his characteristics, but it must also be pointed out that rarely are these to be found combined in a single individual. Features that are marked in some might be less prominent or marginal, or even have disappeared in others. As a general rule, the Jewish parvenu exhibited the following characteristics:

– he was obsessed with the desire to be accepted by the social world around him;

– he sought to adapt to the prevailing system without ever challenging it;

– he tried to repress his Jewish identity. His relationship to Judeity could vary considerably – from that of Theodor Herzl, leader of the Zionist movement, to Otto Weininger, a Jew and an anti-Semite who ended his agonizing ambivalence through suicide – but as a rule it was problematical and full of conflict;

– his difficulty in accepting his own Judeity led to dissimulation or, sometimes, self-denial, which might then take the well-known form of Jewish self-hatred [*jüdischer Selbsthass*];

– a revealing element in his identity crisis was the rejection of East European Jewish immigrants, whose language, appearance, habits, attachment to a religious tradition; in short, national characteristics, projected an image of Judeity diametrically opposed to the one he had built up over a century of assimilation. The parvenu wanted it to be possible for anti-Semites to accept him, but he could not tolerate the *Ostjuden,* because all his efforts of integration were suddenly nullified by the appearance on the scene of this disturbing emblem of Jewish otherness, as fundamentally alien in the German context as it was, on a much larger plane, to Western bourgeois rationalism.[8]

## From Bleichröder to Wendriner

Gerson Bleichröder was a perfect example of the economic parvenu. Bismarck's banker continued to hide behind his patron, even though he was one of the principal sources of the latter's power and played a decisive part in assuring the Prussian chancellor's success. As Fritz Stern, his biographer, stresses, they were complementary figures. Thanks to Bleichröder's capital and the effectiveness of his financial management, Bismark had the necessary means at his disposal to win his victories (in 1866 against Austria and in 1870 against France). For his part, Bleichröder, Berlin's chief banker at the end of the nineteenth century and a key figure in international finance, acquired respectability and a social position that, in effect, no Jewish subject of the German Reich had ever known before.

Bismarck's mentality was that of a Prussian aristocrat – a Junker: investment and the accumulation of capital did not give him the same material and psychological satisfaction as did great landed estates. He was imbued with an aristocratic and precapitalist consciousness typical of the Prussian elite that was dominant in a Germany now expanding industrially and commercially. On the other hand, Bleichröder's economic practices were inspired by an entirely capitalistic, modern rationalism – for the Romantic nationalists and German anti-Semites, he personified the detested spirit of *Manchestertum*. However, it was his deepest wish to be admitted into the Prussian elite. When he was ennobled, in 1872, he held a fabulous reception to which he invited the entire diplomatic corps and 'upper crust' of the Berlin court, but not his own family, which, by its presence, would clearly have spoiled the celebrations and offended the illustrious personages present. Instead of gratifying him, his title, *von*, made him even more acutely aware of his parvenu status in the Prussian aristocracy.

Relations between Bismarck and Bleichröder were based on respect and collaboration, and even, up to a point, on friendship, but the Jewish banker never abandoned a sort of servility and dependency deriving from his condition as a Jew. 'Bleichröder,' wrote Fritz Stern, 'did not try to create a patrician style suitable to him and preferred to imitate, as best he could, the representatives of a class that traced its ancestry back to feudal times. And this world that owed him so much taunted him with being a parvenu, with lacking "authenticity." '[9]

Another type of economic parvenu, this one not so much tragic as comical, was Herr Wendriner, the character created by Kurt Tucholsky to satirize the behavior, vices, and mediocrity of the Jewish bourgeoisie in the Germany of the twenties. A grasping businessman, utterly conformist, vulgar, and narrow-minded, Wendriner was a caricature of the parvenu.[10] When he returned to Berlin from vacation in Paris, all he could speak about was what his wife had spent. If he went to a funeral, he seized the opportunity to discuss his dealings on the stock exchange. At the barber's, he described the Russian Revolution as the work of a 'bunch of loafers.' Clearly he regarded reading as a waste of time and if a friend suggested he read *The Magic Mountain*, he would reply that he had not yet begun Wagner's *Memoirs* which he had received as a Christmas present. At the theater, he thought he had seen an East European Jew, which sent him into hysterics: 'Just look at that darky over there! Probably an East European Jew. . . . You know, with fellows like that, you can understand anti-Semitism. What a sight! Disgusting, that fellow.'[11] This vitriolic portrait of Herr Wendriner accounts for the complaint of 'Jewish anti-Semitism' that several critics have leveled at Tucholsky. However, if it would certainly be misleading to identify all German Jews in the Weimar Republic with the caricature of Wendriner, which Tucholsky did seem at times to be trying to do, it would be just as wrong to try to deny its reality.[12]

For instance, an attitude worthy of Wendriner was adopted by certain leading individuals of the German Jewish community in 1933, after Hitler's rise to power. How other than as a political parvenu can an individual like Hans-Joachim Schoeps be described? This young leader of the Nationalverband deutscher Juden [National League of German Jews], whose watchword was 'Ready for Germany! [*Bereit für Deutschland!*],' wanted to put at the disposal of the Nazi regime an 'assault force' of young Jewish fighters. In 1936, the *Pariser Tagblatt*, organ of the anti-Fascist émigrés, conveyed the distress and irony that the antics of the Jewish pan-Germanists aroused among exiles: 'German Judaism dressed in brown behind its would-be *Führer* H.-J. Schoeps, quite apart from the sorry spectacle this represents, is a comedy, or rather a tragic farce.'[13] H.-J. Schoeps was a borderline case, certainly not very representative of the attitude of German Jews. Nevertheless, the position taken by Rabbi Leo Baeck, president of the Reichsvertretung der deutschen Juden (National Agency of German Jews, the new name for the Zentraverein after 1933), adopted, if not Schoeps's language, at least his basic orientation. While the pariahs – the anti-Fascist Jews – were leaving Germany or were being imprisoned, the parvenus declared their loyalty to the Nazi regime. In late March 1933, Leo Baeck announced that the 'national revolution' aiming to combat bolshevism and to bring about 'the renewal of Germany,' could only be supported by the Jewish community. As an 'atheistic movement [*Gottlosenbewegung*],' bolshevism was the enemy of the Jews, who, for their part, saw the new Germany as 'an ideal and an inspiration.'[14]

But the positions taken were not entirely opportunistic. H.-J. Schoeps and Leo Baeck regarded themselves as deeply Jewish and would never have agreed to compromise with the new authorities at the cost of renouncing their faith. It was not a question of suddenly capitulating to the new order, but of totally identifying with Germany and its civil authorities, which could only perpetuate a tradition – that of the political parvenus of Central European Judaism. During World War I, the newspaper that preached the most extreme German chauvinism and which gathered together all the annexationists and pan-Germanists was *Die Zukunft*, edited by the Jewish intellectual Maximilian Harden.[15] During the Habsburg monarchy, the praises of Emperor Franz Joseph were sung by Rabbi Adolf Jellinek, Jewish leader of Austrian liberalism, who swore eternal allegiance to the state and to its dynastic symbols. Deeply grateful to the emperor who had granted them full citizenship, the Jews 'are thoroughly dynastical, loyalist, Austrian. The Double Eagle is for them a symbol of redemption and the Austrian colours adorn the banner of their freedom.'[16] As against the Russian Zionist Leo Pinsker, for whom the pogroms of the Czarist Empire signalled a new wave of anti-Semitism which might overtake the Habsburg monarchy, Jellinek, as a good progressive liberal, replied that the pogroms sprang from obscurantist prejudice that was unknown in enlightened Austria.

## A Patriotic Jew: Ernst Kantorowicz

Not all parvenus were like the Wendriners. Among them were individuals with wide-ranging minds, morally upright and intellectually consistent. Their tragedy sprang often from the impossibility of combining Judeity with allegiance to Germany, which they regarded as a mission and a moral duty, though the country was determined to reject them. A typical example of the intellectual parvenu is the historian Ernst Kantorowicz, author of *Frederich the Second* (1927). He was the perfect antithesis of the *schlemihl*, whom Yiddish tradition honors for pacifism and antimilitarism. When an officer asked him why one had to die for one's country, the soldier Schlemihl replied candidly: 'You are right, Sir, why?'[17] But the title of one of Kantorowicz's most celebrated studies, written in 1949, is precisely *Pro patria mori* and opens by recalling the 1914 war, in particular with an ultrapatriotic quotation describing the soldier who dies for his country as a martyr.[18]

Born into a family of assimilated Poznan Jews, Kantorowicz went to business school in Hamburg, before joining the imperial army during World War I. An ardent nationalist, he became a member of the circle around Stefan George, whose vision of the heroic individual's role in history profoundly influenced his biography of the medieval emperor Frederick II. This innovative, scholarly work enabled him, in 1932, to obtain a university position, in Frankfurt. His problems started in 1933, when the Nazis expelled Jews from the universities. At first exempted as a veteran—he was finally to be expelled only in 1935, on account of the Nuremberg Laws — Kantorowicz protested vigorously to the Ministry of Education, not against the anti-Semitic measures adopted by the government but against there having been the slightest suggestion of anything anti-German in his unblemished patriotic record. In other words, what shocked him was not the anti-Semitic legislation as such, but the fact that it was applied to him – he who had been a volunteer in 1914, who had fought in the *Freikorps*, putting down the Spartacist Revolt in January 1919 and who a few months later had taken part in the Bavarian Volkswehr (militia) to crush the Soviet Republic of Munich. His political conduct, as much as his historical writings, testified to his deep loyalty to the German fatherland. 'I need no guarantees, neither past nor present, to vouch for my feelings for a Germany with a new national sense of direction,' he wrote, not neglecting to add that his 'enthusiasm' for the new regime far exceeded that of the 'general' public.'[19] In 1938, after the pogroms of *Krystalnacht*, Kantorowicz decided nevertheless to leave Germany and emigrate to the United States. His subsequent opposition to McCarthyism, insisting on the independence of universities – paradoxically he was the only conservative and anti-Communist intellectual to adopt this nonconformist attitude – shows that he was no coward, but a convinced and consistent nationalist. His biographer, Alain Boureau, well describes the neverending agony of a man 'constantly persecuted, but yearning for order and loyal to established institutions.'[20]

*Pan-Germanism and Zionism: Theodor Herzl*

Paradoxically, Zionism, a movement which for so many Jews seemed the occasion for the restoration of dignity and national identity, was directed by a man whose psychology, culture, and political inclinations appeared to fit him perfectly for the role of parvenu. As Carl E. Schorske has quite correctly pointed out, Theodor Herzl 'embodied in his person the assimilationist ideal.'[21] Born into a family of middle-class, Hungarian, German-speaking Jews (his father was a well-to-do merchant), he left Budapest in 1878 to go to university at the age of eighteen. Quite detached from the Jewish tradition, which for him represented no more than a vague family connection, his career as a journalist and writer reflected the conformist mentality of a large section of the liberal Viennese-Jewish intelligentsia. 'I believe in the ascent of man to higher and yet higher grades of civilisation; but I consider this ascent to be desperately slow,' he wrote at the outset of his 'revolutionary' work, *The Jewish State (Der Judenstaat).*[22]

Herzl's burning ambition was to become an officer or senior civil servant, and to achieve this he would have been willing, in his youth, to sacrifice the Hebrew religion (an action which his parents kept him from doing). Nevertheless, throughout his life he was to suffer from an insatiable yearning for greatness and fame. When he was appointed Paris correspondent of the *Neue Freie Presse,* the principal Austrian liberal newspaper, he wrote to his parents that he would try to turn this job into a 'springboard to higher things.'[23] His private journal is crammed with revealing comments about his ambitions and even his letters often reflected his narcissistic personality. In 1895, he wrote that he aspired to become 'a member of the Prussian nobility'[24] and the German aristocracy remained, in fact, his ideal and his model even after his conversion to Zionism.

Contrary to widespread belief, his conversion to Jewish nationalism was not a result of the Dreyfus Affair, of which there is no mention at all in his journal.[25] Of course, he could not remain indifferent after he had witnessed, in 1895, the Captain's dismissal – in his opinion, an intolerable assault on the honor of an innocent man, an insult that was the more unacceptable in that it concerned a Jew respected in society and highly placed in the military hierarchy, with whom he no doubt felt a deep affinity. The Dreyfus Affair was only one element in Herzl's turn toward Zionism, as too were the Viennese elections, a few months later, which marked the victory of Karl Lueger's Christian Socialist movement. Driven by anti-Semitism to rediscover his Jewish roots, he was aware of the impasse the assimilationist process now found itself in and he began to formulate the notion of a *national* solution to the Jewish question. Profoundly ignorant of the tradition and religion of his people, he wrote *The Jewish State,* in his eagerness to pass on to the world the revelation he had had, without realizing that there had been numerous predecessors, even in Vienna (the Kadimah circle, whose moving spirit was Nathan Birnbaum). But Herzl reinterpreted the Zionist idea in the context of his own liberal, assimilated, Viennese, Jewish culture. With him, the hope for a return to Palestine lost its religious and mystical character and became the basis for a modern, secular, political project: the creation of a Jewish national state. In this sense, he was the true originator of political Zionism. In this secularized form, Jewish nationalism was modelled on the codes of that pan-German culture that was his. His attitude expressed simultaneously the desire to break with assimilationism and the impossibility of abandoning a culture inherited from assimilation, with which it was utterly imbued and which shaped its entire thought. The Jews had henceforth to rid themselves of the illusion of being Germans or Austrians, but Germany remained the model for the state and nation which it would be their mission to build in Palestine.

Having become the undisputed leader of the Zionist movement, he hoped to be accepted by heads of state and the imperial authorities on their own level. Between 1896 and 1904, the year of his death, he devoted most of his time to trying to enter into negotiations with Jewish bankers and high state officials. He succeeded, in fact, in meeting a large number, from the German kaiser to the Ottoman sultan, Abdul-Hamid II; from the person responsible for the British colonies, Joseph Chamberlain, to the Czarist ministers Plehve and Witte; from Pope Pius X to the Italian king, Victor Emmanuel III. Each of these encounters was scrupulously recorded in his diary as a solemn event in his life and in the history of the Jewish people. In 1895, he described himself, in a letter to Baron Hirsch, as a '*condottiere* of the mind,' whose destiny it had been 'to emerge at the beginning of a new era,' adding that he should not be accused of presumptuousness, since at his age, thirty-five, Napoleon was already emperor of France.[26] He imagined himself as chancellor of the future Jewish state and hoped that his descendants would put up a 'more artistic' statue to him than that raised by the French in the Tuileries to honor Gambetta.[27] But in order to realize his plan, which he believed depended almost entirely on his titanic energy, it was absolutely necessary that he 'secure the highest decorations,' an essential prerequisite if he was 'to make a proper impression at the European Courts.'[28] Only a few months before he died, in January 1904, he was writing in his journal that he had dreamed of the German emperor. They were alone together, out at sea, in a boat.[29]

The evolution of his attitude to the Jewish question shows both disjunction and continuity: disjunction, represented by the passage from German nationalism to Jewish nationalism; and also a basic continuity, to the extent that this change took place within the framework of the same assimilationist culture. In 1882, he described the Jews as a 'wretched race' doomed to oblivion.[30] He reacted with hostility to the anti-Semitic writings of Eugen Dühring, but he also acknowledged that there was some 'value' in them. In his opinion, German racist ideology was quite right to condemn the 'lack of morals' among the Jews, who would certainly have profited from reading the first chapters of his book *Die Judenfrage* ('they are so instructive that every Jew should read them').[31] In 1882, Herzl was a member of the pan-Germanist Viennese Albia association, from which he was obliged to resign the following year because of its increasingly open anti-Semitism. He was deeply disappointed when he learnt that his letter of resignation had been accepted.[32] But this did not shake his radical assimilationism. Two years later, he still regarded the Jews as a 'race' that had been physically and intellectually debilitated as a result of society's hostility. At that time he saw the solution of the Jewish problem in 'the crossbreeding of the occidental races with the so-called oriental one under the aegis of a single state religion.' 'We must merge with the people,' he wrote,[33] envisaging a mass conversion of Jewish children. Naturally, he was to head the movement. He imagined being received by the archbishop of Vienna and then by the pope himself, who would guarantee their support in the battle against anti-Semitism in exchange for an 'honorable and voluntary conversion to Christianity.' On the appointed day, with all due solemnity, he would lead a procession of Jewish children to Saint Stephan Cathedral, in the center of Vienna, for the ceremony of baptism. Benefactor and leader of the conversion movement, he would nevertheless remain faithful to the creed of his fathers, which would demonstrate even more clearly the humanitarian and disinterested nature of his enterprise. If anti-Semitism did not at once disappear, he would not hesitate to fight a duel with the mayor of Vienna, Karl Lueger, or the pan-Germanist leader Georg von Schönerer.[34] Any solution of the Jewish question must come about as a result of his personal initiative, as trustee par excellence of the intelligence and courage of his people.

Witnessing the anti-Semitic wave that swept through France during the Dreyfus trial, he was in no doubt as to the Captain's innocence. He was too familiar with the psychology of the assimilated Jew, being himself a notable Austrian example of the type, to suspect him of treason. In this regard he wrote that 'a Jew who has opened a career avenue of honor as general staff officer cannot commit such a crime. . . . As a consequence of their long civic dishonor, Jews have an often pathological desire for honor; and a Jewish officer is in this respect a Jew raised to the $n$th power.'[35]

In reality, even after his Zionist metamorphosis, Herzl remained at heart an Austrian assimilationist. He wanted to build a Western state in Palestine, based on the European model. In his view, the return of the Jews to Palestine was in no way a messianic event but had more to do with colonization. To realize this, it was necessary to obtain money from Jewish capital, the support of the great powers, and even the cooperation of 'honest anti-Semites,' 'partners' in this enterprise in order to insure its accountability.[36] It is interesting to note that he became a Zionist once he had abandoned any hope of combating anti-Semitism. He did not see the latter as an obstacle, but rather as an ally in the realization of his state-building plans. In 1903, soon after the Kishinev pogrom, when the Jewish workers' movement was organizing the self-defense of Jewish villages and the Jewish quarters, and European Socialists were conducting campaigns against anti-Semitism, Herzl held talks with Plehve, the Czarist minister of the interior and the one principally responsible for the pogroms, proposing a mutually advantageous arrangement: the Russian government should support the Zionist movement, which wanted to help rid Russia of its Jews, and he, Herzl, would undertake to call off all revolutionary activity on the part of Russian Jews.[37] When he related these talks to Chaim Zhitlowsky, a Russian Jewish Socialist leader, the latter was so amazed that, at first, he thought he had misunderstood what Herzl was saying.

Bringing progress to the backward territories of Palestine, Zionism aimed to transform the Eastern Jews into good Europeans. In *The Jewish State*, Herzl wrote that 'we should there form a portion of the rampart of Europe against Asia, an outpost of civilisation as opposed to barbarism.'[38] A convinced exponent of the virtues of liberal bourgeois society, he declared that, in the future Jewish state, private property would establish itself 'free and sacred.'[39] The most desirable political system, in his view, was 'democratic monarchy,' or rather, the 'aristocratic republic,' which better suited the character of the 'modern' Jewish people. The official language of the Zionist state could only be German,[40] as the Jews will have abandoned Yiddish once and for all, 'those miserable, stunted jargons, those Ghetto languages which we still employ.'[41] In short, the Jewish society he wanted to create in Palestine was an exact replica of the Germany and Austria he was urging the Jews to flee. If they were victims of a Europe founded on the system of nation-states, they ought not to combat the system that excluded them but to adapt completely to it, by creating their own nation-state. Eurocentric prejudices strongly rooted in the culture of the nineteenth century made Palestine seem, not a part of the Arab world but, simply, an area to be colonized.[42] A child of the nineteenth century, Herzl could think only in terms of the political culture of nationalism. His notion of a Jewish state, evidently so disturbing for official Jewish circles in Germany and Austria, in fact showed a deep desire for assimilation. The point was to 'normalize' the Jewish condition, not as something distinct from but within the framework of the existing order. The creation of a Jewish State represented for Herzl the means of achieving a radical and definitive elimination of Jewish *otherness*.

### An Admirer of 'Nordic Beauty': Walther Rathenau

The same all-consuming ambition, linked to a personality and mind of quite another caste, is found in Walther Rathenau — industrialist, intellectual, and future minister of foreign affairs of the Weimar Republic, who fell victim to an anti-Semite's bullet. The son of Emil Rathenau, founder of the Allgemeine Elektrizität Gesellschaft (AEG), one of the principal German enterprises of the turn of the century and unquestionably the largest company owned by a Jew, Walther Rathenau belonged to a privileged class called at that time the 'Jewish patriciate.' He attended the Wilhelms Gymnasium, the most prestigious school in the capital, where the Prussian aristocratic ideal obsessed him. His dream of becoming an officer was not realized: experience of military service, in 1890–91, made him aware of the difficulties in the path of a Jew trying to penetrate the innermost recesses of the state bureacracy. He turned to a diplomatic career, at the same time participating in the industrial and banking activities of his family. His relations with Judeity went through two major stages: the years of youth and the entire first phase of his literary work, roughly up to the eve of World War I, characterized by a fairly obvious form of *jüdische Selbsthass;* and the last decade of his life, when he tried to reconcile German patriotism and Jewish identity.[43] A wealthy and influential industrialist, a talented writer, a celebrated intellectual endowed with strong artistic sensibility, Rathenau was probably the model for Robert Musil's character Arnheim, in his novel *The Man without Qualities.*

Even though he denied it later, it seems that he abandoned the Jewish community without going so far as to convert. What is certain is that he was very early on attracted by pan-Germanist literature. A great admirer of the racist theories of Gobineau, as he was later to admit in his correspondence, he was also excited by the anti-Semitic works of Houston Stewart Chamberlain.[44] He confessed to his friend Alfred Kerr that, as a Jew, therefore belonging to a minority detested for centuries, he would have preferred 'never to have been born.'[45] The piece in which his 'self-hatred' was expressed most openly and strikingly is undoubtedly 'Höre Israel!' an article composed in violent, impassioned prose that appeared in 1897, under the revealing pseudonym, Walther Hartenau, in the magazine *Die Zukunft,* edited by his friend Maximilian Harden. He defined the Jews as an 'Asiatic horde' living in the midst of the German nation as a 'population of foreign stock [*fremdartiger Menschenstamm*].' They had been abandoned by their God, who would take no further interest in a band of 'merchants and usurers [*Krämern und Maklern*]' and they lived despised by all and sundry. Using the common clichés of *völkisch* literature, based on the racial opposition between 'Aryans' and 'Semites,' he exalted the beauty and nobility of the Germanic spirit, as against the ugliness and debility, physical and moral, of the Jews: 'Look at yourself in the mirror! This is the first step toward self-criticism,' he wrote. Compared with the 'Germanic tribes . . . a race raised on a quasimilitary discipline,' the 'southern' traits of the Jews seemed to him frankly 'ridiculous.' His erotically colored exaltation of 'Aryan' aesthetic types led him to paint an alarming picture of the Jewish type: 'Look at your unharmonious constitution, your elevated shoulders, your clumsy feet and feminine curves: if you recognize there the signs of your physical degeneration, then you can work toward a renewal of your appearance over sev-

eral generations.' Marked by the stigmata of 'two thousand years of destitution,' the Jewish people could not rid itself of these external signs of misfortune simply by applying 'a little eau de cologne.'[46]

This 1897 article already included a theme Rathenau was to develop
in subsequent writings: the 'spiritual polarity [*Polarität des Seelenzu-
standes*]' between Jews and Germans. Displaying a Romantic sensibility
which was to find its theorist, with regard to the Jewish question, in Werner
Sombart, he tended to identify Judaism with the spirit of rationalism and
calculation, linked to preeminently modern values as opposed to the traditional values of German culture. The conflict between aristocratic virtues
and plebeian ways, courage and weakness, passion and coldness, loyalty
to principles and opportunism, conservatism and liberalism, tradition and
modernity, was symbolized in his view by the contrast between German
*Mutmenschen* and Jewish *Furchtmenschen*.[47]

Nevertheless, in contrast to the anti-Semitic ideologues, Rathenau did
not find this conflict unresolvable. The Jews could redeem themselves, not
by imitating the Germans but through a long process of self-education and
regeneration, with the object of creating a *jüdisches Patriziertum* meriting a
place in the German nation. Once their faults had been acknowledged, they
would have broken through the barriers of the 'invisible ghetto' which separated them from Germanic civilization, drawing spiritual as well as physical nourishment from 'the free air of the German forests.' Gradually his
writings were to present a less negative image of Jews. In an article of 1904,
'Von Schwachheit, Furcht und Zweck' ('On Weakness, Fear, and Intention') – again published in *Die Zukunft* – the weakness of the *Furchtmenschen* was accompanied by a feeling of 'anxiety and hope.'[48] He saw in it the
seed for a possible rebirth of the Jewish people. In *Staat und Judentum*,
written in 1911, Rathenau even highlighted certain positive traits of the
'Semitic races'; for instance, that 'ingratitude' was still a foreign emotion for
them. He no longer hated this people which had nothing to hope for from
baptism, an illusory 'admission ticket' to society, and each of whom was
aware of being 'a second-class citizen,' but he proposed now to lift it up from
the German nationalist point of view.[49]

Rathenau's reconciliation with his Judeity was more clearly evident from
his correspondence. His German patriotism was not diminished, since he
continued to frequent Prussian nationalist circles and to have many friends

in the pan-German movement. What he had given up was not the criticism of Judaism, but the racist mythology and the self-hatred which hitherto had so painfully obsessed him. To Wilhelm Schwaner, the ultranationalist editor of the *Volkserziehr* who, in his letters, did not fail to allude to his correspondent's 'Semitic' origins, he wrote that he had 'no other blood than German blood, no other origin, and no other people than a German origin [*Stamm*] and people [*Volk*].' The 'mixture of blood [*Blutmischung*]' characteristic of Jews did not prevent him from feeling German to the core, from belonging to the German people and spirit.

> My people is the German people and no other. The Jews [he added] in my view are of German stock, in the same way that the Saxons or Bavarians are. In the light of racist theories, you will find this absurd. But that science does not trouble me at all. Science, which changes from one day to the next, can tell us nothing about feelings and about the ideal of transcendence. . . . For me, belonging to a people and a nation is determined only by the heart, the mind, the soul, and the feelings.[50]

At the end of the war, he addressed an appeal to young people in which he presented himself as a German 'of Jewish stock [*jüdischen Stammes*].'[51]

This reconciliation with Judeity no doubt reflected a psychological shift in Rathenau, but it was inscribed also in the development of his thought, characterized by the search for a synthesis that could overcome the Romantic opposition between *Kultur* and *Zivilisation*. Rathenau's writings on technology – notably *Die Mechanisierung der Welt* (1912) – bear witness to a deep fascination with the esthetic and cultural authenticity of preindustrial society, a Weberian nostalgia for the values of a world that was not yet 'disillusioned.' However, as a banker and industrial entrepreneur, he had to balance and reconcile the cult of *Gemeinschaft* – which he identified with the aristocratic ideals prevailing in Germany – with professional activity that related totally to the sphere of the *Gesellschaft*. An advocate of economic rationalization, and responsible, during World War I, for the reorganization of production for military purposes, Rathenau developed a scheme for a planned economy and 'organized capitalism' that attempted to reconcile the spiritual values of the German nation and industrial modernity.[52] It is in this context that he envisaged the regeneration of the *Furchtmenschen* and allotted the Jews a place in the Germany of the future.

The transformation of the Jews into Germans nevertheless remained a contradictory process. In 1917, he again criticised the concept of conversion as the sole means of redemption for the Jews, the ideal being that of 'reconciliation,' not that of the mingling of religions.[53] But, at the same time, this did not prevent him from regarding Christianity as a religion theologically superior to Judaism and on several occasions from praising the virtues of the Gospels.[54] In a letter of 1917 to von Jagow, former secretary of state for foreign affairs, he divided the Jews into three categories: those who were completely assimilated and had been 'regenerated,' prefiguring the 'Jewish patriciate' to which he aspired; those who belonged to the middle classes, useful to Germany and loyal to liberalism, on the way to being germanized in spite of their 'unpleasant' and often irritating external traits; and finally, the Jewish proletariat, still imbued with 'medieval' prejudices and bound to a ritual, totally alien to the traditions of Germany.[55]

Rathenau's ambiguous relations to Judeity were probably reenforced by his homosexuality, which lay at the root of his 'Nordic' esthetic ideals, drawing on the *Männerbund* culture very widespread in German society at that time.[56] His correspondence, between 1911 and 1921, with Schwaner, the racist intellectual mentioned above, reveals a homosexual attraction which was probably more than just literary. With the exception of a few manifestations of rediscovered Jewish pride, as in the letter of 1916 quoted above, their entire epistolary relationship depended upon their acting out two quite distinct and stereotyped roles: Rathenau was the 'Jew' and Schwaner the 'Aryan.' Moved by his reading of *Zur Kritik der Zeit*, Schwaner expressed his admiration for Rathenau when he wrote that, by a kind of miracle, 'the "dark" Jew [*der "dunkl" Jude*]' had 'saved the fair-haired, blue-eyed German.' Deeply touched, Rathenau replied: 'I take your hand and join myself to you in a feeling of benevolence and of trust.'[57]

When he was appointed minister of foreign affairs under the Weimar Republic, he was soon forced to acknowledge that his dream of becoming the German Disraeli would not be easily realized. Principal architect of the peace treaty with the USSR, signed at Rapallo in 1921, he was a favorite target of the nationalist and anti-Semitic press, where he was henceforth described as '*Börsen und Sowjetjude* [stock market and Soviet Jew],' if not more crudely as *Judensau* [Pig of a Jew].[58] He did not have to wait long for the hatred to translate itself into action. Rathenau was assassinated on 24 June 1922 by young militants of the extreme nationalist Right. Fritz Stern has shrewdly observed that Rathenau would probably have felt a certain sympathy for the 'blond fanatics' who killed him, while he had always kept his distance from the Left, the only group that organized a protest against his murder.[59] But, at base, Rathenau remained an outsider in spite of all his efforts to germanize himself. He was perceived by the workers as a capitalist, as a Jew and an intellectual by the anti-Semitic Right, and as a Socialist by the conservative bourgeoisie, which disliked his schemes for economic rationalization. Thus, his marginalism made him a prime target for all the enemies of the Weimar Republic.[60]

## A Tragic Epilogue

The creation of a class of Jewish parvenus was only *one* of the consequences of the process of assimilation. The integration of the Jews into German and Austrian society, in most cases, took the form of an entry into the bourgeoisie and the middle classes. Assimilation, thus, meant assimilation into the bourgeoisie, with its cultural standards and value system. To the extent that the appearance of modern anti-Semitism, from the end of the nineteenth century, began to influence peoples' attitudes, and that the culture of the *Aufklärung* was gradually replaced by new principles of nationalist thought, Jewish assimilation found itself at an impasse. Confronted by the impossibility of making Judeity a condition of *normal* life, the Jew turned into a pariah or a parvenu.

These two choices led to diametrically opposed political and cultural orientations: in Germany between the wars, Walter Benjamin embarked on a study of the fragments of a messianic redemption which led to his discovery of the forgotten figure of Louis Auguste Blanqui, hero of all the revolutions of the nineteenth century, while Ernst Kantorowicz, searching for the roots of German greatness, extolled the memory of Frederick II; Franz Kafka was fascinated by *Yiddishkeit*, a Jewish culture preserved and not contaminated by assimilation, while Walther Rathenau could not hide his admiration for the 'Siegfriedian beauty' of the 'Nordic race.'

The fate of the Jewish parvenus could only be a tragic one. Desperately clinging to an idea of Germany embodied in the *Aufklärung* of Lessing, Kant, and Goethe which National Socialism had completely destroyed, they were incapable of understanding the catastrophe which was about to overwhelm them and, in most cases, remained passive in the face of persecution. Those who were not exterminated withdrew, their pride and identity deeply and permanently wounded, into an exile of sorrow and of suffering.

# PART TWO

# From Extermination
# to Memory

# CHAPTER FIVE

# Auschwitz, History, and Historians

IT IS KNOWN that, in 1941, during the first months of Hitler's war against the USSR, the Jewish populations of the Ukraine, from Lithuania and Poland, often refused to flee before the advancing German troops. This is how a million Jews came to be taken captive and massacred by the *Einsatzgruppen* in less than a year. How can one explain this passivity in the face of an unprecedentedly murderous onslaught? One reason for it lies no doubt in the traditional view of Germany as the locus par excellence of emancipation. Eight years of a Nazi regime had not managed to obliterate a perception, going back to the end of the eighteenth century and deeply rooted in people's minds, of the Germanic world as the home of the *Aufklärung*. This delayed collective awareness with regard to political and historical changes underlines one of the most striking contradictions signaling the end of that 'Judeo-German symbiosis' whose course we have attempted to chart in the first part of this book: the steady progress of emancipation and of assimilation was abruptly interrupted, like an ascending curve suddenly breaking off. Germany, in a few years, changed from a symbol of emancipation into the center for the systematic annihilation of the Jews.

The history of the 'Germano-Jewish dialogue' is one of a process of assimilation extending over a century and a half. This development was stopped and then reversed after 1933, with Hitler's rise to power. The Jewish genocide was carried out in a four-year period, between 1941 and 1945, during World War II. This bare chronology forces a radical change of perspective on the historian: the long period of assimilation is negated during the short period of extermination. So, to investigate the end of the 'Judeo-German symbiosis' means to consider the place of Auschwitz in the history of the twentieth century.

## The Jewish Genocide and Others

Auschwitz continues to challenge our consciences and poses a major question to the history of the West. But the perception of its central position in this century's history has not been a simple matter. The facts were already known during the war. In spite of the uninterrupted flow of information reaching the Allies, the latter did not react, taking refuge in a silence that expressed as much their refusal to believe as the desire to keep it all secret.[1] Immediately after the war, the full scale of the tragedy was revealed and the world was shocked, but soon − particularly with the onset of the cold war − trauma gave way to repression. The survivors of the massacre often encountered a world that could not understand, or that listened to them with indifference. In 1947, Primo Levi could find only a small publisher willing to bring out *Survival in Auschwitz* (*Se questo è un uomo*), and the book received very little attention. People wanted to forget, for psychological reasons already noted by Isaac Schipper at the Maïdanek concentration camp, when he asked: 'Who will believe our stories? No one will want to believe because our misfortune is that of the whole civilized world. We will have the thankless task of proving to a world turning a deaf ear that we are Abel, the murdered brother.'[2]

With the birth of the state of Israel, regarded as a kind of 'reparation' for the wrongs inflicted on the Jewish people during World War II, the Western powers imagined they had settled the question of their own responsibility with regard to the genocide. The shame had been washed out and the cost of this did not seem too high.

And yet, from the end of the war, it was clear that the destruction of European Judaism represented not only a huge tragedy for humanity as a whole, but also a unique phenomenon, without historical precedent. To appreciate it, a new conceptual framework had to be created. In 1944, Raphaël Lemkin, a Polish-Jewish jurist who had emigrated to the United States, invented the term *genocide* − from the Greek *genos*, race, and the Latin suffix *coedes*, murder − to describe 'a coordinated and methodical plan' for the annihilation of an entire national or ethnic group. The term *holocaust*, which thenceforth was used to identify the Jewish genocide in popular parlance, was invented toward the end of the fifties. This neologism resurrected a twelfth-century Latin word of Greek origin, *holocaustum*, the literal meaning of which was 'that which burns completely.' For the Jews, this term referred to an offering to God in which the sacrificial victim was cere-monially immolated. The term entered into common use, but the notion that it conveys, apparently giving a religious sanction to genocide, seems highly ambiguous and problematical for historiography.

On the other hand, *Shoah,* a Hebrew word meaning 'destruction,' which gained currency in Europe after Claude Lanzmann's great film, is certainly far more expressive of the uniqueness of the extermination of Europe's Jews.[3] To invoke the uniqueness of the Shoah is not, of course, to want to set up a hierarchy among victims of racist violence. A Jew liquidated at Ausch-witz possesses no particular 'aura,' making his death more significant or more lamentable than that of a black lynched by the Ku Klux Klan in the South of the United States or, to be even less ambiguous, than that of a Palestinian child killed by Israeli bullets in the Gaza Strip or on the West Bank. The fact, nevertheless, remains that the America of the black ghettos is not the Third Reich and that the state of Israel has no plans for the exter-mination of the Palestinian people.

The 'final solution' appears to us today, at one and the same time, as the culminating point in an uninterrupted sequence of violence, injustice, and murder that has characterized Western development and as an unprece-dented *break* in historical continuity. In other words, it is only by setting Auschwitz in a larger context of racist crimes and violence that its unique-ness may be perceived and analyzed. It should not become the excuse for imposing a Judeocentric view of history nor for establishing a 'cult of re-membrance' for the exclusive use of the Jewish people, having the effect of dehistoricizing, sanctifying, and in the last analysis mythifying the gen-ocide, by abstracting it from the memory and critical awareness of society *as a whole.*[4]

First of all, an ambiguity must be cleared up. The distinctiveness of the Shoah is not quantitative, even though the losses inflicted on the Jewish people were enormous. Nor is it exclusively linked to the modern industrial technology employed in its execution. The uniqueness of the Shoah is *quali-tative:* for the first time in history an attempt was made to eliminate a hu-man group for reasons of 'racist biology.' Auschwitz was neither the first nor the last genocide in human history: we have only to recall the massacre of the Armenians in Turkey during World War I and the genocide of the Gypsies, which was carried out contemporaneously with the 'final solution' of the Jewish question in Europe; or again, to go further back in time, the ethnic slaughter that accompanied the Spanish conquest of the New World. However, it certainly marks a turning point and a disruption in this series of violent events. This time the extermination served no social, economic, or political purpose; it served only one end: the destruction of the 'Jewish race.' The Jews of Europe numbered about 9½ million in the interwar period. The Nazis did away with between 5 and 6 million. A few hundreds of thousands managed to leave Europe before war broke out, or to escape to the USSR between 1939 and 1941. The planned and mechanized massacre left only a tiny number of Jews alive in most of the territories occupied by the Third Reich. We might reconsider this figure in the context of a century in which the number of victims caused by wars, political and racial persecution, and actual genocides easily exceeds 100 million human beings.[5] Also, Stalin's forced collectivization of the Soviet countryside, in 1928, took the lives of 10 million people, 5 million of whom were Ukrainian peasants. In 1915, the genocide of the Armenians in the Ottoman Empire accounted for between 1 and 1½ million victims out of an Armenian population of about 2 million. Outside Europe, we are confronted by the Cambodian tragedy, where Pol Pot's regime managed to reduce the population by about 1 million people. A few centuries earlier, during the Renaissance, modern Western civilization for the first time attempted genocide in the conquest of the New World. It is probably there that extermination, from the qualitative point of view, had its most serious and irreparable consequences. The figures are impressive. The Aztecs, Incas, and Mayas numbered more than 50 million at the time of the coming of the *conquistadores*. A century and a half later there were only 3½ million left.[6]

At the beginning of the last century, in the United States, the conquest of the American West was achieved at the cost of the genocide of the Indian tribes. The Frontier, celebrated by Frederick Jackson Turner as the foundation of American democracy, was born in the flames of extermination.[7] In this particular case, the crime was not hidden but was vindicated in Western movies and mythified as a glorious page in the history of America.

But the genocides and massacres just mentioned were profoundly different to the Shoah. In the United States, the basis for the extermination of the Indians was the need to take possession of their lands; WASP xenophobia and anti-Indian racism were grafted onto this murderously violent appropriation of territories, but they were not the fundamental reason for it. In Latin America, the essential aim of the *conquistadores* was not the massacre of the Indians but the colonization of a continent. The destruction of communal native forms of production, the plundering of raw materials, and the introduction of a colonial economic system in the Spanish possessions set the process of capitalist accumulation in Europe going. The Indians, killed by gunfire and decimated by diseases hitherto unknown, were the first non-European victims of Western civilization. For the colonizers, their ethnic and cultural otherness was an incentive and justified the liquidation of these peoples, but it was not the reason for the massacre.

In Islamic Turkey, the Christian Armenians made up a particularly vulnerable minority and became the scapegoat for the contradictions besetting an empire in decline. Their destruction met specific socioeconomic and political needs: by exterminating them, the Young Turks regime intended to rid itself of a national minority which, due to its economic dynamism, was sapping the archaic and now fragile foundations of the Ottoman Empire.[8]

Forced collectivization and the 'dekulakization' of the Soviet countryside during the thirties were the product of an aberrant economic policy, which certainly also reflected the contempt of the Stalinist bureaucracy for the non-Russian nationalities (largely peasant) of the USSR; but it was not the counterpart of a scheme for racial and biological 'purification' of an alleged 'Slav race' (the first victims of collectivization, the Ukrainian peasants, were themselves Slav).[9] In Cambodia, the massacre of a million people was the consequence of three years of domination by the Khmer Rouge, a movement that united fierce nationalism and an authoritarianism of the Stalinist kind radicalized by thirty years of colonial warfare. The evacuation of Phnom Penh, the abolition of the market and of money, the militarization of the economy, and the forced dispersal of the entire Cambodian rural population in the name of an agrarian and bureaucratic 'communism' made an extreme form of Stalinism possible in a backward country, the product of colonial domination and war, and the historical phenomenon exemplified here differs radically from the Jewish genocide.[10] Of course, the Stalinist crimes should not be underestimated, but it is important to recognize that they were qualitatively different from those of the Nazis. Like any other historical phenomenon, each genocide or collective massacre has its own specific character: none should be forgotten, none can be pardoned; but not all mass exterminations can be placed on the same level (explaining them in terms of 'universal' categories, which are highly ideological and not very relevant or operational in historical research, such as the notion of 'totalitarianism').[11]

One of the principal traits of the Shoah is its *modernity*. For the first time in history, a complex administrative, bureaucratic, and industrial system was established for the purpose of destroying a people in a 'rational' and planned manner. To this extent, a gulf exists between Auschwitz and the pogroms which for thirty years had steeped the Czarist Empire in blood and impelled its Jewish population to flee in massive numbers to Western Europe and the United States. A similar gulf separates it from the genocide of the Armenians, which was an immense pogrom organized by the Young Turk regime (the Armenian population was deported before being massacred) but whose methods were primitive compared with those employed in the Nazi death camps.

Nevertheless, the modernity of Auschwitz and Treblinka has probably been surpassed by the atomic bomb dropped on Hiroshima (130,000 dead on the spot, and thousands more in the following years) or the Vietnam War. Between 1964 and 1973, the United States dropped 7½ million tons of bombs (including napalm) and 86 million liters of herbicide and defoliant on Vietnam, adding up to three times the tonnage dropped during World War II. In Laos, a small country of 4 million inhabitants, it used 3 million tons of bombs. The colonial war waged by the United States inflicted between 1.0 and 1.7 million civilian casualties on the Vietnamese population.[12] These figures indicate a policy verging, de facto, on the genocidal. But Vietnam was not Auschwitz. It is true that the American army on several occasions engaged in actions that exceeded the norms of warfare. At My Lai, the conduct of the marines was entirely comparable with that of the *Einsatzgruppen* in the USSR in 1941. But the basic difference is that My Lai did not result from a genocidal plan drawn up by the Pentagon. The massacres of the Vietnamese civil population led to expressions of public indignation in the United States, which were translated into a large-scale anti-war campaign. Can one conceive of a mass movement against the Jewish genocide in Berlin, between 1942 and 1944?

A final comparison remains to be drawn between the Shoah and another genocide carried out in the same period and place in which the Jews of Europe met their death: that of the Gypsies (approximately 200,000 victims). Too often forgotten, the massacre of this ethnic minority represented another 'final solution.' However, the destruction of this group was in a way predetermined by the Jewish genocide. Described as a 'foreign race' in 1935 and finally bracketed with the Jews in 1942, the Gypsies were exterminated as 'antisocial elements' from 1943, when the system of gas chambers was already in place and the Jewish genocide had been proceeding for almost two years. The murderous system devised to eliminate the Jewish 'antirace' could serve also to 'deliver' society from an 'antisocial' and 'parasitic' group. The history of the Gypsy genocide has not yet been studied as rigorously and as closely as the Shoah. The numbers are uncertain and estimates of them fluctuate between a few tens of thousands and 500,000 people. According to the documentation now available, 6,340 Gypsies were killed in the gas chambers of Auschwitz.[13] Up to the start of the war, Nazi policy with regard to the Gypsies differed fundamentally from the measures adopted to resolve the 'Jewish question.' From the time of Hitler's seizure of power, all the gains made by the Jewish emancipation began to be questioned and were finally abolished (in 1935), while the Gypsies were to be 'regenerated,' notably through the adoption of a settled style of life and through methods of productivization. In short, the Gypsies were to be made to abandon their nomadic ways and to adopt the German language (an attitude that recalls in several respects the notion of Jewish emancipation developed by the Enlightenment culture).

Homosexuals were described as an 'antisocial group' in the same way as the Gypsies, their crime consisting in not complying with a fundamental duty of all good Germans to reproduce the 'race.' Up to 1934, Ernst Röhm's SA tolerated homosexuality without any problem. After the 'Night of the long knives,' the Nazi regime began progressively to biologize homosexual prejudice by promulgating discriminatory and persecutory laws which strengthened the repressive measures already in force under the Weimar Republic (clause 175). However, repression of homosexuals cannot be classified as genocidal: homosexuals were actually deported during the war to concentration camps (where they comprised a special category, identified by a pink triangle), but were never the object of a policy of extermination.[14]

Auschwitz was preceded by another form of methodical and planned destruction, carried out in the name of the purity of the 'Aryan race.' The decision to eliminate the handicapped and the mentally ill, described as 'lives not worthy of being lived,' was taken by Hitler in 1939 and gassing was already employed in implementing this decision between January 1940 and August 1941.[15] This was enough time to kill at least 70,000 individuals. But in these circumstances—here it differed fundamentally from the Jewish genocide—the massacre was stopped because of sharply adverse German public reaction, especially from the Protestant and Catholic churches. This shows that, quite apart from the intrinsic gravity of the crime, the extermination of the Jews might have been prevented or stopped and that Christian anti-Semitism colluded with it.

The Shoah, therefore, was neither the first nor the last genocide in the history of humanity, nor did it constitute the largest massacre from a quantitative point of view or the only one that could be carried out thanks to modern technology. Of course, European Judaism was destroyed by means of the instruments of death and destruction at the disposal of an industrialized and economically advanced society, but in fact the novelty and uniqueness of the Jewish genocide lay elsewhere. The Shoah marked the victory of a quite new, allegedly scientific ideology: *biological racism*. The extermination had no other social, economic, or political end in view than that of eliminating the 'Jewish race' and of asserting the superiority of the 'Aryan race.' Auschwitz has shown once and for all that economic and industrial progress is not incompatible with human and social regression.

And yet, there appears to be a connection between the conquest of the New World, realized through the destruction of the native peoples and cultures, and the 'final solution' of the Jewish question in Europe. The latter was none other than the apogee of a historical process initiated by Cortés at the start of the sixteenth century, when, as J. M. G. Le Clézio wrote, man discovered at one and the same time 'the universality of law and the universality of violence . . . the noble ideas of humanism and the dangerous conviction of the inequality of races, the relativity of civilizations, and cultural tyranny'.[16] Racist anti-Semitism, developed in Europe at the end of the nineteenth century and adopted as an official ideology by Hitler and Rosenberg in National Socialist Germany, would be simply inconceivable detached from a long history of oppression, plunder, colonization, and destruction of other cultures. Simultaneously the culmination of an uninterrupted chain of violence and injustice and a phenomenon radically new in the extent of its murderousness, the Shoah recalls the allegory of 'progress' narrated by Walter Benjamin in the ninth of his celebrated *Theses on the Philosophy of History*. This Shoah crowns the mountain of human debris and suffering which the Angel of History, impotent and horrified, sees rising to the sky, unable to realize his desire to redeem humanity.[17] Adorno fully grasped the dialectic of continuity and disruption within which the Jewish genocide must be placed: 'Auschwitz cannot be brought into analogy with the destruction of the Greek city-states as a mere gradual increase in horror, before which one can preserve tranquility of mind. Certainly, the unprecedented torture and humiliation of those abducted in cattle trucks does shed a deathly-livid light on the most distinct past, in whose mindless, planless violence the scientifically contested was already teleologically latent.'[18]

In barely four years, nazism utterly destroyed the Eastern European Jewish world: *Yiddishkeit*, which henceforth survived only in the paintings of Chagall, the novels of Isaac Bashevis Singer, and the photographs of Roman Vishniac. In *Mitteleuropa*, it had worked unceasingly since 1933 toward the destruction of the Judeo-German culture created over a century of emancipation. The significance of this huge loss for humanity has been well described by Michael Löwy in a striking allegorical image: 'This Judeo-German culture, product of a quite unique spiritual synthesis which gave to the world Heine and Marx, Freud and Kafka, Ernst Bloch and Walter Benjamin, now seems to us a vanished world, a continent obliterated from history, an Atlantis swallowed up in the ocean with its palaces, temples and monuments.'[19] The deserted Jewish cemeteries of Berlin, Prague, Vilna, or Warsaw recall a world that no longer exists, but which was still alive, embodying a vast human and cultural wealth, sixty years ago; a world which was not slowly caught up in the inescapable transformations of society, but which was killed off at a time when it was still making great strides.

The Shoah represented a sudden and violent break, which it would be wrong to interpret as the culmination of an inevitable historical process (the natural outcome of an everlasting Judeophobia). It is certainly possible to detect a logical and progressive sequence connecting Auschwitz and a millenial anti-Semitic Christian past. Paul Hilberg summed up this process perfectly in his response to Claude Lanzmann's questions: 'Since the fourth century, the fifth and sixth centuries, Christian missionaries had been saying to the Jews: "You can no longer live among us as Jews." The secular leaders who followed them from the high middle ages then decided: "You can no longer live among us." Finally the Nazis decreed: "You can no longer live." '[20] However, as Hilberg himself emphasizes, the Nazis were also capable of 'inventing' something of their own. Their entire literature and anti-Semitic legislation had precedents in the long tradition of Christian anti-Judaism, but Auschwitz presented something absolutely new. To reach this point, it was necessary to take a huge step forward; it required a *qualitative leap*. Nothing expresses the reality of Christian anti-Semitism so well as the words of the Polish peasants, interviewed by Lanzmann in *Shoah* as they came out of church. They declared that the Jews were murdered because they 'had condemned Christ to death.'[21] These words bear witness to the enormous cultural and political hiatus between their feelings and their association with the 'scientific' and 'rational' plan of extermination implemented by the Nazis.[22] Auschwitz was a violent break, so deep a 'disruption of civilization'[23] that, as Günter Grass wrote, 'one is tempted to date the history of humanity and our notion of human life by events happening before and after Auschwitz.'[24]

The speed with which the collective murder of six million Jews was accomplished leads us to reflect not only on the enormous potential for destruction of modern society, but also on the very 'meaning' of history. The Shoah represents a major break in our century, brought about in a quite negligible amount of time. This casts doubt on a notion of history based on 'the long view' (Fernand Braudel), where the 'event' is deemphasized and is incorporated into the overall social dynamic of each period.[25] But the long view enables us to get the background to the Jewish genocide into perspective (in this case, the extended history of anti-Semitism), not to grasp the sudden, irreversible historical break that occurred.

## *Interpretations of the 'Final Solution'*

How could it have happened? The first reaction to the vastness of the catastrophe is one of helplessness, incomprehension. Elie Wiesel, for instance, wrote: 'Auschwitz defies imagination and perception; it submits only to memory.'[26] For others it is an utterly impenetrable suprahistorical phenomenon, a sort of 'no-man's-land of the understanding,'[27] and even a Marxist historian like Isaac Deutscher wondered 'whether even in a thousand years people will understand Hitler, Auschwitz, Majdanek, and Treblinka better than we do now. Will they have a better historical perspective? On the contrary, posterity may understand it all even less than we do.'[28] The problem lies, above all, in the anomalous fusion of modernity and archaism, of industrial society and romantic mythology, of bureaucratic rationalism and Teutonic frenzy that is found in the Nazi system and in its anti-Semitic ideology, a contradiction which is extremely hard to resolve.[29]

Acknowledging an inability to understand Auschwitz, which implies recognizing the enormity of the Jewish tragedy, no doubt bespeaks a more honorable attitude than to offer the ready-made explanations, be they economic, sociological, political, or even psychoanalytical, which over the course of the years have flourished in all the ideological pastures (Marxist, liberal, conservative). It is not a question of regarding nazism as the irruption of a 'demoniac' force that distorted the natural development of German society, as Meinecke supposed in 1946;[30] it is more one of acknowledging the difficulty in attempting to *historicize* a phenomenon as complex and also as far from the 'normal' as National Socialism. The difficulties historians encounter when they study the Shoah relate to an intrinsic contradiction in any attempt to explain the crime rationally. The Jewish genocide belongs to history; we can describe its progress and uncover its causes, yet it remains forever a zone of darkness, before which we are helpless. Traditional historical discourse is not able to penetrate this zone. Historical thought has, therefore, to be lent a further dimension, that of *memory*, which does not pretend to explain the event but supplies us with 'a view from the inside.' Forty years of historical research into the 'final solution' have not produced more poignant testimony than the words of Simon Srebnik, the child singer of Chelmno; or those of Abraham Domba, the barber of Treblinka; or of Simha Rottem, the survivor of the Warsaw ghetto who appears in the film *Shoah*.

It is now customary to divide the different analyses of the Jewish genocide into two main schools, which are generally described as *intentionalist* and *functionalist*.[31] The former is extremely heterogeneous, to the extent that it is problematical whether it should be called a 'school,' since it brings together a number of research workers of different backgrounds and ideological orientation. The only element their work has in common is in treating the Jewish genocide essentially as the product of a methodical plan conceived, prepared, and finally implemented at Hitler's command. Focusing attention on the biography of the führer and assembling excerpts from his speeches and writings, they reach the conclusion that the plan for the extermination of the Jews was formulated by Hitler after World War I. Differences arise as to the date that this decision was taken, which some place as far back as 1918 and others at the end of the twenties.[32] A tendency typical of this current of opinion consists in attributing to Hitler a central and sometimes even exclusive role in the Nazi system. According to Andreas Hillgruber, who proposes no specific dates, Hitler bears the sole and total responsibility for the genocide and his radical anti-Semitism was neither shared by the masses nor by the elite of the National Socialist movement. From this point of view, anti-Semitism becomes a particular characteristic of Hitler's and no longer has much to do with German society.[33]

In general, with a few exceptions, the intentionalist interpretation of the Jewish genocide is influenced by the theory of totalitarianism, which to a large extent dominated political science and the historiography of nazism during the fifties. The most important representative of this current in the field of historiography, Karl D. Bracher, rejects the definition of the Nazi regime as Fascist, and classifies it along with Stalinism under the heading of contemporary totalitarian regimes, though he handles the concept flexibly and intelligently, stressing the differences between these two regimes and avoiding any facile attempt to treat them as identical. Avoiding the thorny question as to when the 'final solution' was formulated and when the order to carry it out was given, Bracher insists throughout his work on the Nazi regime's 'blind fixation on ideology,' which first was to impel Hitler into waging war and then into exterminating the European Jews.[34] If for all intentionalist historians the Shoah represents the fulfilment of a program, Bracher has based this point of view on the most thorough analysis of the Nazi system. The National Socialist state seemed to him a monolithic and hierarchical structure, at the center of which was the führer. However, he also takes into account the internal struggles between the different institutional authorities in the Nazi state, even if these do not alter the basic centralism, typical of any totalitarian state.

The functionalist school is composed of German historians who for the most part entered university during the sixties, no longer attracted by philosophy or political science but rather by social history [Sozialgeschichte]. Central to their analysis are the complex structures of the Nazi state apparatus, rather than the figure of Hitler and his obsession with anti-Semitism. According to Martin Broszat, author of *Der Staat Hitlers,* the centralization of the Nazi regime was a purely formal matter. The apparently all-powerful führer fulfilled an essentially symbolic role, behind which, in fact, was a system of power in which the numerous constituent parts tended toward autonomy, increasingly evading Hitler's central control.[35] In his celebrated work *Behemoth* (1942), political economist Franz Neumann of the Frankfurt school had already developed a theoretical model which presented Hitler's Germany as a fragmented state, torn apart by centrifugal forces and polarized around four main centers of power: the army, heavy industry, the territorial organizations of the Nazi party (the *Gauleiters*), and finally the political police (the ss).[36] Broszat has formalized this interpretative model by means of the notion of 'polycracy.' If the Nazi system of power did not derive exclusively from the führer but from a polycentric and fragmented structure, made up of several power sources sometimes opposed to one another, the Jewish genocide could not be attributed to a decision taken centrally. If Nazi policy was the result of a balance of forces within the National Socialist system, then genocide had not been *planned* but followed rather from an empirical choice, made almost spontaneously at the time when the German offensive in Russia was halted by the resistance of the Red Army. Suddenly a chaotic situation was created in Poland, where the Nazis continued to deport Jews by the hundreds of thousands without being able to settle them and above all without being able to exploit them in a productive manner. The 'final solution' would seem then to have resulted from this particular unforeseen combination of circumstances. Hitler, according to this view, simply formalized an empirical choice made on the spot.[37] This explanation seems somewhat flimsy, to the extent that the physical liquidation of the Jews had already begun in the summer of 1941, with massacres on a vast scale carried out by the *Einsatzgruppen* – massacres which could not have been a matter of chance, and which could be carried out the following year due to the introduction of the death camps, when the Nazi leadership did not yet expect a Soviet counteroffensive. For Broszat, Hitler's anti-Semitism was one of the factors that helped create a climate in which the Jewish genocide could take place, although it was not its primary cause.

The functionalist interpretation of the Shoah is primarily associated with the work of Hans Mommsen, for whom the Judeocide was not the result of a plan but the consequence of 'total improvization.' Following in the footsteps of Broszat, he interprets Nazi anti-Semitism as 'metaphorical' and demagogic verbiage. According to him, Hitler saw the Jewish question in a 'propagandistic' perspective, regarding the struggle against Judaism as belonging to 'an almost metaphysical objective.'[38] To implement the 'final solution,' Nazism had to make use of an extremely complex and extensive bureaucratic machine, comprising different branches of the police and army, the transport system, the banks, industry, diplomacy, and the administration of the occupied territories. Without such machinery, genocide would not have been possible. However, as Mommsen emphasizes, the large number of officials who helped to perpetrate these killings acted as tiny components in a huge anonymous system that could not be grasped. This is typified by individuals like Walter Stier, ex-Nazi party member and former head of department 33 of the Reichsbahn, which coordinated the transport of deportees to Auschwitz and Treblinka, who now declared ingenuously: 'I never set foot in Treblinka. I remained in Cracow, in Warsaw, nailed to my desk . . . I was purely and simply a civil servant.'[39] The difficulty comes when Mommsen asserts that not only the officials of the bureaucratic extermination machine, but Hitler himself, in a sense, participated in the genocidal policy without ever having decided to do so. Accordingly, when confronted by the reality of the extermination of the Jews, he reacted 'exactly the same way as his subordinates, by attempting not to be aware of the facts or suppressing his knowledge.' In effect, for Mommsen, the Shoah was not the product of a program, but the inevitable result of a progressive radicalization of the system [*ein zwingendes Resultat des Systems kumulativer Radikalisierung*].[40] No conscious choice lay behind the extermination, since Hitler confined himself to sanctioning and, a posteriori, to shielding with his authority a policy that derived from a polycentric system, obeying its own dynamic and becoming increasingly uncontrollable. The genocide, thus, was carried out in a context of 'collective suppression' of the crime, typical of all types of 'ideological fanaticism.'

A central element in the functionalist interpretation is the absence of any formal order from Hitler or any other Nazi leader regarding the physical liquidation of the Jews. There are a certain number of declarations by Hitler referring, in a quite explicit manner, to the 'annihilation' of the 'Jewish race.' The intentionalist historians never fail to stress the significance of his

speech of 30 January 1939, in which he declares that, 'if international financial Jewry within and outside Europe should succeed once more in dragging
the nations into a war, the result will be, not the Bolshevization of the world
and thereby the victory of Jewry, but the annihilation [*Vernichtung*] of the
Jewish races in Europe.'[41] We should not underestimate the significance of
this declaration, which today appears as a grim prophecy, but it is also true
that the entire history of German anti-Semitism is marked by threats and
invective of this type, which have to do with verbal or literary demagogy
rather than a genuine program of extermination. On the other hand, it is
undeniable that those responsible for planning the 'final solution' tried, as
far as possible, to implement it under conditions of the utmost secrecy. The
murder was cloaked in coded, bureaucratic language, vague and allusive,
the sole object of which was to disguise the genocide. Even in the death
camps themselves, executions were called 'special treatments' [*Sonderbe-
handlung*] and the gas chambers 'special installations' [*Spezialeinrich-
tungen*]. In 1943, in an address to SS generals, Himmler said that the extermination of the Jews must be 'a glorious page in our history never written
and never to be written.'[42] This is another of the distinguishing features of
the Shoah: its *anonymous* nature. The genocide was to be 'an event without
witnesses.'[43]

To the credit of both intentionalist and functionalist schools, it can be
said that they deal with actual problems, but both also unilaterally fix on
one aspect of the question to the detriment of others, and so promote a distorted reading of the historical process. The intentionalists ascribe to Hitler's policy a coherence and linearity that fail to take into account both its
contradictions and the significance of the governmental and other structures involved in the genocide. To see Auschwitz as the culmination of a
plan that had been carefully laid by Hitler since the twenties means to raise
him to the level of a demiurge, which is not really acceptable: the Shoah as
a historical phenomenon clearly cannot be reduced to the paranoiac obsessions of an individual. After all, in the Germany of the early twenties,
shaken by the Spartacist revolt and the Munich commune, Kapp's putsch
and the revanchist movements of the Reichswehr, the French occupation of
the Ruhr and the great inflation, there was nothing particularly exceptional
about Hitler. Rabid nationalists ready to take up arms to combat the *Juden-
republik* that emerged from the defeat could be numbered in the thousands;

and there were several hundred demagogues anxious to place themselves at the head of these movements.[44] To exterminate six million human beings, racist passion alone does not suffice. Material structures (a state) are also needed; and social conditions that will allow such a murderous enterprise to be carried out. In other words, a wholesale crisis of German society was necessary for the NSDAP to take power; and a war for the anti-Semitism of the Nazi regime to be transformed into active genocide.

In general, intentionalists devote a great deal more attention to the central position of anti-Semites in the National Socialist movement and in Hitler's biography than to the actual evolution of Nazi policy with regard to the Jewish question. In reality, the three great waves of anti-Semitism in Germany between 1933 and the start of the war – the first discriminatory measure of April 1933, the Nuremberg Laws of 1935, and finally the pogroms of *Kristallnacht* in spring 1938 – were basically aimed at expelling the Jews from the Third Reich. The German Jewish population was halved (from 500,000 to 230,000) between 1933 and 1939. The pogroms that took place in Vienna after the *Anschluss* had precisely the same objective and led to the departure of about 200,000 Jews from the Austrian territories incorporated into Greater Germany. This internal policy, terrorizing the Jews into emigrating, led to a tactical collaboration initially with the Zionist movement (for different reasons, the Nazis and the Zionists had a common interest in seeing Germany stripped of its Jews), culminating in the 'Madagascar' project, to create a huge ghetto on the African island.[45] These attempts do not tally with the notion of the existence of a blueprint for the extermination of the Jewish people. In effect, the intentionalist approach fails to appreciate or minimizes the disruptions in the process leading to the 'final solution,' in particular those caused by the war, which suddenly gave to Nazi anti-Semitism a new dimension, and lent it its deadly character.

But the intentionalist interpretation also contains a grain of truth, since it is undeniable that, if one ignores ideology – in other words, the central place of anti-Semitism in the National Socialist *Weltanschauung* – the Jewish genocide seems an utterly inexplicable phenomenon. This point should be stressed, since it constitutes one of the major weaknesses in the functionalist interpretation. The obstinate denial of the existence of a plan for genocide can only facilitate a 'relativistic' reading of the Nazi phenomenon and of its crimes (which is not to accuse the functionalist historians of 'revisionism').[46]

Martin Broszat and Hans Mommsen develop a model which, in view of the absence of a written order emanating from Hitler about the 'final solution,' arbitrarily dates the beginning of the genocide from the time when the extermination camps started operating, avoiding an examination of the entire first phase of the *Endlösung*, which began in the summer of 1941 with the attack on Soviet Russia. Between the summer of 1941 and the spring of 1942, the *Einsatzgruppen* massacred almost a million Jews in the territories occupied by the Wehrmacht. This killing was quite unlike the traditional pogroms of the Czarist Empire. The special ss units did not loot the Jewish *shtetlakh* of the Ukraine and Lithuania, did not rape Jewish women (the most heinous crime for 'Aryans'), nor did they try to terrorize their victims. The means used to carry out the massacres were methodical, bureaucratic, and military, even 'rational,' which enabled the ss to liquidate up to 100,000 Jews a month.[47] The establishment of extermination camps represented no more than a qualitative leap in the context of a process already underway since the beginning of the invasion of the USSR. On the other hand, the view of genocide as an empirical and improvisational solution to deal with contingent and unforeseen circumstances does not explain the relentlessness of the Nazi authorities in carrying out the deportation to the death camps of all the Jews remaining in the territories occupied by the German armies (for example, it does not explain the complexity of the economic, diplomatic, and military measures put into effect in 1944 to deport and exterminate the Hungarian Jews).

But the main limitation of the functionalist approach is that it underestimates the enormous pressure of the history of anti-Semitism (namely, a very long tradition of Christian Judeophobia and, especially, the sixty years of modern anti-Semitism, which became more and more openly racist) behind the decision to embark on the 'final solution.' It would be too facile and simplistic to reduce the causes of the Shoah to the history of German anti-Semitism, but it is certain that the latter provided the essential historical premise for it.[48] It is not a marginal element.

On the other hand, criticism of a monolithic vision of the Hitlerite state is an indispensable condition for understanding the contradictions affecting the implementation of the 'final solution.' No doubt it would be misleading to deny the existence of a plan and of an extermination decision, but this plan and this decision, conceived during the war, were not put into effect without meeting with resistance on a number of occasions (for different reasons, which in general were not humanitarian), nor without passing through an experimental phase before they culminated in the death-camp system (first the slaughters carried out by the *Einsatzgruppen,* then the mobile gas chambers, and finally the extermination camps). In this sense, the Shoah was in effect a *process.* The fact that the death camps were under the control of the Central Office for Economic Administration [Wirtschafts-Verwandlungshauptamt, wvha] of the ss, headed by Oswald Pohl, indicates no doubt a certain empiricism in the actual implementation of the genocide. Resulting from a fusion of two previously existing systems, the gas chambers and the concentration camps, the extermination camps reflected a basic contradiction between the desire rationally to exploit Jewish labor for the war economy and the desire to liquidate indiscriminately all the Jews. Evidently, it was the second solution that prevailed, but this was not clear from the start. The Ministry of the Occupied Territories had to insist repeatedly that 'economic questions must not be taken into account in respect to the solution of the Jewish question.'[49] This contradiction also marked the 'final solution' program that emerged from the Wannsee Conference, in January 1942. In fact, the genocide took place against a background of permanent tension between the desire to bring about the total extermination of the Jews and the need to exploit them for production purposes.[50]

These considerations show that criticism of the intentionalist and functionalist interpretations ought not to throw the baby out with the bathwater. In other words, it should integrate their contributions and transcend their contradictions. Raul Hilberg's monumental work, *The Destruction of the European Jews,* to a large extent avoids the traps of the controversy we have just described in general terms. In the first chapter he seems to be adopting a radically intentionalist position, where the Shoah is seen, more or less explicitly, as the logical outcome of a millenium and a half of anti-Jewish persecutions. Genocide appears to be the result of an inevitable process, the different stages of which succeed each other in a progressive and linear manner. He identifies four basic phases in the National Socialist policy as regards the Jewish question: first the Jews had to be *defined* by means of precise and 'scientifically' rigorous legislation; then the Nazis proceeded to the *expropriation* of those they had described as the antirace of *Unter-*

*menschen;* in the third phase, the Jews were *deported* and *concentrated* in the ghettos of Eastern Europe; finally, in the last stage, that of the *Endlösung,* their *extermination* was carried out. In addition, Hilberg notes two key points in the liquidation process: the 'mobile operations,' entrusted to the *Einsatzgruppen* from the summer of 1941 to the spring of 1942, and then, up to the beginning of 1945, the 'centers of execution.' But this is to talk of a diabolical rationale which may be detectable a posteriori but which relates to no preestablished plan.[51] Without the first three phases there would have been no mechanized massacre, but to get to this point a qualitative leap was necessary, coinciding with a major swing in Nazi anti-Semitism, turning from a policy that encouraged *emigration* to one of *destruction.*

In subsequent chapters, Hilberg becomes a functionalist and examines in detail the extremely complex structures of the genocide. The extermination process required the coordinated activity of four main groups: party, army, economic managers, and bureaucracy. The administrative system and conduct of the policy of anti-Semitism underwent a gradual qualitative change, passing from discrimination sanctioned by law to extermination based on an unwritten command.[52] After exhaustive research, Hilberg succeeded in breaking the crime down into its smallest components. He described its machinery, identified those who were responsible for it, distinguished between the different stages, and uncovered its underlying dynamic.

Both a history and an inquiry into the causes of Auschwitz, the recent work by Arno J. Mayer, *Why Did the Heavens Not Darken?,* though not comparable to Hilberg's as regards documentation, has the advantage of approaching the question from a more general historical point of view. The genocide is no longer studied in vitro, as an isolated phenomenon, but in its historical context, which is that of war. Mayer stresses the fundamental role of anti-Semitism in the Nazi *Weltanschauung,* but does not fall into the trap of seeing that as its sole distinguishing feature. The Nazi ideology was 'syncretic,' composed also of symbols and rituals which were often significant as written texts, and comprising, as well as anti-Semitism, elements of irrationalism, of geopolitics (expansion eastward), of social Darwinism, and of anti-Marxism.[53] All these elements played their part, during the war, in radicalizing Nazi policy up to its culmination in Auschwitz. The 'total war' against the USSR enabled these elements to overlap and fuse in a unique process: the struggle for 'living room,' the destruction of 'Judeo-bolshevism,' and the extermination of the Jews became completely indissociable. At the outset of 1941, Hitler had not yet abandoned the plan to deport Jews to Madagascar; in January 1942, at the Wannsee Conference, in Hitler's absence, the 'final solution' envisaged by Heydrich now related to the Jews as a whole, but was rife with contradictions (notably, as has already been mentioned, between exploitation and extermination). If, up to the start of the war, the Nazi regime, helped by the territorial conquests achieved between 1939 and 1942, did its utmost to render Germany *judenrein* through emigration, the Third Reich found itself again with a Jewish population of several million, concentrated mainly in the East. And it is in the East that the nature of the war changed, becoming 'total.' It was no longer a matter of defeating Belgium or France, but of destroying the USSR, of acquiring *Lebensraum* for the 'Aryan race' by means of a fight to the death against 'Judeo-bolshevism.' Operation *Barbarossa* began to look like a modern 'lay crusade,' a kind of secularized 'holy war' against Soviet communism seen as the true embodiment of the Jewish spirit. 'All in all,' wrote Mayer, 'the "Final Solution" may be said to have been forged and consummated in the crucible of the abortive crusading war against Soviet Russia and "Judeo-bolshevism," which in eastern Europe created the context of extreme cruelty and destruction apart from which the Judeocide would have been unthinkable and impracticable.'[54]

If Raul Hilberg's research has cast light on the internal dynamic, even the stage-by-stage process whereby National Socialism planned and carried out the 'final solution,' Arno J. Mayer has explained the historical conditions which permitted this process to take place and which expanded this dynamic. There are the elements here for a wholesale interpretation of the Jewish genocide, which might take as much into account the history of anti-Semitism, the pressure of ideology and of intellectual attitudes, as the evolution of the Nazi system of domination, with its multiple, and sometimes contradictory, centers of power; it might also illuminate the interaction of these different factors in the crucial situation of World War II and especially the attack in 1941 on the USSR, which made it possible to combine a radicalized anti-Semitic discourse (in the framework of the campaign against 'Judeo-bolshevism' and for the conquest of 'living room') with an enormous destructive potential that had already been unleashed. In short, the elements exist for a synthesis between 'intention' and 'structures,'[55] while avoiding the traps of the two interpretations, opposed but equally reductive and in great danger of relativizing the Nazi crimes, either by attributing them solely to Hitler, or by considering them as the product of a 'subjectless process,' of a blind engine without a driver. It would be just as reductive, and in the final analysis misleading, to explain the Shoah in terms of a teleological vision of history, as to see in it a tragic accident. It was the product of a *plan of extermination*, which however was set in motion in entirely exceptional circumstances – the war – without which it would quite simply have been inconceivable.

## The Aporias of Marxism

In a letter to Walter Benjamin, dated 13 April 1933, Gershom Scholem described the rise of Nazi Germany as 'a catastrophe of world-historical proportions' which permitted him for the first time 'to comprehend deeply' the expulsion of the Spanish Jews in 1492: 'The magnitude of the collapse of the communist and socialist movements,' he wrote 'is frightfully obvious, but the defeat of German Jewry certainly does not pale by comparison.'[56] These words, written in Palestine by a historian of the Cabbala who had left Germany almost ten years before, seem today a good deal more lucid than any of the Marxist analyses of the time.

In 1933, very few intellectuals were aware of the fact that Hitler's rise to power signified the end of Judaism in Germany. The Jews, as Scholem bitterly observed in this same letter, were powerless and continued desperately to cling to a national identity that had been obstinately constructed over a century of assimilation. The National Socialist laws were soon to abolish at one shot the gains made by emancipation. The great majority of the tens of thousands of Jews who left Germany were intellectuals and left-wing militants, Socialists or Communists, whose Judeity made their position even more hazardous and precarious. The official institutions of the Jewish community, notably the Zentraverein, tried to find a form of coexistence and accommodation with the new regime.[57]

The workers' movement was no more ready to deal with the catastrophe. From the end of the twenties, Trotsky had seen the danger of German fascism: his warnings went unheeded. The KPD and SPD were dismantled without offering any real resistance, after having shown themselves incapable of obstructing the rise of National Socialism and of providing an alternative to the dissolution of the Weimar Republic. However, in 1933, nazism unleashed its attack on the workers' organizations, not on the Jews. Nazi anti-Semitism developed gradually and inexorably, passing through several stages: first discrimination and the questioning of emancipation again (1933–35); then economic depredations and the adoption of a policy of persecution (1938–41); finally extermination (1941–45). The destruction of the workers' movement was not a gradual process: it was, in fact, one of the conditions for the consolidation of the Nazi regime. Paradoxically, while the parties, the press, and the left-wing militants were outlawed and persecuted, Hitler was establishing and encouraging the development of Jewish institutions. His object was to drive a wedge between the 'Aryans' and the Jews and to eradicate any sentiment of belonging to the German nation that the latter might still entertain. The result was that the anti-Semitism seemed superficial and transitory by comparison with the absolute opposition of National Socialism to the workers' movement. In other words, nazism was perceived as a regime that was far more antiworker than anti-Semitic.

Marxist literature of the interwar period tended to explain Nazi anti-Semitism as a 'tool' of the ruling classes, without seeing in it a new phenomenon. The Jews allowed Hitler to depict himself as an anticapitalist, even as he defended the power of the great economic monopolies. The policy of economic 'Aryanization' (which in effect benefited some of the principal German trusts) was an expression of the growing concentration of monopolistic capitalism as it clashed with Jewish commercial capitalism. This thesis, originally propounded by the Comintern press in a language often bordering on the anti-Semitic, occupied a central position in the writings of Max Horkheimer from 1939–42 (his point of view was to change in the *Dialectic of Enlightenment*).[58] The only noteworthy exception was that of Trotsky, who grasped the modern and qualitatively new character of Nazi anti-Semitism and in 1938 raised an alarm that was truly *prophetic* about the danger of a policy of 'extermination' of the Jews in the event of another war.[59]

Their analysis of anti-Semitism – or silence about it – constituted a major weakness in the works of Daniel Guérin, Arthur Rosenberg, Otto Bauer, and August Thalheimer on German fascism.[60] In 1942, the year in which the death camps began to operate, Franz Neumann published *Behemoth*, where he categorically denied any possibility of a Jewish genocide. In view of its 'instrumental' character and political value, Nazi anti-Semitism could not 'permit a total extermination of the Jews.' 'The internal political value of Anti-Semitism,' wrote Neumann, 'will, therefore, never allow a complete extermination of the Jews.' The foe cannot and must not disappear; he must always be held in readiness as a scapegoat for all the evils originating in the socio-political system.'[61] Behind these words, written by a sociologist who was both Marxist and Jewish, lay not only a false analysis of reality, but also a psychological attitude, a desire to banish the nightmare of the immense danger that loomed more and more clearly on the horizon. It is the combination of this false analysis and psychological attitude, shared at that time by the Left as a whole, that explains why the appeal made by Samuel Zygielbojm, leader of the Bund, who commited suicide in London in 1943 to 'protest the extermination of the Jewish people' and expose the passivity of international public opinion, went unheeded.

In the postwar period, Marxism seemed to have forgotten Auschwitz. Works devoted to the analysis of fascism did not discuss the Jewish genocide. On the other hand, a strictly economic notion of anti-Semitism reemerged in the rare publications on the Jewish question by historians of the GDR. According to the arguments advanced by them, it was not the Nazi regime but the great monopolies that stood behind the genocide (still depicted as a marginal event as against the persecution of insurgent Communists): Eichmann was the representative of 'German monopolistic capitalism as a whole' and in particular of the chemical combine IG-Farben.[62] Of course, 'analyses' such as these were no longer the result of a tragic failure to understand, but rather of a conscious mystification of reality.

Since the sixties, more responsible studies have begun to appear, some very well documented, but the basis for an understanding of the Jewish genocide is still the notion of Nazi anti-Semitism as the 'economics' of German imperialism. In an article of 1987, Kurt Pätzold accepts the 'singularity' of the genocide [*die Singularität des Judenmords*], which he attributes to three factors: the 'barbarous role of the state,' the number of victims, and the modernity of the means of destruction, but concludes by reaffirming that the extermination was consistent with 'the interests of German imperialism, oriented toward a policy of world domination.'[63]

Though the motivation is different, an altogether analogous attitude is now discernible among certain West German Marxist historians – Karl-Heinz Roth, Götz Aly, and Susanne Heim. They see a basic 'economic rationality' behind the Jewish genocide which is underwritten not by Nazi anti-Semitism but mainly by the plan to conquer Eastern Europe and create a new world order. They try to show that the *Endlösung* was planned by numerous Nazi technocrats (economists and especially demographers), exponents of a neo-Malthusian concept that regarded a policy of extermination as necessary in order to restore the balance between productivity and population. According to this view, racism is simply an aspect of 'economic computation' and the two million Russian prisoners of war who died in the Nazi camps are not so much victims of the living conditions, or of excessively hard labor together with malnutrition, including a lack of basic medical care, as of a policy of *extermination* fully comparable with that carried out against the Jews.[64] Götz Aly and Susanne Heim resurrect once again a single-cause, economics-based interpretation of the Jewish genocide. As Christopher Browning has stressed in his criticism of their theses, they are unwilling to admit that 'racism was neither a diversionary manoeuvre, nor a myth behind which real economic interests hid,' but rather 'the fixed point of the system.'[65] The Nazi 'scientists' did not decide on extermination, but simply tried to 'rationalize' it by means of arguments which, in the whole historical context, could not disguise its fundamental irrationality.

To think in terms of 'final solution economics' also means to deprive the Shoah of its historical distinctiveness, by denying a qualitative difference between losses inflicted as a result of overexploitation of enslaved prisoners of war and the bureaucratic and mechanized *racial* extermination of the Jews. However, the struggle for *Lebensraum* in Eastern Europe presupposed the colonization, even reduction to slave status, of the Slav populations, though it in no way implied the wholesale liquidation of the Russians or Poles. According to Götz Aly and Susanne Heim, the Jewish genocide, far from appearing as a unique historical event, simply adds itself to the long list of violent and murderous crimes perpetrated by imperialism.[66] This thesis might be said to represent the culmination of a strong tendency among the new German Left of the sixties and seventies which, cut off from any memory of the Shoah, avoided dealing with the Jewish question.[67] It

Univer    Nebras

(201) 592-2000

(800) 223-6834

(516) 734-5724

(703) 448-1260

(516) 734-7920

often stressed the continuity between National Socialism and the Federal Republic of Germany, two states resting on the same capitalist foundations, and conceived of fascism in extremely abstract terms, reduced to a few basic traits that applied to any authoritarian regime. For Rudi Dutschke, a charismatic figure in the West German alternative movements, the basic character of fascism was preserved by the FGR in the form of anti-Communism. It is clear that this approach could only underestimate the significance of anti-Semitism as a central element in the ideology and practice of the Nazi regime. This cultural legacy is no doubt present in the recent discussions of Götz Aly and Susanne Heim.

It should be remembered that since the sixties some Marxist historians had criticized the notion of an intrinsic economic rationale underlying the National Socialist system. For Tim Mason, the basic choices and overall operation of the Nazi system could be explained only in terms of the 'primacy of politics.'[68] However, if this interpretation of the general dynamic of National Socialism appears somewhat problematical, it also turns out to be more useful than 'materialist' explanations as a means of getting to the roots of the Shoah. Economic anti-Semitism of the traditional kind, based on the myth of the Jew as banker, moneylender, and starver of the people (a type of anti-Semitism that was exploited on a large scale in the past by various political regimes), might lead to the pogroms of the Czarist Empire but it was not about to be transformed into a mechanized massacre organized by a state. An element that strikes and disconcerts historians studying the Jewish genocide is its essentially antieconomic nature. Where was the economic rationality of a regime which, to kill six million men, women, old people, and children, created, in wartime conditions, an administrative system, transport network, and extermination camps, employing human and material resources which would certainly have been put to better use in industry and on the increasingly depleted war fronts?[69]

It should be emphasized that the notion of the Jewish genocide as a kind of 'economics' of German imperialism was developed only by Stalinist historiography. The analyses of fascism developed by Trotsky, Thalheimer, or Gramsci were infinitely more subtle and profound than the progandistic formulae of the Third International of the thirties. Fascism for them was not the result of a big-business initiative but sprang from a mass movement of the petite bourgeoisie destabilized and radicalized by a global crisis in cap-italist society. Hitler had not begun his political career in the pay of Krupp (even though it was not long before the latter was making financial contri-butions), but at the head of a movement of *lumpen* and *déclassés*. The Fas-cist regime was regarded by Trotsky and Thalheimer as a distinctive form of Bonapartism, while Gramsci, in his *Prison Notebooks,* adopted the defi-nition *caesarism.* These analyses took into account the relative political au-tonomy of the Fascist system of power (and of its ideology) in relation to its economic bases. Centered around the figure of a charismatic leader, the Fascist regime had a tendency to elevate itself above the classes so as to 'embody the nation,' which could come together as a unified whole for the mortal struggle against the Jews, enemies of the 'Aryan race.'[70] A nondog-matic, open, Marxist approach might have tried to find a place for Ausch-witz among these theoretical categories without having recourse to the most grotesque forms of economic determinism.

## Archaism and Modernity

How is the technologized barbarism of Auschwitz to be reconciled with the obscurantist cult of the Aryan *Volk?* Historians and sociologists have fre-quently avoided the problem by trying to explain Nazi anti-Semitism in terms of a single conceptual category: modernity or the obscurantist rejec-tion of it.

In 1955, Herbert Marcuse wrote: 'Concentration camps, mass extermi-nations, world wars, and atom bombs are no "relapse into barbarism" but the unrepressed implementation of the achievements of modern science, technology, and domination.'[71] According to this, it might be appropriate to return to the sources of the emancipation process in order to discover the roots of the perception of the Jew as an outsider in modern society. Eman-cipation signaled the emergence of the Jews into 'a world that did not accept them,' where Jewish otherness survived in a new form. Parvenu or pariah, the Jew remained a foreigner, *Other,* and his difference always bore a nega-tive stamp, the indelible traces of a despicable past and a despicable nature. The emancipated Jew was a fully fledged citizen, but could not aspire to becoming a member of the *Volk.* National Socialism pushed the logic of 'nonacceptance' to its outer limits: the suppression of otherness through the physical liquidation of the Jews. According to Detlev Claussen, one of the last representatives of the Frankfurt school, 'extermination for extermination's sake did not derive from anti-Semitism, which needed the eternal Jew, but from the logic of nonacceptance, which cannot admit of any peaceful end, but only of destruction. . . . In the concentration camps, the logic of nonacceptance celebrated its triumph.'[72] The drastic nature of this formulation, which seems to regard Auschwitz as a direct outcome of the *Aufklärung*, raises some doubts. But Claussen's analysis has the virtue of stressing the aporias of emancipation, which helped to crystalize Jewish otherness and allowed anti-Semitism to make it the catalyst for society's destructive impulses. The intellectuals of the Frankfurt school were the first to discover a fundamental key to the understanding of Auschwitz: its modernity and *instrumental rationality*. But they were limited in that they grasped only one side of the question.

Next there is the view of nazism as an *incomplete form of modernization* — economic but not cultural — where anti-Semitism would express the rejection of modernity and the survival of an archaic ideology. In that case, attention is drawn to the *völkisch* ideology, which was the source of Hitlerite nationalism and anti-Semitism.[73] The myth of the German *Volk* (the origins of which go back to Herder) related not only to the 'people' in an ethnographic sense, but more generally to a system of typically German values. If for Herder, this romantic notion of a German soul had no anti-Jewish and racist connotations, contamination by social Darwinism, from the second half of the nineteenth century, transformed volkism into a kind of racist and anti-Semitic nationalist philosophy. The dissemination of this ideological current can be explained in the context of Bismarck's Germany, where it took the form of an irrationalist reaction to the advent of modernity as a result of an extremely swift and harrowing process of industrialization and urbanization. Frustrated national aspirations — the absence of a colonial empire, the 'penalties' imposed at Versailles, and so on — as well as particular aspects of German history — the continuation of an absolutist authoritarian regime (the Prussian *Obrigkeit*) fundamentally opposed to liberal democracy — combined to lend this current of thought a nationalist and aggressive character.

Rejecting the values embodied by modern industrial, urbanized society, polarized between the bourgeoisie and the proletariat, the *völkisch* ideology took refuge in tradition, extolled the land, sun, and the spiritual values of a people that had emerged from the 'Teutonic forests.' According to the clichés of nationalism, the Jew was the embodiment of modernity, city, and the cult of money; he was rootless and cosmopolitan, and as a result was the absolute antithesis of the German *Volk*. Heinrich von Treitschke spoke of an 'intrusion [*Einbruch*]' of Judaism into European civilization and called for the defence of the Christian character of the German nation. Julius Langbehn was horrified by commerce and the technology which threatened traditional German civilization; in his view, it was the Jews above all who embodied this mortal danger: 'The vulgar cult of money, the North American and at the same time Jewish character are increasingly in the ascendent in Berlin,' he wrote in 1890.[74] For Werner Sombart, it was the Jews, due to their 'calculating spirit,' rather than the Protestant ethic, as Max Weber thought, who were at the roots of capitalism. Houston Stewart Chamberlain, who liked to throw Kant and Gobineau, Wagner and Darwin into the same bag, saw the world as divided into hostile races and regarded it as his mission to defend the purity of German blood against the destructive influence of Catholicism and the Jews. If German perceptions with regard to the Jewish question are reduced to the elaborations of *völkisch* thought, everything becomes quite simple: deeply rooted in the landed aristocracy, the university world, youth, and literary circles, anti-Semitism adjusted itself to the general pattern of the Romantic paradox, pitting community [*Gemeinschaft*] against society [*Gesellschaft*], values that were increasingly identified with two other categories, Germanity and Judeity. Having rid itself of all contradictions, nazism amounted simply to a 'wholesale rejection of the Enlightenment.'[75]

Thus, social Darwinism, social anthropology, biological racism become marginal elements in the formation of the Nazi *Weltanschauung*, which might pass as a conservative and antimodern ideology. This interpretation fails to grasp the ambiguity of a doctrine which, in spite of its incoherence and its irrational aspects, tried to integrate industrial modernity into a conservative vision of the world. Joseph Goebbels, a master of mass communication, described this century as a period of *stahlernde Romantik* [steel romanticism]. If Nazi anti-Semitism was the expression of an ancestral hatred, Zyklon B [gas] was the product of German chemical industries.

The interpretation of nazism as a backward-looking social, political, or ideological phenomenon in general is based on a concept of history and a notion of progress that seems outdated, but it must be admitted that neither can nazism be understood exclusively in terms of modernity. Its ideology and practices derived from the overlapping and merging of contradictory elements: biological racism, industrial society, and 'instrumental rationality'; but also *völkisch* nationalism, Teutonic mythology, the cult of the ancestral *Gemeinschaft*, and rejection of urban life. On the one hand, Albert Speer's technocracy; on the other, Martin Heidegger's philosophy. In other words, Nazi ideology represented a mixture, sui generis, of modernity and the rejection of modernity, synthesized in a concept of *reactionary modernism*.[76] This latter notion was the product of an accommodation between a conservative line of thought and modern industry and technology. Anti-Semitism was the indispensable link between the two: technology and industry could be reconciled with the German soul only after they had been cleansed of the Jewish spirit; liberated from the corrupting influence of the Jews, capitalism could serve the German people; industry could become a positive element for the 'Aryan race,' if it was protected from the calculating, mercantile spirit of the Jewish bourgeoisie; capitalism could be national and creative, if it resisted parasitic, monopolistic Jewish capitalism. This idea, already present in the work of certain theorists of the 'conservative revolution,' was deeply imbedded in the ideology of National Socialist Germany. If the Jews were the embodiment of capitalism in an abstract sense (not of industry, but finance; not of production, but of currency speculation and economic parasitism), anti-Semitism could be transformed into a sort of 'anticapitalist rebellion.' This rebellion linked the rejection of (Jewish) modernity and the acceptance of (Aryan) technology. The Jewish people was destroyed in the name of a *Gemeinschaft* founded on blood, land, and nature, by means of industrial technology and rationality.[77]

Nazism essentially amounted to a radicalization, from a biological and rational point of view, of *völkisch* nationalism. From *cultural pessimism* (Lagarde, Langbehn, Diederichs, etc.) it inherited its crusading spirit directed against the West ('Judaized' and denying traditional Germanic values); from the *conservative revolution* (Möller Van der Bruck, Spengler, Schmitt, Jünger, etc.) it had learned to reconcile industry and technology with the criticism of modernity and the urge to 'restore' an eternal order; finally, it borrowed from biologism its concept of the 'Jewish race,' which was at the very root of its *Weltanschauung*. All these currents of thought, although in different degrees, rejected democracy, liberalism, and especially Marxism, and embraced pan-Germanism, nationalism, and anti-Semitism.[78] In this sense, it can be said that nazism, due to the particular historical circumstances of Germany between the wars, summed up the entire history of the reaction in German culture.

Should nazism – in the light of the uniqueness of the Shoah – be seen as the end result of a particular German line of development, of a *deutsche Sonderweg?* It is enough to point out here that the Shoah was not the consequence of incomplete secularization, of the 'industrialization without political renewal' of German society.[79] National Socialism came to power in a highly advanced country, where the workers' movement – Social Democracy and the Communist party – possessed powerful and evidently unassailable organizations, and the bourgeoisie dominated not only the economic and social life, but also the political institutions (the constitution of the Weimar Republic, resulting from the 1918 revolution, was one of the most progressive in Europe). It was also a country whose culture had influenced the whole of Europe for over a century. Germany had not only produced the Krupp plants, the chemical installations of IG-Farben, and Oswald Spengler's and Alfred Rosenberg's ideology; it had also given birth to Immanuel Kant and Friedrich G. Hegel, Karl Marx and Heinrich Heine, Thomas Mann and Bertolt Brecht, Max Weber and Walter Benjamin. In the Wilhelminian Empire and the Weimar Republic, racism and humanism, cosmopolitanism and pan-Germanism, expressionist rebellion and conservative thought rubbed shoulders and coexisted. Furthermore, anti-Semitism was certainly not exclusively a German phenomenon.

From 1946, Hannah Arendt was stating quite precisely that the 'scientificality' to which nazism appealed, 'coupled with efficient modern technique,' lay behind the creation of the 'death factories.'[80] The Shoah was the product of the encounter between modern anti-Semitism (racist and biological, no longer aiming to expel and discriminate against Jews but to annihilate them) and a Fascist state, in a highly industrialized country with modern technology at its disposal. For this encounter to take place, the workers' movement had first to be crushed and the masses – the *Volk* – to be controlled by an authoritarian system. The two elements, anti-Semitism and fascism, entered into a symbiosis in Germany but, taken separately, they were widespread in Europe between the wars. France possessed a tradition of anti-Semitism – from Eduoard Drumont to Vacher de Lapouge – just as significant as that of Germany and which manifested itself on at least two occasions: at the time of the Dreyfus Affair and in the statute on the Jews promulgated in October 1940 by the Vichy regime.[81] Need one recall that fascism came to power in Italy before Germany and that, for many years, Mussolini seemed to Hitler a model ruler? National Socialism was certainly the product of German history, with all its distinguishing marks, but it can be understood only in a larger context, that of Europe between the wars. Auschwitz is not only about Germany but about humanity as a whole: it is on that scale that it must be seen, as a *unicum* [unique event] of history.

# CHAPTER SIX

# History and Memory

*The 'Jewish Question' in Germany after Auschwitz*

IN *THE REAWAKENING,* the moving account of his odyssey through war-torn Europe after his liberation from Auschwitz, Primo Levi has recreated the psychological climate that prevailed in Germany in 1945:

> As I wandered around the streets of Munich, full of ruins, near the sta-
> tion where our train lay stranded once more, I felt I was moving among
> throngs of insolvent debtors, as if everybody owed me something, and
> refused to pay. I was among them in the enemy camp, among the *Her-
> renvolk;* but the men were few, many were mutilated, many dressed in
> rags like us. I felt that everybody should interrogate us, read in our
> faces who we were, and listen to our tale in humility. But no one looked
> us in the eyes, no one accepted the challenge; they were deaf, blind and
> dumb, imprisoned in their ruins, as in a fortress of wilful ignorance,
> still strong, still capable of hatred and contempt, still prisoners of their
> old tangle of pride and guilt.[1]

This 'deliberate forgetfulness' which made any dialogue with the survivors of the genocide impossible was to become one of the pillars of postwar Federal Germany's political consensus and stability.

Of the world of German Judaism, which numbered 500,000 men and women in 1933, there remained, after the war and the historical cataclysm that bears the name of Auschwitz, only the ruins of a few synagogues. In 1945, 3,000 Jews were living in Berlin, 1,000 of whom had returned from the concentration camps, others having remained there in hiding or carrying false papers.[2] The following year, Germany in defeat received 200,000 Jews who had survived the extermination camps, a mass of displaced persons consisting essentially of Eastern European Jews who were soon to leave the continent, particularly after the birth of the state of Israel. In 1955, only 15,000 of them remained.[3]

It is hard to imagine a more fundamental change: having for a century embodied the assimilationist model, Germany had become the symbol of the rejection of the Jews by Europe and the paradigm of a new Jewish identity based on the memory of genocide. Germanity and Judeity had been definitively separated. The idea of a 'Judeo-German symbiosis' was now no more than a grim joke. The state of mind of the survivors of the Shoah was expressed in a declaration, written in Yiddish, by the committee of Jews of the American zone of occupation: 'What is to be done? Work in German factories? Build German houses? Cultivate German land? No Jew wants that, because it is not possible for him to take part in the reconstruction of the economy of a country that has annihilated the Jewish people. The Jews cannot contribute toward the reconstruction of the German economy: it would be an absurdity.'[4]

In 1950, the Jewish Agency closed its offices in Munich and urged those Jews remaining in Germany to leave the country within six weeks. The following year, the World Jewish Congress broke off relations with the West German Jüdische Gemeinde [Jewish community], which henceforth existed only formally, under the patronage of the federal authorities.[5] Initially the occupation authorities invoked the notion of 'collective guilt' – punishments included the expulsion of several million Germans from the annexed territories of Poland and the USSR – and, after the birth of the state of Israel, any Jew remaining in Germany seemed like a 'traitor.' This was the climate that prevailed throughout the fifties.

## The GDR or Memory Manipulated

In the East, the birth of the GDR was experienced as a *Neuanfang*, a new beginning. The purge of former Nazis was a radical one: in 1948, 520,000 former members of the NSDAP had been discharged and nearly 13,000 sentences had been pronounced for war crimes (in the Federal Republic, where former Nazis were far more numerous, there were only 6,450 convictions and in 1949 only 300 war criminals remained in prison).[6] The purge was particularly extensive in the universities and the several domains relating to 'ideology.'

On this point, the contrast with the Federal Republic, where former Nazis were reappointed to their posts in the state apparatus and those with an anti-Fascist past (notably Communist militants and sympathizers) were regarded as more suspect, was striking. Erected on fragile foundations (in response to the establishment of the Federal German Republic) by the Soviet Union, whose forces occupied the Eastern part of Germany, the GDR could nevertheless appeal to the tradition of the workers' movement, which had offered the only social and political opposition to the Nazis. After all, Hitler's regime had sentenced, imprisoned, or deported a million Germans who were represented only by the SED. Ernst Thälmann, who died in Buchenwald, had become the martyr of anti-Fascist Germany, eclipsing the memory of the excoriater of 'social-fascists,' for whom Hitler had seemed the 'lesser evil' in 1933. A claim to historical legitimacy drawing on the anti-Fascist struggle remained the foundation for the GDR throughout its short life. Initially, at least until the worker's revolt of June 1953, there were many whose hopes lay in the rebirth of a Socialist Germany. The total ascendancy of Stalinism over the new state did not prevent its gaining the sympathy of a large number of intellectuals, from those who settled there (Ernst Bloch, Bertolt Brecht, Stefan Heym, Alfred Kantorowicz, Hans Eisler, Anna Seghers, Arnold Zweig, etc.) to those who, without sharing the same ideology, for some time maintained a benevolent neutrality toward it (Thomas Mann, Peter Weiss).

But the anti-Fascist legitimacy claimed by the GDR served only to perpetuate one of the historic defects of the German workers' movement: its repression of the Jewish question. The latter entered not at all into the cultural and political discussions (a situation that continued until the middle of the sixties, when the first serious historical studies of anti-Semitism appeared).[7] According to the official ideology, nazism had only one enemy, the working class, and anti-Semitism constituted only a marginal and secondary ideological element in its history. Commemoration of the Jewish victims of nazism found no place alongside the vast 'Socialist-Realist' literature that celebrated the Communist resistance. Up to 1988, Herbert Baum, the moving spirit behind the sole *Jewish* group active in the anti-Nazi struggle, who was executed in 1942 for having organized the boycott of an anti-Soviet exhibition in Berlin, was remembered each year as a Communist martyr and never as a Jewish insurgent.[8] Ruling over half a nation which, in the eyes of the whole world, was still under a curse, Walter Ulbricht had the good sense not to organize sensationalistic trials of 'Zionist spies,'[9] as did his Czech and Soviet counterparts. Initially, roughly up to the death of Stalin, the East Berlin Jüdische Gemeinde was subject to a great deal of pressure, which persuaded many Jews to cross to the West. It was forced to condemn Zionism, to break all relations with equivalent bodies in the Federal Republic, and to declare its allegiance to the 'Socialist' regime.[10] From the mid fifties, the climate began to improve: disguised anti-Semitism that prevailed at the height of the cold war, when any Jew could be suspected of organizing a 'Zionist plot,' was abandoned, being replaced by a commemoration of the Jews, organized and controlled by the state, that ran the gamut from restoration of cemeteries to an annual ceremony to remember *Kristallnacht*. Once the 'worker and peasant' state had settled its account with nazism, the 'Jewish question' had no further raison d'être. The courageous attitude of some leaders of the SED, like Paul Merker, who regarded aid for the reconstruction of a Jewish communal life as a moral duty in a Germany guilty of a massacre for which there could be no possible 'reparation,' was swiftly marginalized.[11] It was preferable to ignore the problem, which, far from resolving it, quite simply meant that it had been 'repressed.'[12] From then on, the GDR oscillated between, on the one hand, a radical condemnation and banning of anti-Semitism, and on the other a ritualistic and obsessive denunciation of Zionism (particularly under pressure from the USSR), which depicted every practicing Jew (of two thousand Jews in East Berlin, only two hundred belonged to the Jüdische Gemeinde) as a potential 'imperialist agent.'

The attitude that prevailed for forty years in East German institutions was summed up quite succinctly, in 1983, in this comment by Peter Kirchner, president of the Berlin Jewish community: 'In the GDR, we live in the knowledge that the Nazis are in the West. That is how we solve the problem.'[13] It is significant that, from winter 1952–53, the Association of Individuals Persecuted by the Nazi Regime (Vereinigung der Verfolgten des Naziregimes), which included many Jews among its members, was renamed the Committee of Anti-Fascist Combattants [Komitee der antifascistichen Widerstandskämpfer].[14] Anti-Fascism, imposed by decree, did not seek to commemorate the victims of nazism but rather to celebrate the heroes of the resistance, this becoming the underlying myth of the new 'Socialist State' (later of the East German 'nation,' heir to Luther and Goethe). Detaching the crime from the history of the nation and attributing it solely to the misdeeds of the imperialist system, of which the Federal Republic was the continuation, anti-Fascist Germany was thus able to dissociate itself from this crime. The memory of Auschwitz and, especially, of the consensus in German society with regard to the persecution and genocide of the Jews was of minor importance when set beside the memory of the vanquishers of nazism: the Soviet Union and the German Communist resistance. According to this doctrine, the whole of East German society had been redeemed by the SED and the heroic builders of the new state. The monolithic unity of the regime could not admit of the fact that the actual number of former resistance fighters among the population of the GDR was utterly derisory when compared with the mass of those who had identified with nazism.

In the face of this officially manipulated memory, noninstitutional memory had neither a voice nor a place. It began to find an outlet for itself, toward the end of the sixties, in literature. At times explicitly, more often in allegorical form, the novels of Christoph Hein and Christa Wolf, to mention only the two best-known authors of the new East German literature, did not hesitate to interrogate the past again. In her autobiographical novel *Kindheitsmuster* (*Patterns of Childhood*) Christa Wolf described the normal daily life of a German (now Polish) village under nazism, a 'normality' that could not ignore the discrimination and persecution taking place, that was aware of the criminal reality of the Nazi regime, did not challenge it, and adapted to it.[15] In an interview about this novel, Wolf raised the question of the individual's responsibility with regard to nazism. If the GDR regime thought it had settled accounts with the Hitlerite period, the East Germans themselves could not escape their individual responsibility. 'In my opinion,' she declared,

> literature should dig down into the 'layers' within us, to discover what is not as clean and orderly, as catalogued and 'overcome' (*bewältigt*) as we should like. In this sense, I do not believe that we have 'overcome' the period of fascism, even if, in our case, the problem poses itself in a different manner and cannot be compared, for instance, with the FGR. I am speaking now of another type of 'mastery' [of the past]: the struggle of each individual with his own past, that is to say with what each has done or thought which he cannot blame on anyone else or justify by saying that the mass of the people did likewise or worse.[16]

The consequences of this purely bureaucratic settling of accounts with the Nazi past have been very serious, as has become clear since the reunification. Along with the SED regime, the East German population has also rejected en bloc the anti-Fascism of which it had claimed to be the sole representative. The collapse of the state has brought with it the end of institutionalized anti-Fascist memory, the only permitted and supported one. The proliferation of neo-Nazi movements and racist demonstrations in the former GDR certainly reveal a hatred deeply rooted in the German past, but also the sad legacy of a *memory manipulated* during the forty years of Stalinist domination.

## Adenauer or the Era of Forgetfulness

Born out of defeat and the new climate of the cold war, the Federal Republic of Germany (FRG) was a state built on a void. Having rejected anti-Fascism as a Soviet ideology, the FRG tried at first to substitute for historical legitimacy, so blatantly absent, adherence to the West and its anti-Communist profession of faith. It was in this context that the *era of forgetfulness* took shape under Adenauer. The West German authorities did not favor *denazification* – a solution that was regarded as too costly and destabilizing – but rather *integration*. The theory of totalitarianism, which soon became a kind of state ideology, in the same way as Stalinism did in the GDR, allowed the West Germans to dedicate themselves to the work of reconstruction without suffering any pangs of conscience. Since nazism and communism were nothing but embodiments, in different forms, of the same 'totalitarian' evil, the new German state allied to the West gained legitimacy and settled its account with the Nazi past by fighting communism in the present. It was no longer a question of 'collective guilt,' because the task of the hour – the 'defence of the free world' – demanded the support of all Germans. But for many among them, the struggle against communism was nothing but the continuation of a struggle already initiated by Hitler in 1941. Implicitly, the cold war rehabilitated the Nazi past. Suddenly, the former Nazis became Germans who had 'done their duty' as soldiers or civil servants. This attitude was deeply internalized and even today is strongly in evidence when the proposal to erect a monument to the thousands of deserters of the *Wehrmacht* executed by Hitler provokes indignant reactions.[17] Need one recall that, in Austria, the majority of the population was proud of its president, a former *Wehrmacht* officer who 'did his duty' when the Yugoslav Jews were deported to the death camps and who lied shamefully when he should have acknowledged his personal responsibility?

But to return to postwar Germany. Symbolically, in 1951, the policy of *Wiedergutmachung* (the decision to pay reparations to the Jews who had been persecuted)[18] coincided with the reintegration of former Nazis into public service, thanks to the adoption of article 131 of the Basic Law [*Grundgesetz*].[19] If for Kurt Schumacher, principal leader of the SPD, reparation was a moral duty for Germany ('The Third Reich tried to exterminate European Judaism. The German people is under an obligation to indemnify and to make amends')[20] Adenauer saw the *Wiedergutmachung* treaty as a necessary measure for the new German state to gain international legitimacy and recognition of its sovereignty. In an official declaration of September 1951, which has since become celebrated, he explained the decisions of the government in terms that were far more suggestive of a bloc absolution for Germans than an assumption of collective responsibility: 'The great majority of the German people condemned the crimes perpetrated against the Jews and took no part in them. There were many Germans who, under National Socialism, for religious reasons or reasons of conscience, and exposing themselves to great danger, helped their Jewish fellow citizens, washing out the shameful deeds committed in the name of Germany.'[21] A year later, as if to lay bare the essentially instrumental nature of the policy, he defended the reparations treaty in the Reichstag, referring to 'the great economic power of the Jews in the world.'[22] Far from confronting the nation with the legacy of the 'Jewish question,' *Wiedergutmachung* served only to relieve the conscience of those who wanted to forget. The chapter of Nazi crimes seemed thus to have been closed once and for all.[23] The Jews had, yet again, played the part of scapegoat, indispensable for Germany in recovering its national peace of mind. By means of a small financial effort – the payments made by way of reparations represented 0.22 percent of GNP in 1954 and 0.30 percent in 1966[24] – Germany had been freed of a very heavy burden.

Thus, 'collective memory,' pluralistic by definition and made up of different and often contradictory representations of the past, has had quite a distinct fate in Germany, where it has been isolated, frozen and enclosed in proceedings that shared no common dialectic since henceforth they were socially, politically and even geographically cut off. Jewish memory was sustained abroad, especially in the United States and Israel, by the survivors of the genocide and by the émigrés who had managed to leave Nazi

Germany before 1939. The memory of anti-Nazi resistance had been manipulated and transformed into a State ideology in the GDR. In the Federal Republic, only forgetfulness remained, alongside the silent memory of a considerable number of former Nazis reintegrated into civil society. If the Shoah became at once an unavoidable locus of memory for the Jews, for a long time it remained a *nonevent* for the Germans. This forgetfulness was encouraged as much by the absence of a Jewish memory in the two states that emerged after the defeat of the Third Reich as by the old rejection of Judeity by the German nation as a whole. In a country in ruins, the only victims were those who had lost their homes in the allied bombardments or who had been expelled by the Red Army from the Eastern provinces. It was that much easier to obscure the memory of those who were deported in cattle cars and exterminated in the gas chambers insofar as, for many Germans, they had never been perceived as forming part of the nation and in that no trace of their existence remained. The frantic speed with which the Germans cleared away the war ruins is not due solely to their love of work and order, but also to the desire to repress what had happened. According to psychoanalysts Alexander and Margarete Mitscherlich, this was above all the expression of a genuine 'collective negation of the past.'[25]

The motto for the fifties was 'return to normality.' Thanks to the restoration of economic prosperity, society rediscovered its identity, more in contrast to the terrible war years than in contrast to National Socialism.[26] Expansionism had given way to the battle against time, in a frenzied rush toward modernization and economic growth. The *Volk ohne Raum* had been transformed into a *Volk ohne Zeit* and this metamorphosis left hardly any room for memory. For young West Germans, Auschwitz was an unfamiliar word. As Lothar Baier recalled, the memory of nazism continued to haunt society, 'in the form of unaccountable taboos and impenetrable prohibitions,'[27] but never appeared on the surface. It was scrupulously removed as much from official political discourse as from daily life. Seeking to vindicate the Adenauer era, certain conservative intellectuals today insist on the merits of this abortive denazification. According to the historian Hermann Lübbe, after the war 'a certain social, psychological, and political silence' was needed so as to integrate the body of the German population into the new institutions of the FGR.[28] A few voices, breaking this silence, were raised against the new conformism that smothered society and stood in the way of a critical appraisal of the past: Eugen Kogon, Heinrich Böll the writer, Pastor Martin Niemöller, and especially, from 1946 on, Karl Jaspers.[29] In December 1953, Arthur Koestler was writing indignantly:

> The truth has not penetrated the nation's consciousness, and probably never will – because it is too terrifying to face. If admitted to consciousness, the load of guilt would be too heavy to carry, and would crush the nation's pride, frustrate its effort to rise again as a great European power. Many intelligent and well-meaning Germans react, when Auschwitz and Belsen are mentioned in their presence, with a stony silence and the pained expression of a Victorian lady confronted with a rude reminder of the Facts of Life: that they happen to be facts, never enters her head; they are just unmentionable, and that is all there is to them.[30]

Recalling the state of 'moral confusion' characterizing Germany after the war, Hannah Arendt had pointed out that, paradoxically, the only ones to acknowledge collective guilt were those who themselves were innocent, whereas the mass of those who, in different degrees, were politically, ideologically, even criminally implicated in the Nazi crimes, rarely felt 'the slightest remorse.'[31] A telltale indication of this state of mind was the enormous success of a work like *Der Fragebogen* (The questionary), written by the conservative intellectual Ernst von Salomon, which in 1951 became the first postwar German best-seller. Deriding the questionnaire devised by the occupation authorities to assess, classify, and 'reeducate' him, the author seemed to spurn, with a mixture of contempt and irony, all attempts to 'render culpable' the Germans.[32] The two decades following World War II were dominated by a sense of 'collective innocence [*kollektive Unschuld*],'[33] as numerous public opinion polls indicate. In 1961, 88 percent of West German citizens regarded themselves as bearing no responsibility for the Jewish genocide and, three years later, half the population believed the Nazi regime guilty of no crime.[34] An arrogance that derived from restored economic prosperity, a new political legitimization based on anti-communism, a 'cold amnesty' which quite openly aimed at anaesthetizing memory: these are the elements contributing to the shared feeling of 'collective innocence.'

## Disputed Memory

The end of the cold war, followed by Willy Brandt's *Ostpolitik*, loosened the consensus imposed by Adenauer during the fifties and created a new climate. The silence about the Shoah was broken, after 1961, by the Eichmann trial in Jerusalem, followed two years later by the Auschwitz trial in Frankfurt, which for the first time confronted Germany with its past,[35] but the period ended only with the student rebellion toward the end of the sixties. A new generation born after the war, made a critical rediscovery of history and began to interrogate its fathers, masters of the art of keeping silent. This rebellion was notable for the strong anti-Fascist sensibility it displayed, but was still incapable of grasping the significance of nazism's anti-Semitic dimension. The latter was becoming an abstract notion, traces of which were discerned in all authoritarian regimes, sometimes even in the FGR, but its details, even its historical uniqueness, were blurred. The past was reexamined; Germany's guilt was recognized and condemned. At the same time, 'Weimar in exile' was discovered and the tradition of the workers' movement, Spartacism, and the Bavarian Soviet Republic, pages of German history that had been obscured during the conformist years of the Adenauer regime. The 'Jewish question,' however, remained shrouded in oblivion. There is no other explanation for the levity with which certain subjects were treated, often resulting in a singularly offhand manner, verging sometimes on the anti-Semitic, as for example in the leaflets against 'Nazisrael.'[36]

Notwithstanding the sometimes considerable differences distinguishing it from the [similarly] West German *Neue Linke*, the RAF [Rote Armee Faktion, aka Baader-Meinhof Gruppe] terrorist group seemed to embody all the contradictions affecting the radical leftist culture of the sixties and seventies in its relations to the Nazi past. On the one hand, the questioning of this past was symbolized by Gudrun Ensslin, who commited suicide in Stammheim Prison in 1977, and who refused to answer her judges, declaring: 'One does not speak to people who created Auschwitz'; on the other hand, one cannot forget the 1976 Entebbe incident, when West German terrorists took part in the selection of Jewish hostages from among the passengers of an airplane hijacked by a Palestinian commando unit. Nor can the considerable impact on the German public, several years later, of a film like *Holocaust* be explained, unless this tendency to repression is taken into account. The stodgy and, in the final analysis, confusing television series, which banalized the crime by trying to portray the unportrayable, nevertheless can claim credit for breaking the silence of the generation which had lived through the war and nazism, of stirring consciences which imagined themselves to be at ease, and of bringing home the reality of the Jewish genocide to generations of Germans born or raised during the age of oblivion.[37] For the young militants of 1968, the decisive experience fueling their rebellion was the search for a new identity based on a rejection of the 'silence' of their fathers, those Germans who had lived under nazism. The motivations and impulses behind the internationalism of this radicalized youth – in the first instance solidarity with Cuba and Vietnam – often went beyond support for the oppressed: it was a form of 'negative patriotism,' a sort of borrowed identity that replaced the rejected German identity.[38]

But rebellion against the father generation did not necessarily imply that responsibility for past history had been assumed. We cannot forget the victims of this problematical confrontation of the youth of the sixties and seventies with history: the case of Bernward Vesper, son of Will Vesper, the celebrated writer of the Nazi period, is emblematic in this respect. Leader of the alternative Left and author of an autobiographical novel that appeared posthumously in 1977, *Die Reise* (The journey), Bernward Vesper commited suicide in 1971.[39] But this work of remembrance, aiming at the critical reappropriation of the past, is far from over. The recent Gulf War sheds light on the Left's incomplete and painful reappraisal. How can one not see the ghosts of the past at work here, when a war waged by a military coalition under the leadership of the West against Saddam Hussein suddenly turns into one in which the state of Israel, threatened with destruction by the chemical weapons of the 'Nazi' regime of Iraq, has to be defended? From the moment when the split is no longer between warmongers and pacifists, but rather between those who wish to expiate the crimes of Germany through the destruction of the Iraqi state and the new accomplices of Hitler and of Jewish genocide via Bagdad's despotic ruler, it becomes clear that the poisoned legacy of the Nazi past, and the long period of repression of the Jewish question and of anti-Semitism by the German Left, constitute a stake left by memory, the consequences of which may turn out to be decisive as regards political action in the present.[40]

Official circles, however, do not agonize over dilemmas of this kind, linked to memory, in spite of the courage and the integrity of a Willy Brandt, who broke official protocol during a state visit to Poland, in 1970, kneeling at the site of the Warsaw ghetto. Their sole concern is to provide the Germans with a new conscience, a new national pride. This implies a 'revision' of history, the groundwork for which was laid during the eighties through a series of symbolic events. The most significant of these no doubt was the visit of Chancellor Kohl and President Reagan to the military cemetery in Bitburg, where forty-seven members of the Waffen-SS, including officers, are buried. The West German chancellor spoke of them as 'victims of nazism,' the same as those who were exterminated at Bergen-Belsen, which was visited by the two statesmen just before they went to Bitburg. After this happy and moving reconciliation of victims and executioners, benefiting the latter and having a negative impact on the memory of the former, the Germans could once more live with their past, in defiance of those vanquished by history, according to a remorseless logic already explicated by Walter Benjamin; namely, that when memory is denied or tarnished, 'even the dead will not be safe.'[41] Bitburg inaugurated a sort of 'negative catharsis' of the German national conscience,[42] which was continued the following year by the quarrel of the historians [*Historikerstreit*], taken up by the media, in which certain intellectuals connected with governmental circles made an open plea for the 'normalization' of the German past.

### To Free Oneself from 'A Past Which Will Not Pass'?
#### THE MEMORY OF AUSCHWITZ & THE HISTORIANS

The eccentric views propounded by a number of individuals of the extreme Right and of the neo-Nazi sects, which persistently deny the historical reality of the Jewish genocide, are generally described as 'revisionist.'[43] But negationism is not the only way of 'murdering memory.' There is another, in certain respects more subtle and more insidious than the lies of a Faurisson, which does not consist in denying Auschwitz but rather in 'relativizing' it, making it a commonplace, if not in explaining it away with arguments that amount to a vindication. The new German revisionists do not deny the existence of the gas chambers and have no problem expressing their moral condemnation of the Nazi crimes. They are 'respectable' conservative historians with comfortable positions in the FGR establishment, where they occupy university chairs, direct research centers, and write for the most prestigious dailies. Their aim is different: they are concerned with reinterpreting nazism and relativizing the Jewish genocide, a task they regard as necessary if Germans are to recover a 'positive' sense of national identity, freed from the specters of a 'past which will not pass.'

As we know, this ideological campaign gave rise to a highly animated debate in Germany, which received wide coverage in the media and was henceforth known as the 'quarrel of the historians' — a somewhat inappropriate name, when one remembers that the principal opponent of the revisionists, Jürgen Habermas, is a sociologist and philosopher, and that the controversy extended beyond specialist circles and reached the general public. The starting point was an article by the conservative historian and former student of Heidegger, Ernst Nolte, which appeared in June 1986 in the *Frankfürter Allgemeine Zeitung*. His thesis is quite clear: the Nazi crimes were simply a response to the 'Asiatic barbarism' of bolshevism; the gulag preceded Auschwitz, and without the gulag the Nazi extermination camps would not have existed. According to Nolte, 'with the sole exception of the technical process of gassing' the genocidal policy of nazism had a precedent in the 'extermination of entire groups' carried out by the Bolsheviks, whose actions 'had already been described in the voluminous literature of the late 1920s.'[44] The evidence, irrefutable in his opinion, on which he bases this argument is extremely weak and inconsistent. In the first place there is the 'rat cage,' a form of torture which Chinese elements in the Cheka (the Soviet political police) had used during the civil war. However, as Hans-Ulrich Wehler easily demonstrated, Nolte's source is none other than an anti-Semitic and anti-Communist pamphlet, published in Berlin in 1924, by S. P. Melgunov, a Russian exile and White Guards sympathizer.[45] The other argument, which Nolte had already put forward in a 1985 essay, bases itself on a letter sent in 1939 to British Prime Minister Chamberlain by the Zionist leader Chaim Weizmann: this is supposed to demonstrate that Hitler could legitimately consider himself to be at war with 'international Judaism.' The fact that Weizmann was not a head of state and could in no way claim to represent Germany's Jews is of only minimal significance to Nolte. This is another way in which the historian, instead of analyzing the Nazi point of view, simply accepts it, drawing conclusions which can only be described as vindicatory.[46] On this extremely flimsy basis, Nolte constructs a theory of the Jewish genocide as a 'pre-emptive massacre,' provoked by the threat of destruction coming from Bolshevik Russia. Between the two forms of extermination – 'of class' by the Bolsheviks and 'of race' by the Nazis – a 'causal link' is supposedly established which must 'logically and factually' lead back to the October Revolution. This analysis concludes by denying the unique character of the Shoah, the ultimate responsibility for which does not lie with the Nazi regime but rather with the October Revolution, which inaugurated an era of totalitarianisms. After the outbreak of the *Historikerstreit*, Nolte's views grew even more radical, as evidenced by a ponderous and confused ideological study that appeared in 1987, entitled *Der europäische Bürgerkrieg* (The European civil war), in which he openly declared that what defines the nature of National Socialism is neither its 'destructive tendencies' nor its 'anti-Semitic obsessions' but its relationship to communism and especially to Russian bolshevism. In his opinion, Hitlerite anti-communism was not only entirely comprehensible but also, 'up to a certain point justified.'[47] To get at the underlying motivations of the Hitlerite regime – the struggle against communism and the Bolshevik gulag – with which he is to a large extent in sympathy, he thus dissociates himself from those historians – 'in most cases Jewish writers'[48] – who place Auschwitz at the center of the history of nazism.

Nolte's ideological offensive was taken up by another historian of nazism, Andreas Hillgruber, in a book with the highly significant title, *Zweierle Untergang* (Dual decline), in which the Jewish genocide is treated in the same manner as the collapse of the Third Reich. For Hillgruber, the 'end' of Judaism in Central and Eastern Europe was a tragedy comparable to the 'destruction' of Greater Germany, victim of a plan by the great powers to eliminate its hegemonic role in the center of Europe. He described the last battles of the Wehrmach as heroic attempts to defend the German civilian population from 'the vengeful orgies of the Red Army, mass rapings, arbitrary murders, and indiscriminate deportations,' and ended by declaring his moral support not of those who struggled against Hitler (including the German resistance), but of the soldiers who defended the frontiers of the Reich.[49] Quite apart from the comparison (utterly revealing) between the 'end' of Judaism, the Shoah, and the 'destruction' of the Hitlerite state, Hillgruber's argument does not escape an intrinsic contradiction: to treat two 'catastrophes' like the Jewish genocide and the German defeat in the same manner – even suggesting, through his historical empathy with the soldiers of the Wehrmacht, that the second should be regarded as the more serious –

is to forget that it was the defence of the Reich in the face of the Soviet and allied advance that permitted the massacre to be carried out.

In Nolte's case, the ideological discourse is based on a historical analysis entirely lacking in rigorousness. Resurrecting McCarthyite language and arguments, he makes no distinction between bolshevism and Stalinism, between the early years of the Soviet regime and the Stalinist dictatorship. The repressive measures adopted by the Bolsheviks with regard to opposition movements (including those of the Left) after the October Revolution, starting with the political imprisonments already started under Lenin after the crushing of the 'counterrevolutionary' Kronstadt rebellion, show that Soviet Russia of the twenties was no idyllic socialist utopia. But neither was the Red Terror of 1918–22 the totalitarian hell described by Solzhenitsyn. It is pure fabrication to depict Bolshevik authoritarianism as a forerunner of 'class extermination.' In the language of the Bolsheviks, 'elimination of the bourgeoisie as a class' meant its expropriation, not its physical liquidation. Is the execution of the Czar 'class extermination' in an embryonic form? One might as well go further back still and look for the roots of Auschwitz in the Jacobin Terror. As for the Bolsheviks, the example is a very poor one. Every serious work on Soviet Russia shows that, during the civil war of 1918–21, the Red Army defended the Jewish population of the Ukraine against the extremely violent pogroms of the White Guards.[50] Can this be seen as 'a logical and factual precedent' for the Jewish genocide?

Of course, there is no question as to the murderous nature of Stalin's 'Thermidor.' During the thirties, collectivization of the Soviet countryside (preceded by massive confiscation of crops) took the form of a genuine extermination in which millions of peasants perished. The mass deportations and executions of opponents destroyed an entire generation of revolutionaries. However, the nature of this extermination was qualitatively different from the Jewish genocide. With the collectivization of the countryside, social opposition to the ascendancy of the bureaucracy was put down, and with the Moscow trials and subsequently the gulags Stalinism eliminated its political adversaries: these two phenomena cannot be equated with the liquidation of millions of human beings as members of an 'inferior race' and as 'subhumans [Untermenschen].' Primo Levi, that great writer indelibly marked by Auschwitz, expressed this difference quite unequivocally: 'Unpaid work, in other words, slave work, was one of the three objects of the concentration camp system, the two others being the elimination of political opponents and the extermination of the so-called inferior races. It should be said, incidentally, that the Soviet concentration camp regime differed in essence from the Nazi system in the absence of the third of these and the dominance of the first'[51] (in my view it would be, rather, the second). Clearly this observation is not an attempt to whitewash Stalinism, the crimes of which remain monstrous, but only to prevent its being used as a pretext for the relativization of nazism.

Nolte calmly (and deliberately) ignores a basic fact: Hitler's anti-Semitic obsessions preceded the October Revolution. His hatred of the Jews originated in Austria, before World War I, under the influence of the demagogic populism of the Catholic leader Karl Lueger and the pan-German movement of Georg von Schönerer, whose anti-Semitism was already tinged with open racism. The frustrations of an unemployed and failed artist, in a cultural milieu profoundly influenced by Vienna's Jewish culture, only strengthened the conviction that he was the victim of a 'Judaized' world. Germany's defeat and the 1919 Munich revolution, in which several Jews played leading roles, radicalized his anti-Semitism still further.[52] He was not the only one, in any case, in the early days of the Weimar Republic, to regard the Jews as responsible for the catastrophic situation in which the country found itself. Anti-Marxism and anti-communism, which were certainly constituent parts of the National Socialist *Weltanschauung,* were grafted onto a preexisting anti-Semitic mentality. If, in Hitler's eyes, Judaism and Marxism were practically indistinguishable (hence the neologism 'Judeo-Bolshevism'), it is because his racist anti-Semitism led him to regard Marxism and Soviet Russia as Jewish creations. One need invent no theory of 'class extermination' to explain the psychological mechanism affecting broad social strata of the population (bourgeoisie and petite-bourgeoisie) in Germany as it emerged from the war. As Hans Mommsen explicitly pointed out, Hitler simply took over 'the anti-Bolshevism of the German right,' in which 'the equation of Bolshevism and Jewry' had become a commonplace after 1918.[53]

Nolte's thesis, which represents Auschwitz as the traumatic consequence of the 'Gulag Archipelago,' utterly detaches the question from the history of German anti-Semitism. Behind Hitler was not the Bolshevik with a knife between his teeth – as the propagandistic clichés which agitated Nolte had it – but a long tradition of *völkisch* nationalism and German anti-Semitism. Hitler and Rosenberg were preceded by Wilhelm Marr, Heinrich von Treitschke, Julius Langbehn, Paul de Lagarde, Houston Stewart Chamberlain, Arthur Möller Van der Bruck, and Oswald Spengler, to mention only the most important among a quantitatively significant number of anti-Semitic writers. Here is an eloquent extract from a 'scientific' work by Paul de Lagarde, *Juden und Indogermanen,* of 1887: 'One must have the hide and heart of a rhinoceros. . . . not to hate the Jews, not to hate and despise those who, in the name of humanity, speak for the Jews or who are too cowardly to crush this pullulating vermin. One does not negotiate with thread worms and bacillae. One does not educate thread worms and bacillae, one exterminates them as swiftly and as totally as possible.'[54] At the turn of the century, writing of this kind was current in many mass-circulation periodicals. The biological racism of the Nazi regime focused a whole cultural movement that was increasingly influential in Germany from the end of the nineteenth century: nationalism impregnated with the Aryan myth of the *Volk* and obsessed by the image of the Jew as an element foreign to Germany. This is where the roots of Nazi anti-Semitism must be sought.

Joachim Fest, Hitler's biographer and coeditor of the conservative daily, *Frankfurter Allgemeine Zeitung,* as well as the Bonn historian Klaus Hildebrand intervened in the debate in defence of Nolte. Hildebrand resurrected the theory of totalitarianism to bolster the argument that genocide was a policy pursued simultaneously by the USSR and Nazi Germany.[55] Fest's argument was somewhat more subtle. He attacked the notion of the historical uniqueness of the Jewish genocide, insisting that, in spite of their different motivations – 'in the one case class, in the other race' – the 'liquidations' carried out by the Bolsheviks were quite as bureaucratic, impersonal and 'reproducible' as those of the Nazis. He acknowledged the 'repugnant' character of the 'technologized barbarism of the Hitler regime,' symbolized by the gas chambers, but added, 'Can it really be said that the mass liquidations by a bullet to the back of the head, as was common practice during the Red terror, are qualitatively different?'[56] The objection raised to this that the Nazi genocide took place in an economically advanced country with 'an old culture' seems inconsistent to him, because all it does is to repeat the distinction made by the Nazis themselves between advanced and backward peoples. His conclusion is that the notion of the uniqueness of the Nazi crimes 'rests on shaky ground.' An excellent response to Fest came from the historian Eberhard Jäckel, who retraced the path of Hitlerite anti-Semitism and reaffirmed that 'the National-Socialist murder of the Jews was unique because never before had a nation with the authority of its leader decided and announced that it would kill off as completely as possible a particular group of humans, including old people, women, children and infants, and actually put this decision into practice, using all the means at its disposal.'[57]

Three basic themes inform the *Historikerstreit:* denial of the unique nature of the Jewish genocide (Nolte, Fest), which, except for a few marginal innovations (the gas chambers) is no more than a copy of the original model: the Bolshevik gulag; identical treatment of the perpetrators of the crime and of its victims, linking the Germans in the territories occupied by the Red Army with the Jews exterminated in the Nazi death camps (Hillgruber); and finally, normalization of the German past by treating the National Socialist ideology as typical of an 'age of tyrants' (Hildebrand) where it not only loses its murderous uniqueness but even acquires a certain historical legitimacy in the struggle against communism. What is at stake in the 'quarrel of the historians' thus becomes clear: it concerns the relationship of Germany to its past. Behind the revision of history lies a political objective, in the achievement of which the Bitburg episode already represented a significant stage, aiming to reconcile Germany with its past, in order to return to it, in Michaël Stürmer's words, a 'positive' sense of national identity.

In the end, Nolte's thesis must be given the right epithet: anti-Semitic.[58] The wish to 'normalize' the German past, by representing the Nazi period as one historical stage among others, implies indifference to the victims of genocide. The idea that nazism was no more than a response to the 'Asian barbarism' of the Bolsheviks (a response to the threat of 'class extermination') simply recapitulates a theme typical of Nazi propaganda; namely, the need to protect the German *Volk* and 'Aryan civilization' against 'Judeo-Bolshevism.'

## An Amnesic Reunification

If what was basically at stake in the *Historikerstreit* was the relativization of Nazi crimes and the normalization of the Jewish question in Germany, this implies the end of forgetfulness, or at least of the earlier forms that it assumed. In this connection, one must remember that the *Historikerstreit* took place more in the daily press than in specialist magazines and was widely discussed in the media. Auschwitz is no longer a taboo subject, as in the fifties. The attempts to relativize its significance involve talking about it. It has become impossible to forget the Shoah and now an effort is being made to substitute for it its relativization, even its banalization.

At the same time, Germany seems finally to have discovered the importance and vast richness of the Jewish contribution to its culture. The works of thinkers and writers often described, before the war, as representatives of an *undeutsch* spirit, fill the shelves in libraries and bookshops of the Federal Republic today. Studies dealing with the history of the Jews in the Germanophone countries have proliferated in the last decade or so: Frankfurt has seen the appearance of *Babylon,* the first Jewish cultural magazine to be published in Germany since 1933. Berlin, again the capital of a reunited nation, would have its museum of Jewish history. Anti-Semitism, openly preached only by neo-Nazi groups of, after all, marginal importance, is no longer acceptable and even the verbal sideslippings of a Jenninger (who, wishing to evoke the atmosphere of the thirties, indulged in bathos that was immediately and wrongly perceived as an apology for nazism)[59] were immediately penalized. On the other hand, after the democratic revolution of 1989, one of the last official acts of the GDR was the recognition of 'the responsibility of the German people as a whole' for the crimes perpetrated against the Jews by the Nazi regime.[60] In short, Germany seems to have acknowledged its crimes. Contrary to the wishes of the Nazis and their epigones who try to destroy the memory of it, the Jewish genocide is not going to be, as Himmler wanted, 'an unwritten page of history.'

The fact remains, however, that the function of museums is often to embalm the past rather than bring it to life and that ritual condemnation of anti-Semitism by institutions smacks primarily of an official expression of regret. There is nothing to suggest that Germany has learned to live with the memory of its 'Jewish question.' The latter remains unfinished business for historiography and, in a general sense, for civil society, a wound which is far from having healed over. It is the object of various strategies aiming at 'mastering the past [*Vergangenheitsbewältigung*]' which, as we have seen, in connection with the *Historikerstreit,* are sometimes totally incompatible.

But the paths of memory are tortuous and painful. Since the nineteenth century, historiography has no longer been coincidental with memory: the one tries to recreate and interpret the past rigorously and scientifically, while the other studies it from the inside and develops a subjective point of view. However, they may interact with one another and are equally subject to the vagaries of the present, which modify our way of studying the past as much as they do of remembering it. Nevertheless, the jumble of history and memory is quite a distinct one in Germany, a country which, at each turn in its social and political life is having to rediscover its past and, at the same time, is exposed to the ever growing temptation of amnesia. Henry Rousso's observation with regard to his research on Vichy France — 'the corpse was still warm: it was not a time for the forensic pathologist but for the doctor pure and simple, even the psychoanalyst'[61] — is perfectly valid for Nazi Germany. National Socialism constitutes a basic and unavoidable stage in the German past and to speak of National Socialism means also, and above all, to recall the German attitude to the Jewish question. This burdensome legacy must today be shouldered by a nation in which a large part of the population — the nearly three generations born during and after World War II — is confronted by contradictions that spring from a double impossibility: the impossibility of *remembering* and the impossibility of *forgetting.*[62] But if the former impossibility is simply a fact, the second is experienced by some as a moral duty and by others as a paranoid obsession, even as a handicap which they would like to get rid of as soon as possible. One should add to this the absence of a Jewish memory that might have been able, from within, to help develop a national conscience (the approximately 35,000 Jews living in Germany today nearly all hail from Eastern Europe and do not come from the pre-1933 community). In such conditions, the dangers of amnesia remain considerable, particularly if they are reinforced by a conscious strategy aiming to repress in the collective memory the Nazi crimes; to normalize German history through the elimination of these zones of darkness; in short, to classify 'a past which will not pass' as again part of the natural order of things.

The 'quarrel of the historians' might, therefore, appear as a symbolic event indicating a simple *transformation of forgetting,* final stage in the flight from a past too dire to contemplate and the beginning of a new form of repression, based on the 'normalization' of a past, which now becomes nonproblematical. The banalization of the crime in the national consciousness provides the indispensable passage from one forgetting to another. The Shoah is no longer hidden away; Auschwitz is no longer a nonevent. Quite simply, they will not become a locus for memory: Germany will be able to do without them. This can only open the way as much to an absolutory presentation of the past as to new forms of collective amnesia.

Memory, writes Pierre Nora, 'is in a permanent state of evolution, open to the dialectic of recollection and of amnesia, unaware of its successive deformations, vulnerable to all the ways in which it is used and manipulated, susceptible to long periods of latency and of revitalization.'[63] If, as Freud has taught us, the loss of memory is not due to the slow workings of time but mainly to the work of the unconscious, which hides unpleasant experiences and memories in the shadows of forgetfulness,[64] and if, as Yosef Hayim Yerushalmi has emphasized, the identity of each people is based on the selective preservation of certain mythical or historical elements from the past designed to nourish the 'tradition,' while the rest of its 'history' is abandoned and lost,[65] then German reunification appears as a typical example of collective amnesia. History is not a supermarket in which we can choose what suits us and leave the rest; history is a process, and the historian who wishes to study the German past today cannot finesse twelve years of Nazi rule, since it is precisely this terrible period that connects him to the German past as a whole.[66] On the other hand, memory can fairly be said to resemble a supermarket. It is subject to no scientific criterion, is selective, and is wholly unconcerned about its contradictions. Just as the memory and traces of a past that historiography cannot recover with its traditional tools, or that is concealed by official institutions, can be preserved, so forgetfulness in the face of a past already largely surveyed by historians can also be perpetuated. German reunification appears as a paradigmatic example of the gulfs that may open up between history and memory. The joy in national unity recovered and, for the East Germans, liberation from forty years of cultural and political oppression, seem to have put an impermeable lid on any critical appraisal of the past and the causes of the division of the country. Everything passed off as though there were only one reason for the separation of Germany into two states, 'communism,' and as though the war and nazism had nothing to do with it. 'The ninth of November will become part of history!' Walter Momper, burgomaster of West Berlin, announced triumphantly on the day the Wall fell, conveniently forgetting that, on this same date, Berlin had already been the scene of another historical event: *Kristallnacht*, 9 November 1938, which was marked by horrible pogroms and the destruction of all that was left of Jewish institutions in Germany. A highly symbolic coincidence, which reveals the present amnesia and, at the same time, shows how impossible it is for Germany to free itself from its past. The 'sense of guilt,' remarked a German-American writer, Irene Dische, has suddenly vanished: 'Like a historical catharsis, the opening of the Wall has eradicated the Second World War from their consciousness.'[67] Historian Michael Schneider sees reunification as a 'collective flight from the past' – as a desire once and for all to turn the German past into a tabula rasa.[68]

It is perhaps in reaction to this repression of memory that Günter Grass courageously defended a position radically hostile to reunification: 'Auschwitz speaks out against every passionate current of opinion, reinforced by the appeal to the passions, against the purchasing power of the West German economy – we can pay for unity with the hard cash of the DM – even against a right to self-determination unreservedly enjoyed by other peoples, because one of the premises for this horrific crime – alongside other, older motive forces – was a united Germany.'[69] This position might appear to be extreme, but it remains eloquent as testimony and as a historical reminder, because the existence of two German states was a permanent evocation of a history that remained an open wound, a neverending rift, a reminder of nazism and its crimes.

The forms assumed by the process of reunification reveal, too, the weakness and intrinsic contradictions in Jürgen Habermas's attitude.[70] He fought against the 'vindicatory tendencies' of so many conservative West German historians and argued for a 'posttraditional' national identity: the memory of Auschwitz and the assumption of the 'divided legacy' which flows from it would be inescapable constituents of this identity; but at the same time he stressed the anchoring, necessary in his opinion, of this identity in a 'constitutional patriotism' and loyalty to the West, which, in fact, was one of the premises for the amnesic reunification we recently witnessed.

The conservative historians and statesmen seem, therefore, for the moment to have won their battle for a 'mastery of the past' that takes the form of a 'reconciliation' of Germany with its history, smoothing out its roughnesses, eliminating its black holes, and above all returning to the Germans a 'positive' national consciousness. This is a long way from building a re-unified nation, as Karl Jaspers hoped after 1946, on a consciousness critical of the past, capable of integrating the dire legacy of Nazi crimes.[71] What he called 'metaphysical culpability,' and which we might more simply describe as 'collective responsibility,' did not intend to hold all Germans – still less those who were born after the war – accountable for the crimes for which only the Nazi regime had to answer, but stressed the duty to become fully aware of belonging to a nation and of being the heirs to a history that had produced National Socialism and perpetrated the genocide of the Jewish people. From the end of 1944, Hannah Arendt was putting the question in perfectly clear terms. Of course, the Germans were not 'potential Nazis since the days of Tacitus,' nor had all become convinced Nazis, but the division between guilty and innocent had been so blurred that it became ex-tremely difficult to establish the correct and necessary distinctions. The punishment of war criminals (which was carried out only to a very limited extent) could not resolve the problem, because

the number of those who are simultaneously responsible and guilty must be relatively small. There are many who are partly responsible without there being any indication of their guilt. More numerous still are those who became guilty without being in the least responsible. Among those who are responsible in the larger sense, must be included the ones who showed themselves to be well disposed toward Hitler for as long as it was possible to be, those who assisted him in his rise to power, and those who approved him in Germany as in the rest of Europe.[72]

There is the responsibility of the ruling elites that helped Hitler to gain power, of 'national' parties which did not try to stop him but rather tried to ally themselves with him, of the workers' movement which was unable to find sufficient unity to block the spread of the brown plague and went down without a fight, of the churches which sought a compromise with the Nazi regime and, in spite of several individual acts of resistance, did not mobil-ize as institutions to try to prevent the extermination of the Jewish people. After the war, the ruling elites reestablished their economic power, the par-ties were reconstructed, and the churches reorganized. All these institutions share a significant political responsibility before history and must acknowledge it. But there is also another responsibility: that of all Germans who knew and who kept silent or who, while remaining glued to their desks, fulfilled their role in the administrative and bureaucratic apparatus that was needed for the work of extermination to be carried out; the responsibility of all those one sees, in photographs of the thirties, calmly smiling in front of a poster that proclaims 'Jews Out.' This awareness of our *historical responsibility* for the Jewish genocide ought to be extended to the whole of Europe, because the work of extermination required collusion that goes beyond Germany and because Auschwitz represents a breakdown of civilization which concerns and challenges us all.

On the other hand, the only 'culpability' the authorities of the Federal Republic seem disposed today to recognize is that of having been members of the SED. The Stasi, the former political police of the GDR deservedly hated by the citizens of East Germany, is in danger of becoming the scapegoat that allows the memory of the Gestapo to be repressed.[73] The identity of present-day Germany relies largely on a single negative force: *anticommunism*. In the eyes of government representatives and conservative intellectuals, anti-Fascism was nothing but an ideology invented in Moscow, suspect and not to be taken on board. Hitler, they say, belongs to the past, to the period of totalitarian regimes, to an 'age of tyrants' inaugurated by the Red Terror and of which Germany, according to Ernst Nolte, was the unhappy victim. This attitude which, in the name of the struggle against 'totalitarianism,' equates the GDR and National Socialism, simply perpetuates a practice tried and tested in the Federal Republic. A few years ago, the Rote Armee Faktion, a terrorist group, was routinely compared with nazism – which meant, on the occasion of the kidnapping of the industrialist Hans-Martin Schleyer, that his active Nazi past had to be cloaked under the strictest censorship. The former SS officer thus became a martyr of democratic Germany.[74] Since 1991, the voices of those demanding a new Nuremberg trial for the 'criminals' of the SED and who would like to turn Bautzen, the 'gulag' of the GDR, into a 'museum of totalitarianism' in the same way as Auschwitz or Buchenwald, have been growing louder. Legal writers raise not only the question of reparations for the victims of Stalinism (*SED-Opfern*) – and that is perfectly justified; they also describe the expulsion of the Sudeten Germans after 1945[75] in terms of 'genocide [*Völ-*

*kermord*].' Others add that, given the equally criminal nature of the two regimes, the GDR was certainly worse than nazism, because it managed to survive for forty years, whereas Hitler's Germany constituted a brief paren-thesis of only twelve years.[76] It is not the East German intellectuals and oppositionists, censored, monitored, sometimes persecuted or even expelled (Wolf Biermann) by the authorities of the former GDR who indulge today in this visceral anti-Communist prose, but the leaderwriters of the large dailies of the Federal Republic. It is not hard to understand that hiding behind this apparent desire to break radically with Stalinism, in fact, lies the desire to free themselves from the Nazi past.[77] The GDR is just the latest scapegoat for the insuperable German *Schuldfrage*.

### Sham Memory

This new form of historical revisionism, which is not a matter of denying Nazi crimes but rather of relativizing and banalizing them, avoids all crit-ical reflection upon the legacy of the 'Jewish question.' When Joachim Fest, who sees no qualitative difference between the Red Terror of the twenties and the mechanized extermination of the Jews in Auschwitz, speaks of a 'century-old German-Jewish symbiosis, a process that belongs among the great cultural achievements of history,'[78] it is evident that he does not feel challenged by the tragic end of this same 'symbiosis,' an end which in his opinion is not 'historically unique.' In a Germany that has been 'reconciled' with its past, the German-Jewish dialogue becomes an object of study with-out any significance for the present. 'Hitler's empire,' wrote Jean Améry,

> will first continue to pass as an accident in the workings of history. But, finally, it will be regarded as history pure and simple, neither bet-ter nor worse than any other dramatic historical period. Even stained with blood, the empire will have had its daily life, its family life. The picture of grandfather in SS uniform will be hung in the place of honor, and schoolchildren will hear less about the selections that took place on the ramps than about the surprising victory over an all-pervasive unemployment. Hitler, Himmler, Heydrich, Kaltenbrunner will be names like those of Napoleon, Fouché, Robespierre, and Saint-Just.[79]

After all, the recovery of national pride in the democratic Federal Re-public can be accompanied by the restoration of several synagogues and even the opening of a new museum of Jewish history. Every provincial *Volkshochschule* has already organized its exhibition of the 'vanished world of the Shtetl' or its concert of Jewish popular music and, as Henryk M. Broder has sarcastically and bitterly remarked, the new Germany has demonstrated its 'incurable love for the Jews, provided that they are dead.'[80] Though it comes late in the day, the highlighting of the Jewish contribution to German culture is certainly a positive factor that no one can regret. But this idealization of a mythical 'Judeo-German symbiosis' is often not so selfless. Politicians who had felt that 'a certain silence' about the Nazi past was necessary in order to conciliate the nation, but who now want to make an example of former Communist leaders, display an enthusiasm in inaugurating synagogues, or opening exhibitions and conferences on the 'Judeo-Christian dialogue' that is too openly opportunistic not to appear suspect. Heedless of the pervasive conformism, the film director Hans-Jürgen Syberberg no doubt reflects a widely held point of view when he refers bluntly to 'the fatal alliance of the Left and the Jews,' which in his opinion stifled the creative spirit of the nation in the postwar period.[81] Ignored for decades, the anniversary of *Kristallnacht* is now commemorated more as a crime committed against 'a part of the German nation' than as a purely anti-Semitic act. The 35,000 Jewish citizens of today's Federal Republic, nearly all hailing from Eastern Europe, can hardly identify with this type of commemoration; if they left their country of origin, it is precisely because nazism destroyed Jewish communities which did not belong to the 'German nation.'

In 1946, in a letter to Karl Jaspers, who had just published *Die Schuldfrage,* Hannah Arendt stressed the absolute necessity of sending a clear and unmistakable signal to indicate the 'rejection of anti-Semitism in remembrance of what has happened to the Jews through the Germans.' She proposed that a future German republic 'constitutionally renounce anti-Semitism, stipulating, for example, that any Jew, regardless of where he is born, can become a citizen of this republic, enjoying all rights of citizenship, solely on the basis of his Jewish nationality and without ceasing to be a Jew.'[82] This was not possible in 1946, as Jaspers painfully acknowledged in his response. And even today, in spite of the protestations of Heinz Galinski, the representative of the Berlin Jewish community, the unification treaty contains no reference to the Jewish genocide.[83] On the other hand, any Pole, Rumanian, or Russian whose ancestors were citizens of the Reich is today warmly welcomed in the Federal Republic, and automatically acquires German citizenship; whereas asylum is denied or doled out in driblets to Kurdish refugees. The *völkisch* ideology is no longer acceptable but, in practice, some of its principles remain valid in defining what constitutes belonging to the nation. Nor should what Theodor W. Adorno called the possibility of a 'displacement of what exploded at Auschwitz'[84] be forgotten either; that is to say, the substitution of other targets as the object of hatred already directed against the Jews, a hatred turned today on immigrants, taking the form of violent attacks against Vietnamese or African homes and which is expressed, on the walls of Berlin, Hamburg, and Leipzig, in slogans like 'Destroy the Turks' or 'Strangers Out.' Reunified and amnesic, Germany is far from having overcome its past, which remains a cultural and political consideration for the future of the nation.

The nation, it should be remembered, is not a metaphysical entity, with roots in a 'spirit' or in an 'ethnic group' – in this case a Germanic *Geist* and *Volk* above history. The nation is not a monolith, but a historic structure joined to the past by a complex web, dense and subtle, often tangled or broken. However, the German past crystallizes into a set of irreconcilable and contradictory memories: that of the émigré Jew who, notwithstanding his exclusion from the *nation*, belongs to German *history* and who lives now in New York or in Tel Aviv; that of the anti-Fascist resistance fighter who has retired to Berlin or Leipzig; that of the former Nazi who has comfortably managed his Munich or Hamburg brewery for forty years; finally, that of the mass of people who threaded their way between the shoals of history, who did not choose sides and so submitted to the conquerors. The Germans of today, men and women for the most part born after the war, are linked to the German past, not through their identification with the preceding generations but through a shared legacy, which imposes on them the duty to preserve the memory. There is no 'collective guilt' inherited from the past weighing on the Germans, but neither does the 'grace of a belated birth' (Helmut Kohl) shelter them from history. That nation is guilty which refuses to shoulder the responsibility of memory, the only way to prevent a recurrence of the crimes of the past. Posthumous atonement for this 'Judeo-German symbiosis,' dreamed up, idealized, and finally recognized as an illusion, might start with the introduction into the German language of a Hebrew word: *Zakhor,* 'remember.'

# Notes

INTRODUCTION

1. The essay by Arthur Eloesser, 'Literatur,' in the collection assembled by Kaznelson, *Juden in deutschen Kulturbereich*, pp.1–67, is still an extremely useful, indeed indispensable repository of information, giving some idea of the breadth and richness of Judeo-German culture in the realms of literature and the social sciences.

2. See introduction by Löwy to his fascinating study *Redemption and Utopia*.

3. See this letter, dated 7 October 1916, in Kafka, *Letters to Felice*, p.517.

4. Quoted by Herbert Kaiser, 'O jüngster Tag. Jüdische Dichter des deutschen Expressionismus,' in Schörken and Löwitsch, *Das doppelte Antlitz*, p.139.

5. See Arendt, *La tradition cachée* and *The Jew as Pariah*.

6. Bourel, 'Les Juifs et l'Occident,' pp.54–59.

1. THE 'JUDEO-GERMAN SYMBIOSIS'

1. See the letter from Benjamin to Scholem dated 20 February 1939 and the latter's 30 June 1939 reply, in Benjamin and Scholem, *Correspondence*.

2. Caullery, *Le parasitisme et la symbiose*, p.21. See also Bein, 'The Jewish Parasite,' pp.3–40.

3. See Ilsar, 'Zum Problem der Symbiose,' pp.122–172.

4. Ernst Pawel, 'Franz Kafka Judentum,' in Grözinger, Zimmermann, and Moses, *Kafka und das Judentum*, p.253. Pawel's *The Nightmare of Reason* is a remarkable biography of the author of *The Trial*.

5. See the full title (in Bibliography) of a collection of studies on the Jews in German culture, edited by Bronsen, *Jews and Germans from 1866 to 1933*. In this connection, Julius H. Schoeps has described the 'Judeo-German symbiosis' as a 'dream' born of 'failed emancipation' ('Die missglückte Emanzipation. Zur Tragödie des deutsch-jüdischen Verhältnisses,' in Schörken and Löwitsch, *Das doppelte Antlitz*, p.21).

6. On the problem of assimilation in the United States, see the classic work by Higham, *Strangers in the Land*, as well as Gordon, *Assimilation in American Life*. It is interesting to note that the concept of 'Judeo-Arab symbiosis' has been employed by the Austrian historian Bunzl in *Juden im Orient*, p.19, and by Halevi, *Question ju'ive*, p.87. On assimilation in France, see Marrus, *Les Juifs de France à l'époque de*

*l'affaire Dreyfus*, as well as Vidal-Naquet, 'Le privilège de la liberté,' *Les Juifs, la mémoire et le présent*, pp.59–84.

7. See the now classic work by Weinrich, *History of the Yiddish Language* and Robin's very fine *L'amour du yiddish*.

8. Scholem, 'Against the Myth of German-Jewish Dialogue,' in *Jews and Judaism in Crisis*, pp.61–64.

9. Mann, *Der Hass*, p.102.

10. Arnold Zweig, *Bilanz der deutschen Jedenheit*, p.303.

11. Mosse, *German Jews beyond Judaism*.

12. Adler, *Die Juden in Deutschland*, p.162. See Theodor Fontane's well-known comment: 'I like the Jews, provided I am not dominated by them.'

13. Susmann, 'Vom geistigen Anteil,' pp.17–25.

14. Buber, 'Das Ende der deutsch-jüdischen Symbiose,' p.644.

15. Baeck, 'The German Jews,' p.35.

16. Quoted in Borries, *Selbstzeugnisse*, p.54.

17. Leschnitzer, *Saul und David*, p.146.

18. Diner, 'Negative Symbiose,' in Diner, *Ist der Nationalsozialismus Geschichte?*, pp.185–197.

19. On Heine's Judeity, see Rosenthal, *Heinrich Heine als Jude*.

20. See Bourel's introduction to Mendelssohn, *Jérusalem*, pp.23–50.

21. Dohm, *De la réforme politique des Juifs*, pp.63 and 85.

22. Berding, *Moderner antisemitismus in Deutschland*, p.25.

23. Arendt, *Rahel Varnhagen*, p.58. On the Jewish salons of Berlin, see Herz, *Jewish High Society*, and Meixner, 'Berliner Salons,' pp.97–106.

24. See Scholem, 'The Science of Judaism – Then and Now' in *The Messianic Idea in Judaism*, pp.304–313.

25. Quoted by Kaser, 'Berthold Auerbachs Traum einer deutsch-jüdischen symbiose,' in Hermand and Mattelklott, *Jüdische Intelligenz in Deutschland*, p.41.

26. Quoted by Adler, *Die Juden in Deutschland*, p.71.

27. See Laqueur, *Weimar*.

28. See Arendt, *La tradition cachée*, p.166.

29. The definition of the 'non-Jewish Jew' is one of the central themes in Deutscher's collection, *The Non-Jewish Jew*. On Deutscher's Judeity see also, in the same work, the preface by his wife, Tamara.

30. Preface to the Hebrew edition of *Totem and Taboo*, quoted by Bourel, 'Les Juifs et l'Occident ou la métaphore impossible,' p.57. In 1918, in a letter to a Swiss friend, Oskar Pfister, Freud defined himself as a 'Jew without God.' See Gay, *Ein gottloser Jude*.

31. Katz, *Out of the Ghetto*, ch.4.

32. Quoted by Arendt, *Rahel Varnhagen*, p.120.

33. Marx, 'On the Jewish Question,' in *Early Writings*, pp.236ff., and Hess, 'Über das Geldwesen,' p.167. For a discussion of Hess and Marx, see the first chapter in Traverso, *The Marxists*.

34. Volkov, *Jüdisches Leben*, p.136.

35. Rozenblit, *The Jews of Vienna*, p.49.

36. Katz, *Out of the Ghetto*, p.230.

37. Ibid., p.221. However, it should be pointed out that there was a net increase in mixed marriages during the Weimar Republic, reaching a figure of 33.4 percent between 1925 and 1934 (see Della Pergola, *La transformazione demografica*, p.193).

38. Mayer, *Ein Deutscher auf Widerruf*, p.61.

39. Quoted by Bourel, 'Un soupir de Rosenzweig,' pp.176–177.

40. Benjamin, 'A Berlin Chronicle,' pp.339, 344–45.

41. Scholem, *From Berlin to Jerusalem*, pp.10–11.

42. Volkov, *Jüdisches Leben*, p.128.

43. G. Mosse, 'Jewish Emancipation. Between *Bildung* and Respectability,' in Reinharz and Schatzberg, *The Jewish Response to German Culture*, pp.1–16. On the importance of the *Bildung* for the Judeo-German culture of the emancipation, see Sorkin, *The Transformation of German Jewry*.

44. See the biography of Bleichröder by Stern, *L'or et le fer*. We shall return to Bleichröder as the epitome of the parvenu Jew in chapter 4.

45. See Mosse, *Jews in the German Economy*, p.28.

46. Lessing, *La haine de soi*, which examines the cases of Paul Rée, Otto Weinger, Arthur Trebitsch, Max Steiner, Walter Calé, and Maximilian Harden.

47. See Gay, 'Hermann Levi,' in *Freud, Jews and Other Germans;* on Kraus, see Le Rider, 'Karl Kraus ou l'identité juive introuvable,' *Modernité viennoise*, pp.298–320.

48. We take this definition of the emancipation (*ein Welt ohne Anerkennung*) from Claussen, *Grenzen der Aufklärung*, p.82.

49. On the immigration of the Eastern European Jews to Germany, see especially Aschheim, *Brothers and Strangers*, and Wertheimer, *Unwelcome Strangers*.

50. No doubt the best survey of anti-Semitism in Germany is Berding's *Moderner Antisemitismus in Deutschland*. For anti-Semitism in a late nineteenth-century German context, see Fritz Stern, *Politics of Cultural Despair*.

51. See Dupeux, 'L'antisémitisme culturel de Wilhelm Stepel,' in the collection edited by Dupeux under the title, *La 'Révolution conservatrice' dans l'Allemagne de Weimar*, pp.253–260.

52. Volkov, 'Antisemitismus als kultureller Code,' in *Jüdisches Leben*, pp.13–36.

53. Heinrich von Treitschke, 'Unsere Aussichten,' in Böhlich, *Der Berliner anti-*

*semitismusstreit*, p.13. On Treitschke, see Liebeschutz, 'Treitschke and Mommsen,' *Leo Baeck Institute Year Book* 7 (1962), pp.153–182, and Kurt Lenk, 'Der Antisemitismusstreit oder: Antisemitismus der "gebildeten Leute," ' in Horch, *Judentum, Antisemitismus und europäische Kultur*, pp.23–34.

54. Theodor Mommsen, 'Auch ein Wort über unser Judentum,' in Böhlich, *Der Berliner*, pp.219–226. On Mommsen, see also Herzig, 'Zur Problematik,' *Menora*, pp.216–217.

55. Kautsky, *Rasse und Judentum*, p.108. On Kautsky, see Traverso, *The Marxists*, pp.104–109.

56. Katz, *Wagner et la question juive*, p.56.

57. See S. E. Aschheim, ' "The Jew Within": The Myth of "Judaization" in Germany,' in Reinharz and Schatzberg, *The Jewish Response*, pp.212–241.

58. See Hans-Peter Bayerdörfer, ' "Vermauschelt die Presse, die Literatur": Judische Schriftsteller in der deutschen Literatur zwischen Jahrhundertwende und Erstem Weltkrieg,' in Horch, *Judentum*, pp.207–231. For a more general treatment, see the now classical work by Poliakov, *Histoire de l'antisémitisme 2*.

59. Quoted by Le Rider, 'Karl Kraus,' in *Modernité viennoise*, p.215. 'Hep, hep, hep' (*Hyerosolima est perdida*) was the slogan of the 1819 German pogroms. See parody of this speech early in Bettauer's novel, *The City without Jews*.

60. On Chamberlain, see the important biography by Field, *Evangelist of Race* (on *Die Grudlagen*, see in particular ch.5).

61. Sombart, *Les Juifs et la vie économique*. On Sombart, see in particular Raphael, *Judaïsme et capitalisme*.

62. See Katz, *Wagner et la question juive*, p.98.

63. Ludwig Bamberger, 'Deutschum und Judentum,' in Böhlich, *Der Berliner*, p.167.

64. Moritz Lazarus, 'Was Heisst national?'; *ibid.*, p.26.

65. Quoted by Reinharz, *Fatherland or Promised Land*, p.81.

66. Bernstein, 'Wie ich al Jude,' *Der Jude* vol.2, p.194.

67. Quoted by Norbert Altenhofer, 'Tradition als Revolution: Gustav Landauers "geworden-werdendes" Judentum,' in Bronsen, *Jews and Germans*, p.191.

68. Quoted by Ellbogen and Sterling, *Die Geschichte*, p.279.

69. Oppenheimer, 'Stammesbewusstsein,' *Die Welt*, no.7, quoted by Reinharz, *Fatherland or Promised Land*, pp.130–132.

70. Herzl, *Diaries*, p.41.

71. See Stephen Magill, 'Defense and Introspection: German Jewry, 1914,' in Bronsen, *Jews and Germans*, p.214. On the attitude of German Jews during World War I, see also Goldmann, *Autobiographie*, pp.54–57.

72. Ibid., p.220.

73. Quoted by Reinharz, *Fatherland or Promised Land*, p.223.

74. Hermann Cohen, 'Germanité et judéité,' in *Pardès* 5, p.41. According to Micha Brumlik, Cohen was far more representative of a 'Jewish symbiosis with reason' than of a 'German-Jewish symbiosis' (see his study 'Zur Zweideutigkeit deutsch-jüdischen Geistes: Herman Cohen,' in Grözinger, *Judentum in deutschen Sprachraum*, pp.371–381). See also Steven Schwarzschild, ' "Germanism and Judaism": Cohen's 'Normative Paradigm of the German-Jewish Symbiosis,' in Bronsen, *Jews and Germans*, and especially Zimer, 'Judentum und Deutschum,' *Revue d'Allemagne* 13, no.3, pp.473–479.

75. Quoted by Moses, *Système et révélation*, p.263.

76. Quoted by Raphaël, *Judaïsme et capitalisme*, p.338. On the controversy stirred up by Sombart, see Kampmann, *Juden und Deutsche*, pp.426–428, and Baioni, *Kafka e l'ebraismo*, pp.117–118.

77. 'Deutsch-jüdischer Parnass' (*Kunstwart* 25, no.11 (1912), now in Goldstein, *Berliner Jahre*, pp.214–221. Goldstein has traced the evolution of this essay in 'German Jewry's Dilemma before 1914,' *Leo Baeck Institute Year Book* 11 (1957), pp.236–254.

78. Quoted by Itta Schedletzky, 'Ludwig Jacobowski (1868–1900) und Jakob Loewenberg (1856–1929),' in Moses and Schöne, *Juden in der deutschen Literatur*, p.197.

79. See the letters of Benjamin to Strauss in Puttnies and Smith, *Benjaminiana*, pp.46–54. See also Brodersen, *Spinne im eigenen Netz*, pp.52–56. On Benjamin's Judeity, see also Traverso, 'Il materialismo messianico,' *Il Ponte* 46, no.2, pp.47–70.

80. Kafka, *Letters to Friends*, p.289. This famous passage is quoted in several biographies of Kafka.

81. Kafka, *Letters to Milena*, p.219.

82. Wassermann, *Mein Weg*. On Wassermann, see also Azuelos, 'Judéité et germanité,' *Pardès*, no.5, pp.159–177.

83. See Zweig, *The World of Yesterday*, p.22. On the history of the Jews of Vienna, see Wistrich, *The Jews of Vienna*, and Beller, *Vienna and the Jews*.

84. Stern, 'Le poids de la réussite,' in *Rêves et illusions*, p.149.

85. See Buber's collection *On Judaism*. On the rebirth of messianic Judaism in Germanophone *Mitteleuropa* at the turn of the century, see Löwy, *Redemption and Utopia*.

86. On Birnbaum, see Goldsmith, *Modern Yiddish Culture*, ch.4, pp.99–120.

87. Quoted by Walter Zwi Bacharach, 'Ignaz Zollschans "Rassentheorie," ' in Grab, *Jüdische Integration*, p.186. On the appropriation by German Zionists of certain categories of *völkisch* thought, see Niewyk, *Jews in Weimar*, pp.129–131.

88. See Poppel, *Zionism in Germany*, pp.127–130. See especially Buber in *On Judaism*.

89. On Dinter's novel, see Berding, *Moderner Antisemitismus in Deutschland*, p.182; on Heck's, see Hermand, *Der alte Traum vom neuen Reich*, p.135. More generally, on anti-Semitic literature in Germany, see Poliakov, *Histoire de l'antisémitisme 2*, pp.263–283.

90. Jünger, 'Über Nationalismus und Judenfrage,' *Süddeutsche Monatshefte*, no.27, p.845. Cf. Jost Hermand, 'Juden in der Kultur der Weimarer Republik,' in Grab and Schoeps, *Juden in der Weimarer Republik*, p.12.

91. Benno Jacob, 'Krieg, Revolution und Judentum,' in Borries, *Selbstzeugnisse*, pp.43–44.

92. Franz Rosenzweig, 'Briefe,' *ibid.*, pp.45–46.

93. Quoted by Helmut Gollwitze, 'Postface,' *ibid.*, p.281.

94. Toller, *I Was a German*, pp.281–282.

95. Gay, *Weimar Culture*.

96. See Stéphane Moses, *L'Ange de l'Histoire*, pp.34, 245.

97. Berlin, 'Les Juifs: de la servitude à l'émancipation,' *Trois essais*, p.173.

98. Grunfeld, *Prophets Without Honour*, p.5.

99. Moshe Zimmermann, ' "Lessing contra Sem". Literatur im Dienste des Antisemitismus,' in Moses and Schöne, *Juden in der deutschen Literatur*, p.182.

100. Brecht, *Work Journals, 1938–1955*. See also observations by Brecht on the nonexistence of a 'national' Jewish culture and on the need for Jews to 'emancipate themselves from capitalism' instead of seeking refuge in the 'old culture' (22 April 1944).

101. See Alexander Altmann, 'Franz Rosenzweig et Eugen Rosenstock-Huessy,' in Bourel, *Franz Rosenzweig*, pp.187–204.

102. See especially Kohn, *Martin Buber*, p.239.

103. On relations between Benjamin and Lieb, see Chryssola Kambas, 'Actualité politique: le concept d'histoire chez Benjamin et l'échec du Front populaire,' in Wismann, *Walter Benjamin et Paris*, pp.273–284.

104. See the texts collected by Bourel and Le Rider in *De Sils-Maria à Jérusalem*. According to André Comte-Sponville, Nietzsche felt 'at the same time admiration, gratitude, fear, horror and disgust' with regard to the Jews ('Nietzsche et Spinoza,' *ibid.*, p.65).

105. See Julius Schoeps, 'Erwacht aus dem Traum der Assimilation: Max Liebermann,' in Volkov, *Jüdisches Leben*, pp.6–9. Another example is provided by Sigmund Freud, who wrote as follows: 'My language is German. My culture, my connections are German. I regarded myself intellectually as a German before the increase in anti-Semitic prejudice in Germany and in German Austria came to my attention. Since then, I have no longer regarded myself as German. I would rather call myself a Jew.' Quoted by Le Rider, *Modernité viennoise*, p.253.

106. See Jay, *The Dialectical Imagination*.

107. See Benjamin, *Deutsche Menschen*. See also Albrech Schöne, ' "Diese nach jüdischem Vorbild erbaute Arche": Walter Benjamins Deutsche Menschen,' in Moses and Schöne, *Juden in der deutschen Literatur*, pp.350–365.

108. Canetti, *The Human Province*, p.53.

109. Heine, *Sämtliche Schriften* 4, pp.257–258. See also Rosenthal, *Heinrich Heine als Jude*, p.336.

110. Quoted by Habermas, 'The German Idealism of the Jewish Philosophers,' *Philosophical Political Profiles*, p.41.

111. Klemperer, 'Lingua Tertii Imperii,' *Les Temps modernes* no.521, p.107.

112. Améry, 'Zwang und Unmöglichkeit,' *Jenseits*.

113. Quoted by Botstein, *Judentum und Modernität*, p.116.

114. Jack Ziper, 'Die kulturelle Operationen' *Babylon* 8, pp.34–44. The two stories are included in Panizza's collection, *Der Korsettenfritz*.

115. Gramsci, *Quaderni del carcere* 3, p.1801. See also Momigliano, 'The Jews of Italy,' *New York Review of Books*.

116. Rosenzweig, 'Le caractère national juif,' *Cahiers*, pp.184–185.

## 2. THE JEW AS PARIAH

1. See Shmueli, ' "Pariah-People," ' *American Academy for Jewish Research* 36, p.169.

2. Quoted by Lothar Kahn, 'Michel Beer,' *Leo Baeck Institute Year Book* 1967, pp.155–157.

3. Heine, 'Struensee von M. Beer' (1828), *Sämtliche Schriften* 1, p.434.

4. Weber, *The Protestant Ethic*, pp.165–166. On the concept of *pariah* in Weber, see Liebeschutz, 'Max Weber Historical Interpretation of Judaism,' *Leo Baeck Institute Year Book* 9, pp.41–68; Arnaldo Mormigliano, 'Le judaïsme comme "religion-paria" chez Max Weber,' in Olender, *Pour Léon Poliakov*, pp.201–207; Raphael, *Judaïsme et capitalisme*, pp.291–301.

5. Weber, *Ancient Judaism*, p.3.

6. Weber, *Economy and Society* 2, pp.493ff.

7. Weber, *Le savant et la politique*, p.69.

8. Simmel, 'Exkursus über den Fremden,' *Soziologie*, p.510. On Simmel, see Raphaël, 'L'étranger et le paria,' *Archives des sciences sociales des religions* 61/1, pp.63–81 and Karl-Siegbert Rehberg, 'Das Bild des Judentums in der frühen deutschen Soziologie. "Fremdheit" und "Rationalität" als Typesmerkmale bei Werner Sombart, Max Weber und Georg Simmel,' in Horch, *Judentum*.

9. Lazare, *Antisemitism*, pp.82, 90–91.

10. Ibid., p.17.

11. Ibid., p.161.

12. Lazare, *Le fumier de Job*, p.49.

13. Ibid., p.79.

14. Quoted by Wilson, *Bernard Lazare*, p.287.

15. Ibid., p.327.

16. In 1890, Lazare was urging the 'French Jews to stop . . . the continual immigration of these predatory, vulgar and dirty Tartars' (Ibid., p.112).

17. Ibid., pp.198, 240. On this point, see also the chapter on Lazare in Löwy, *Redemption and Utopia*.

18. See Green, 'Socialist anti-Semitism,' *International Review of Social History* no.3, pp.374–399.

19. See Péguy, *Notre jeunesse*, pp.82–90.

20. Quoted by Young-Bruehl, *Hannah Arendt*, p.109.

21. Arendt, *Men in Dark Times*, p.17.

22. Arendt, *The Jew as Pariah*, p.71.

23. Charlie Chaplin's Judeity is a controversial subject. According to his main biographer, Chaplin was not a Jew but probably had Huguenot ancestors (see David Robinson, *Chaplin, His Life and Art*). However, it is as much his name (Kaplan, anglicized) as his work itself that leads one to doubt this hypothesis. What is certain is that the Charlie persona is typically Jewish. On this controversy, see Martin, *Charles Chaplin*, ch.1, 'Le Juif errant.'

24. Arendt, *Men in Dark Times*, p.13. This point has been made by Leibovici, 'Le paria chez Hannah Arendt,' in Abensour, *Ontologie et politique*, p.207, and by Barnow, *Visible Spaces*, p.83.

25. Arendt and Jaspers, *Correspondence 1926–1969*, p.200. On the biography of Rahel Varnhagen, see Plard, 'Hannah Arendt et Rahel Levin,' *Les Cahiers du Grif, Hanna Arendt*, pp.101–117.

26. Arendt, *Men in Dark Times*, p.16.

27. See the 1963 letters between Arendt and Scholem in Arendt, *The Jew as Pariah*, pp.240–251.

28. Arendt, *La tradition cachée*, pp.77–78. The significance of this passage has been stressed by Santini, 'La passione di capire,' Introduction to Hannah Arendt, *Il futuro alle spalle*, p.15. On Rahel's 'shame,' see also Arendt, *Rahel Varnhagen*, pp.216–217.

29. Arendt, 'Organized Guilt,' *Essays in Understanding*, p.131.

30. See Palmier, *Weimar en exil* 1, pp.362–363, and 2, p.203. On the life of German exiles in the United States, see also Heilburt, *Kultur ohne Heimat*.

31. Quoted by Young-Bruehl, *Hannah Arendt*, p.188.

32. Arendt, *La tradition cachée*, p.53.

33. Arendt, *The Origins of Totalitarianism*, p.147.

34. Arendt, *Rahel Varnhagen*, p.25.

35. Arendt, *The Jew as Pariah*, p.78.

36. Ibid., p.60.

37. See Pierre Péju, 'L'ombre et la vitese,' Introduction to Chamisso, *Peter Schlemihl*, pp.57–58.

38. See Stora-Sandor, *L'humour juif dans la littérature de Job à Woody Allen*.

39. Arendt, *The Jew as Pariah*, p.78.

40. See Wisse, 'Lo *Schlemihl* come eroe moderno,' *Comunità* no.172, p.219.

41. Still in the context of German culture, it is interesting to note that the figure of the *schnorrer* took on quite a different significance in Freud, who devoted several pages to it in his work *Jokes and their Relation to the Unconscious*. According to Robert, Freud had 'a weakness for this low character, radiating intelligence, who, in the guise of the *schnorrer*, of the matchmaker or the unhappily married individual, of the commonplace liar or the fabricator of genius, can lay bare or seduce the world with a single word' (Robert, *D'Oedipe à Moïse*, p.62).

42. Arendt, *Penser l'évènement*, p.127. See also Abensour, 'Hannah Arendt et le sionisme en question,' *Passé, Présent*, no.3, pp.17–23.

43. See Arendt, *Auschwitz et Jérusalem*, p.50.

44. Ibid., p.38.

45. Arendt, *The Origins of Totalitarianism*, p.290.

46. Arendt, *On Revolution*, p.1. See the essay on this work by Eric J. Hobsbawm, 'Hannah Arandt über die Revolution,' in A. Reif, *Hannah Arendt*, pp.263–271.

47. See Dal Lago, ' "Politeia," ' *Il Mulino* 33, no.293 (1984) p.430.

48. Jay, 'Hannah Arendt: Opposing Views,' *Partisan Review*, 45, no.23 (1978) pp.350–351.

49. Manès Sperber, 'Mein Judentum,' in Schultz, *Mein Judentum*, p.190. For Sperber, see especially the novel, *Burned Bramble*.

50. Cited by Broué, *Trotsky*, p.131.

51. This idea also lay at the root of the extremely ambiguous position taken by Arendt regarding the question of blacks in the United States. In her 'Reflections in Little Rock' (*Dissent* 6/1 (1959), pp.45–56) she came out clearly against all legislative discrimination with regard to blacks and supported the civil rights movement unconditionally. However, at the same time she declared that 'social discrimination' was inevitable and that it was useless to resist it. In defence of pluralism in American society – and even, one might add, from fear of seeing the well-known dichotomy between pariahs and parvenus establish itself among the blacks – she ended by excusing the social victimization of the Afro-American community. 'The question is not how to abolish discrimination,' she wrote, 'but how to keep it confined within the

social sphere, where it is legitimate, and prevent its trespassing on the political and the personal sphere, where it is destructive' (p.51).

52. See Bloom, *Prodigal Sons*, p.219, and Jay, 'Hannah Arendt: Opposing Views,' p.349.

53. See Varikas, 'Paria: Une Métaphore,' *Sources. Travaux historiques*, no.12.

54. Bock, 'Geschichte,' *Geschichte und Gesellschaft* 14/3, no.188, pp.376–377.

55. See Le Rider, *Le cas Otto Weininger*.

56. Nettl, *Rosa Luxemburg*.

57. Arendt, *Men in Dark Times*, p.44.

58. Quoted by Ettinger, *Rosa Luxemburg*, p.140.

59. Arendt, *Men in Dark Times*, pp.44–45.

60. Quoted by Ettinger, *Rosa Luxemburg*, p.142.

61. Christel Neusüss, 'Patriarcat et organisation du parti. Rosa Luxemburg critique des idées de ses comilitants masculins,' in Badia and Weill, *Rosa Luxemburg aujourd'hui*, p.92.

62. Frölich, *Rosa Luxemburg*, ch.1.

63. Quoted by Ettinger, *Rosa Luxemburg*, p.262. On Luxemburg and the Jewish question, see also Bensussan, 'Rosa ou l'impossible recoin,' *Questions juives*.

64. Ibid., p.102.

65. Arendt, *Men in Dark Times*, p.43.

66. Luxemburg, *J'étais, je suis, je serai*, p.180.

67. Ibid., p.152.

### 3. JUDEITY AS *HEIMATLOSIGKEIT*

1. See Bronsen, *Joseph Roth*, pp.601–604.

2. Roth, *Briefe 1911–1939*, p.95.

3. See Magris, *Lontano da dove*, p.46.

4. Roth, *Hotel Savoy*, p.94.

5. Cziffra, *Der heilige Trinker*, p.28.

6. Roth, *Briefe*, p.164.

7. *Ibid.*, p.257.

8. On the fascination of a sector of German-speaking Jewish intellectuals for Yiddish, see Goldsmith, *Modern Yiddish Culture*.

9. This aspect is stressed by G. Shaked, 'Wie jüdisch is ein jüdisch-deutsche Roman? Über Joseph Roths' *Hiob. Roman eines einfachen Mannes*,' in Moses and Schöne, *Juden in der deutschen Literatur*, pp.281–292.

10. Letter quoted by Bronsen, *Joseph Roth*, p.123.

11. Kafka used the expression *westjüdische Zeit* in a letter to Max Brod in January 1918. On this subject, see Baioni, *Kafka e l'ebraismo*.

12. See Robin, *Kafka*, p.55.

13. Roth, *The Radetzky March*, p.121.

14. Roth, *Juden auf Wanderschaft*, p.289.

15. Ibid., p.848.

16. Ibid., p.830.

17. Roth, *Flight without End.*

18. See Bronsen, *Joseph Roth*, pp.152—153.

19. Roth, *Juden auf Wanderschaft*, p.838.

20. Roth, *Job, the Story of a Simple Man*, p.3.

21. Roth, *Juden auf Wanderschaft*, p.836.

22. Müller-Funk, *Joseph Roth*, p.36.

23. Roth, *Werke* 1, pp.276—277.

24. 'Bekenntnis zum Gleisdreieck,' in Roth, *Berliner Saisonbericht*, pp.295, 298.

25. See Cziffra, *Der heilige Trinker*, pp.58—59.

26. See the 'Berliner Reportagen' in Roth's *Berliner Saisonbericht*, especially 'Jazzband,' 'Wolkenkratzer,' 'Die Toten ohne Namen,' and 'Nachruf auf den lieben Leser.'

27. Quote by Magris, *Lontano da dove*, p.210.

28. Roth's *Der Antichrist* also appears in *Juden auf Wanderschaft*, see p.573 for quotation.

29. See Inka Mülder-Bach, 'Négativité et retournement. Réflexions sur la phénoménologie de la surface de Siegfried Kracauer,' in Raulet and Fürnkäs, *Weimar*, pp.273—285. On Roth and the cinema, see Westermann, *Joseph Roth, Journalist*, pp.173—190.

30. See Cziffra, *Der heilige Trinker*, pp.104—105.

31. Roth, 'The Antichrist,' in *Juden auf Wanderschaft*, p.594. On Benjamin's language theory, see Giorgio Agamben, 'Langue et histoire: Catégories historiques et catégories linguistiques dan la pensée de Benjamin,' in Wissman, *Walter Benjamin et Paris*, pp.793—808.

32. Roth, 'Gruss an Ernst Toller,' *Werke* 2, p.221. On Roth's political involvement during his socialist period, see Schweickert, 'Der rote Joseph' in *Text und Kritik*, special issue devoted to Joseph Roth, 1974, pp.40—55.

33. Roth, *Briefe*, p.91.

34. Roth, *The Silent Prophet*, p.126.

35. Roth, *Flight without End*, p.32.

36. See Benjamin, *Moscow Diary*, note of 16 December 1926.

37. Roth, 'Über die bürgerlichung der russischen Revolution?' *Werke* 2, p.689.

38. Roth, 'Raise nach Russland,' ibid., p.630.

39. Roth, 'Über die burgerlichung der russischen Revolution?' *ibid.*, p.690.

40. For a typology of the romantic critique of modernity, see Löwy and Sayre, *Révolte et mélancolie*.

41. Roth, *Briefe*, p.143.

42. See Roth, 'Das Autodafé des Geistes,' *Berliner Saisonbericht*, p.386.

43. Ibid., p.390.

44. Ibid., p.392.

45. See Scheidle, 'Joseph Roth,' in *Text und Kritik* 1974, p.64.

46. See Bronsen, *Joseph Roth*, p.480.

47. Ibid., p.198.

48. Roth, 'Raise nach Russland,' *Werke 2*, p.593.

49. See Magris, *Il mito asburgico*. See especially the beginning of Stefan Zweig's memoire, *World of Yesterday*.

50. See Bronsen, *Joseph Roth*, p.176; Cziffra, *Der heilige Trinker*, p.9.

51. Roth, *Briefe*, p.240.

52. Roth, 'Die Büste des Kaisers,' in *Erzählungen*, p.177.

53. Magris, *Lontano da dove*, p.19.

54. Roth, *The Emperor's Tomb*, p.17.

55. Ibid., p.32.

56. Quoted by Bronsen, *Joseph Roth*, p.488.

57. Roth, *Juden auf Wanderschaft*, p.641.

58. Roth, 'Ritter Meuchelmord' (1924), *Werke 2*, pp.19–20.

59. Roth, *Briefe*, p.257.

60. See Müller-Funk, *Joseph Roth*, p.118.

61. Roth, *Briefe*, p.449. On this point, see Strelka, 'L'attitude,' *Austriaca*, no.30, pp.33–46.

62. See Magris, *Lontano da dove*, p.41.

### 4. THE JEW AS PARVENU

1. Musil, *Man without Qualities*, p.241.

2. Uhlman, *Reunion*, p.58.

3. Schnitzler, *Road to the Open*. For a more in-depth study of this novel by Schnitzler, see Le Rider, *Modernité viennoise*, pp.217–219.

4. See Cohen, *Variations autour de K.*, pp.97–99.

5. See Mosse, *Jews in the German Economy*.

6. Arnold Zweig, *Caliban*, pp.125–126. See also Jost Hermand, 'Arnold Zweigs Judentum,' in Hermand and Mattenklott, *Jüdische Intelligenz*, pp.70–95.

7. On Moses Mendelssohn and Yiddish, see Robin, *L'amour du yiddish*, pp.36–39.

8. See Aschheim, *Brothers and Strangers*.

9. Fritz Stern, *L'or et le fer*, p.540.

10. Tucholsky, *Gesammelte Werke* 4, pp.431, 203, 221, 393, 560.

11. Tucholsky, 'Herr Wendriner fängt gut an,' *Gesammelte Werke* 4.

12. In his memoirs (*Ein Deutscher auf Widerruf* 1, p.71) Hans Mayer depicts Wendriner as the 'ultra-typical' middle-class Berlin Jew. On Tucholsky and the Jewish question, see Marcel Reich-Ramicki, 'Kurt Tucholsky. Deutscher, Preusse, Jude,' in Strauss and Hoffmann, *Juden und Judentum in der Literatur*, pp.254–272, and ch.6 in Grunfeld, *Prophets without Honor*.

13. Article published as an appendix to the Schoeps's collection, 'Bereit für Deutschland!' *Der Patriotismus*, p.259. On Schoeps, see also George L. Mosse, *German and Jews*, pp.105–109.

14. Quoted in Schoeps, *Der Patriotismus*, p.12.

15. On Maximilian Harden, see Lessing, *Der Judische Selbsthass*.

16. Quoted by Wistrich, *The Jews of Vienna*, p.164.

17. See Wisse, 'Lo *Schlemihl* come eroe moderno,' *Comunità* 172, p.183.

18. Kantorowicz, *Mourir*.

19. The entire text of this letter is to be found in Giesey, 'Ernst Kantorowicz: Scholarly Triumphs,' *Leo Baeck Institute Year Book* 1985, pp.197–198.

20. Boureau, *Histoires d'un historien*, p.132.

21. Schorske, *Fin-de-siècle Vienna*, p.146.

22. Herzl, *The Jewish State*, p.14.

23. See especially Bein, *Theodor Herzl*, p.73.

24. Quoted by Schorske, *Fin-de-siècle Vienna*, p.150.

25. See Beller, *Herzl*, pp.18, 31–32.

26. Herzl, *Diaries*, pp.21, 28.

27. Ibid., p.36.

28. Ibid., p.39.

29. Ibid., p.431.

30. Quoted by Chouraqui, *Theodor Herzl*, p.51.

31. See Bein, *Theodor Herzl*, p.37.

32. See Chouraqui, *Theodor Herzl*, p.52.

33. See Schorske, *Fin-de-siècle Vienna*, p.151, and Chouraqui, *Theodor Herzl*, p.91.

34. See Beller, *Herzl*, pp.21–22.

35. See Schorske, *Fin-de-siècle Vienna*, p.162, and Bein, *Theodore Herzl*, p.189.

36. Herzl, *The Jewish State*, ch.3: 'The Jewish Company.'

37. Herzl, *Diaries*, pp.388–393, and Laqueur, *A History of Zionism*, pp.123–127.

38. Herzl, *The Jewish State*, p.30.

39. Ibid., p.30.

40. Herzl, *Diaries*, p.41. See also Ritchie Robertson's comments in 'The Problem of "Jewish Self-Hatred" ' in *Oxford German Studies* 16, pp.90–91. Regarding this, Le Rider has described Herzl's Zionism as a 'Jewish and "neo-liberal" variant of pan-Germanism,' *Modernité viennoise*, p.258.

41. Herzl, *The Jewish State*, p.71.

42. See Rodinson, *Peuple juif ou problème juif?*, p.142, and Halevi, *Question juive*, pp.182–183.

43. See Ernst Schulin, 'Walther Rathenau und sein Integrationsversuch als "deutscher jüdischen Stammes," ' in Grab, *Jüdische Integration und Identität*, pp.13–38. There are two biographies of Walther Rathenau, but they devote only a few pages to the problem of his Judeity: Count Harry Kessler's *Walther Rathenau: His Life and Work*, and Buglar's *Walther Rathenau: Seine Zeit, Sein Werk, Seine Persönlichkeit*. One imagines that Rathenau would have been happy to learn that an English lord was his biographer, but less so to see that today he is the subject of so many studies on Jewish self-hatred.

44. Rathenau, *Briefe* 1, pp.253–254. See also Carmely, *Identitätsproblem*, p.47. In July 1916, during World War I, when he was the target of attacks in the anti-Semitic press, he [Rathenau] wrote a letter to Houston Stewart Chamberlain in which he defended his conduct in the War Ministry. There was no reply (see Geoffrey G. Field, *Evangelist of Race*, pp.391–392).

45. Rathenau, *Hauptwerke und Gespräche*, p.628.

46. Rathenau, 'Höre Israel!' in Wilde, *Walther Rathenau*, p.23.

47. Ibid.

48. Rathenau, 'Von Schwachheit, Furcht und Zweck' (1918), *Schriften* 4, p.14. See also Robert A. Pais, 'Walther Rathenau's Jewish Quandary,' *Leo Baeck Institute Yearbook* 1968, pp.120–131.

49. Rathenau, 'Staat und Judentum,' ibid. 1, pp.183–207.

50. Rathenau, *Schriften*, p.114.

51. Rathenau, 'An Deutschelands Jugend,' *Schriften* 6, p.99. See also Schulin, 'Walther Rathenau und sein Integrationsversuch,' in Grals, *Jüdische Integration*.

52. See Cacciari, *Walther Rathenau*, pp.31, 65.

53. Pais, 'Walther Rathenau's Jewish Quandary,' p.127.

54. Ibid., p.126.

55. Rathenau, *Schriften*, p.115.

56. See George Mosse, *Nationalism and Sexuality*.

57. Lowenberg, 'Antisemitismus,' *Geschichte und Gesellschaft* 4, 1979, pp.458–459 (correspondence as yet unpublished).

58. See Gay, *Freud, Jews and Other Germans*, p.197.

59. Fritz Stern, 'Walther Rathenau. Une âme divisée,' *Commentaire*, no.51, p.573.

60. See Shulamit Volkov, 'Überlegungen zur Ermordung Rathenaus als symbolischem Akt,' in Raulff, *Ein Mann vieler*, pp.100–101.

## 5. AUSCHWITZ, HISTORY, AND HISTORIANS

1. See Wyman, *The Abandonment of the Jews*, and Laqueur, *The Terrible Secret*.

2. Quoted by Wardi, *Le génocide*, p.22.

3. The history of the neologism 'genocide' has been briefly recounted by Finkielkraut in *L'avenir d'une négation*, pp.146–150.

4. See Mayer, *Why Did the Heavens Not Darken?* p.16. For a criticism of 'Judeocentric' notions of history, see Claussen, *Grenzen der Aufklärung*, pp.61–62, and Rodinson, 'Antisémitisme éternel ou judéophobies multiples?' in *Peuple juif*, pp.264–327.

5. See della Loggia, 'L'olocausto e gli olocausti,' *Il Mulino*, no.321, p.46.

6. See Bernand and Gruzinski, *Histoire du Nouveau Monde*.

7. On the genocide of the North American Indians, see Novak, *America's Revolutionary Heritage*.

8. See Libaridian, 'Répression finale,' *Les temps modernes*, nos.504–505–506, p.8 (special issue dedicated to the Armenian diaspora). On this subject, see especially Chaliand and Ternon, *Le génocide des Arméniens*. For a historical perspective on the Jewish and Armenian genocides, see Vidal-Naquet, 'Et par le pouvoir d'un mot . . .' *Les Juifs*, pp.267–275.

9. The most complete documentation on the number of victims of Stalinism is to be found in the new edition of Medvedev's classic work, *Let History Judge*.

10. On Pol Pot's Cambodia, see Ponchaud's, *Cambodge année zéro*.

11. See Denis Peschanski, 'Le concept de totalitarisme est-il opératoire en histoire?,' in Thanassekos and Wismann, *Révision de l'histoire*, pp.77–93.

12. The estimates of the number of victims of the Vietnam War vary between 1 million, based on official American sources (see Lewy, *America in Vietnam*, p.453; and 1.7 million according to Vietnamese sources (see Harrison, *The Endless War*, p.301. Sartre evidently misused the word genocide with reference to the Vietnam War. See Cohen-Solal, *Sartre*, pp.756–757. This idea crops up again in Aronson, according to whom Vietnam represented a 'variant of genocide,' this being 'disguised by the fact that its object was neither oppression nor extermination but to win the war.' See *The Dialectics of Disaster*, p.163.

13. In totalling the number of Gypsy victims, the figure of 500,000 has been proposed by Joachim S. Hohmann, 'Le génocide des Tsiganes,' in Bédarida, *La politique nazie*, pp.263–277. Kenrik and Puxon, on the other hand, give the figure of

200,000 (see *Destins gitans*, p.241). On the number of Gypsies gassed at Auschwitz, see Uwe D. Adam, 'Les chambries à gaz,' in Colloque de l'EHESS, *L'Allemagne nazie*, p.260. For a comparison between the Jewish and Gypsy genocides, see Dawidowicz, *The Holocaust and the Historians*, p.11.

14. See Traverso, 'Homosexuels et nazisme. Notes sur un crime occulté,' *Raison Présente*, no.96, pp.65–75. See also Plant, *The Pink Triangle*, and Stümke, *Homosexuelle in Deutschland*.

15. See Kogon, Langbein, and Rückerl, *Les chambres à gaz secret d'État*, ch.3, 'L'euthanasie.' The most fully documented study is Bock, *Zwangsterilisation im Nationalsozialismus*.

16. Le Clézio, *Le rêve mexicain*, interromp p.213. It should be added that the 'elective affinity' fabricated by history between Jews and [American] Indians was the inspiration for *Hablador*, a 1987 novel by the Peruvian writer Mario Vargas Llosa.

17. See Benjamin, *Illuminations*, pp.257–258.

18. Adorno, *Minima Moralia*, pp.234–235.

19. Löwy, *Redemption and Utopia*, p.7. On the historical significance of the disappearance of *yiddishkeit*, see 'Reflexions sur le génocide,' Marienstras, *Etre un peuple en diaspora*, pp.9–38.

20. See Lanzmann, *Shoah*, p.95.

21. Ibid., p.125.

22. See Ascherson, 'La controverse autour de Shoah,' in *Au sujet de Shoah*, p.233.

23. See Diner, *Zivilsationsbruch*.

24. Grass, 'Ecrire après Auschwitz,' p.19.

25. See Mayer, *Why Did the Heavens Not Darken?*, p.viii; and Vidal-Naquet, 'Le défi de la Shoah à l'histoire,' *Les Juifs*, p.229.

26. Quoted by Marrus, *The Holocaust in History*, p.2.

27. See Diner, 'Zwischen Aporie und Apologie. Über Grenzen der Historisierbarkeit des Nationalsozialismus,' in Diner, *Ist der Nationalsozialismus Geschichte?*, p.73.

28. Deutscher, *The Non-Jewish Jew*, p.163.

29. See Saul Friedländer, 'Introduction' to Fleming, *Hitler et la solution finale*, p.xxxiii.

30. See Meinecke, *Die deutsche Katastrophe*.

31. See Mason, 'Banalisation du nazisme?' *Le Débat*, no.21, pp.151–166. For a more detailed analysis of the different interpretations of the Jewish genocide based on an intentionalist-functionalist classification, see Friedländer's authoritative work, 'De l'antisémitisme à l'extermination: Esquisse historio-graphique et essai d'interprétation,' in Colloque de l'EHESS, *L'Allemagne nazie et le génocide juif*, pp.13–38.

32. According to Dawidovicz, the plan for the *Endlösung* was formulated between 1919 and 1926 (see *War against the Jews*, p.150). For Eberhard Jäckel, the many allusions in Hitler's letters and speeches after 1919 to the 'elimination of the Jews' make him suspect that already at this time Hitler had in mind 'an extermination plan' (see 'L'élimination des Juifs dans le programme de Hitler,' in Colloque de L'EHESS, *L'Allemagne nazie*, p.102). Taylor, for his part, shifts this fateful date forward to 1927 (see *Prelude to Genocide*, pp.217–218).

33. Hillgruber, *Zweierlei Untergang*, pp.79–81, 83–85.

34. See Bracher, *The German Dictatorship*, p.534.

35. See Broszat, *Der Staat Hitlers*.

36. Neumann, *Behemoth*. The affinity between Neumann's theory and Broszat's historical research was stressed by Ayçoberry in *La question nazie*, p.273.

37. Broszat, 'Hitler und die Genesis,' *Vierteljahrshefte*, pp.759–775.

38. Mommsen, 'The Realization of the Unthinkable,' in Hirschfield, *The Policies of Genocide*, p.112.

39. Lanzmann, *Shoah*, p.169.

40. Mommsen, 'The Realization of the Unthinkable,' in Hirschfield, *The Policies of Genocide*, pp.113, 126, and 128.

41. Quoted by J. P. Stern, *Hitler: The Führer and the People*, p.79.

42. Quoted by Friedländer, *Reflets du nazisme*, pp.103–104.

43. Shoshana Felman, 'A l'âge du témoignage: *Shoah* de Claude Lanzmann,' in Cuau, *Au sujet de Shoah*, p.63.

44. See Mandel, 'Role of the Individual,' *New Left Review*, no.157, p.64.

45. See Burrin, *Hitler et les Juifs*, ch.3.

46. Burrin, 'Hitler dans le IIIe Reich,' *Vingtième siècle*, no.16, p.41.

47. See especially Hilberg, *Destruction of the European Jews*, ch.7 ('Mobile Killing Operations').

48. See Volkov, 'Le texte et la parole,' in *L'Allemagne nazie et le génocide juif*, p.89.

49. Quoted by Hilberg, *Destruction*, p.917.

50. See observations by Mayer, *Why Did the Heavens Not Darken?*, p.289.

51. Hilberg, *Destruction*, p.53.

52. Ibid., p.54.

53. Mayer, *Why Did the Heavens Not Darken?*, p.90.

54. Ibid., p.314.

55. This exigency can be seen, too, in Kershaw, *Nazi Dictatorship*, pp.129–130.

56. Letter of 13 April 1933, from Scholem to Benjamin, in Benjamin and Scholem, *Correspondence*, p.39.

57. See Bolkovsky, *Distorted Image*.

58. On the Frankfurt school analysis of anti-Semitism, see Jay's study, 'The Jews

and the Frankfurt School: Critical Theory's Analysis of Anti-Semitism,' *Permanent Exiles*, pp.90–100.

59. Trotsky, *On the Jewish Question*.

60. For a general synthesis, see the excellent collection assembled by Beetham, *Marxism in Face of Fascism*. On the Marxist analysis of anti-Semitism up to World War II, see Traverso, *The Marxists and the Jewish Question*, ch.9.

61. Neumann, *Behemoth*, p.125.

62. See especially Konrad Kwiet, 'Historians of the German Democratic Republic on Antisemitismus and Persecution,' *Leo Baeck Institute Year Book* 21, p.185.

63. Kurt Pätzold, 'Wo der Weg nach Auschwitz begann. Der jüdische Antisemitismus und der Massenmord an den europäischen Juden,' in Kühnl, *Streit ums Geschichtsbild*, p.194. See especially, Pätzold, *Faschismus, Rassenwahn, Judenverfolgung*, on the period 1933–35. See also the study by Alain Brossat, Sonia Combe, and Jean-Charles Szurek, 'Le génocide vu de l'Est (URSS, RDA, Pologne),' in Thanassekos and Wismann, *Révision de l'histoire*, pp.223–250.

64. See Aly and Heim, *Vordenker der Vernichtung*.

65. See Christopher R. Browning's critique of Aly and Heim, 'Vernichtung und Arbeit: Zur Fraktionierung der planenden deutschen Intelligenz im besetzen Polen,' in Schneider, *Vernichtungspolitik*, p.49.

66. See Ulrich Herbert, 'Rassimus und rationales Kalkül: Zum Stellenwert utilitaristisch verbrämter Legitimationsstrategien in dernationalsozialistischen "Weltanschauung," ' Ibid., p.35.

67. See Rabinbach, 'The Jewish Question,' *New German Critique*, no.44, p.175. See Claussen's interesting comments, 'Ein kategorischer Imperativ: Die politische Linke und ihr Verhältnis zum Staat Israel,' in *Jüdisches Leben*, pp.230–242.

68. See Tim Mason, 'The Primacy of Politics: Politics and Economics in National Socialist Germany,' in Woolf, *Nature of Fascism*, pp.165–195.

69. See Ulrich Herbert's study, 'Arbeit und Vernichtung. Ökonomisches Interesse und Primat der "Weltanschauung" im Nationalsozialismus,' in Diner, *Ist der Nationalsozialismus Geschichte?* pp.198–236, as well as some very pertinent observations in Friedländer, *Reflets du nazisme*, pp.124–127.

70. See Kershaw, 'The Nazi State: an Exceptional State?' *New Left Review*, no.176, pp.47–67.

71. Marcuse, Introduction, *Eros and Civilization*, p.4. Cf. Zvi Tauber, 'Herbert Marcuse: Auschwitz und My Lai?' in Diner, *Zivilisationsbruch*, pp.88–98.

72. Claussen, *Jüdisches Leben*, pp.185–186.

73. See Mosse, *The Crisis of German Ideology*.

74. Quoted by Stern, *Politics of Cultural Despair*, p.151.

75. This is the conclusion Mayer comes to. *Why Did the Heavens Not Darken?* p.90.

76. Herf, *Reactionary Modernism*, and Louis Dupeux, ' "Kulturpessimismus," "Révolution conservatrice" et modernité,' in Raulet, *Weimar ou l'explosion de la modernité*, pp.31–45.

77. Postone, 'Anti-Semitism,' *New German Critique*, no.19, pp.97–115.

78. Dupeux, ' "Révolution conservatrice" et hitlérisme,' *Revue d'Allemagne* 16, no.3, pp.322–336 (now in the collection edited by the same author, *La 'Révolution conservatrice,'* pp.201–214).

79. Kocka, 'German History before Hitler,' *Journal of Contemporary History* 23, pp.3–16.

80. See Arendt, 'The Image of Hell,' *Essays in Understanding*, p.204.

81. On the anti-Semitism of the Vichy regime, see the classic work by Paxton and Marrus, *Vichy France and the Jews*. In this connection, it should be added that even Italian fascism, in which anti-Semitism was not an essential element, passed its own anti-Semitic legislation in 1938 (the notorious *Leggi sulla razza*). If the alliance between Italy and Germany was the determining factor here, it is nevertheless clear that the initiative was taken quite independently by Mussolini's regime (see de Felice, *Storia degli*).

## 6. HISTORY AND MEMORY

1. Levi, *The Reawakening*, pp.370–371.

2. Zipes, 'The Vicissitudes of Being Jewish in West Germany,' in Rabinbach and Zipes, *Germans and Jews since the Holocaust*, pp.27–28.

3. Monika Richarz, 'Juden in der Bundesrepublik Deutschland und in der Deutschen Demokratischen Republik seit 1945,' in Brumlik, *Jüdisches Leben in Deutschland seit 1945*. See also Schoeps, 'Les Juifs dans l'Allemagne,' *Matériaux*, no.23.

4. Quoted by Benz, *Zwischen Hitler und Adenauer*, pp.66–67.

5. Y. Michal Bodemann, 'Staat und Ethnizität: Der Aufbau der jüdischen Gemeinden im Kalten Krieg,' in Brumlik, *Jüdisches Leben in Deutschland*, p.58.

6. See Combe, 'Mémoire,' *Esprit*, no.10.

7. See especially the collective work *Kennzeichen 'J.'* The most recent significant work on the Jewish genocide to appear in the GDR is without question Hirsch and Schuder, *Gelbe Fleck*.

8. See Sonia Combe, 'Des commémorations pour surmonter le passé nazi,' in the collection edited by Brossat, Combe, Potel, and Szurek, *A l'Est la mémoire retrouvée*, p.286.

9. It could be said that the 'raw material' was lacking for this kind of staging (the Jews of the SED were far more numerous than those of the POUP in Poland), but in fact, especially from the end of the sixties, the GDR's attitude with regard to the

Shoah differed noticeably from that of the other Soviet satellites, with research into, publications on, and commemorations of the Jewish genocide.

10. See Ostow, *Jüdisches Leben in der DDR*, pp.16–19.

11. See H. Eschwege, 'Die jüdische Bevölkerung der Jahre nach der Kapitulation Hitlerdeutschlands auf dem Gebiet der DDR bis zum Jahre 1953,' in Schoeps, *Juden in der DDR*, p.87.

12. Peter Honigmann, 'Über den Umgang mit Juden und jüdischer Geschichte in der DDR,' *ibid.*, p.110.

13. Quoted by Combe, 'Mémoire du nazisme et histoire officielle.'

14. Ostow, *Jüdisches Leben in der DDR*, p.16.

15. See Christa Wolf, *Patterns of Childhood*. Hein has described the attitude of the Germans when confronted with Nazi crimes in *Horns Ende*, a novel in which the victims of persecution are represented by the Gypsies.

16. Wolf, 'Erfahrungsmuster,' *Die Dimension des Autors*, p.811. See also Karl-Heinz Harmann, 'Das Dritte Reich in der DDR Literatur. Stationen erzählter Vergangenheit,' in Wagner, *Gegenswartsliteratur*, pp.307–328.

17. See Haase, *Deutsche Deserteure*.

18. On the history of the *Wiedergütmachung* Treaty, see Hilberg, *Destruction*, p.1182.

19. See Rabinbach, 'The Jewish Question,' *New German Critique*, no.44, p.167.

20. Quoted by Kloke, *Israel*, p.43.

21. Quoted by Y. M. Bodemann, in Ostow, *Jüdisches Leben in der DDR*, p.60. See also Rovan, *Adenauer*, pp.107–109.

22. See Wolffsohn, *Ewige Schuld?*, p.108.

23. The Jewish attitude to reparations was ambivalent. An ethical rejection of the entire notion of indemnification was made by Jankélevitch: 'For our part we say to the Germans: keep your indemnities, these crimes cannot be paid for in money; no amount of damages can compensate us for six million tortured victims, there can be no reparations for what cannot be retrieved. We do not want your money.' *L'imprescriptible*, p.59.

24. See Hilberg, *Destruction*, vol.3, p.1182. It should not be forgotten either that reparations for the Jews became a symbolic act which made it possible to forget all the other victims of nazism. The Russian and Polish *Zwangsarbeitern* deported to Germany homosexuals, euthanasia victims, and members of the Communist resistance, none of whom were ever indemnified (only the Gypsies were to be, much later).

25. See Mitscherlich, *Le deuil impossible*, p.37. For the historian Frei it was not so much a question of 'repression' as of an 'inability to endure what might have been expressed and evoked' by any reference to Nazi crimes ('L'Holocauste,' in *Vingtième siècle*, no.34, p.159).

26. See Lutz Niethammer, ' "Normalisierung" im Westen. Erinnerungsspuren in die 50er Jahre,' in Diner, *Ist der Nationalsozialismus Geschichte?*, p.161.

27. See Baier, *Un Allemand né de la dernière guerre*, p.14.

28. See Lübbe, 'Nationalsozialismus,' *Historische*, no.236, p.585.

29. See Bier, *Auschwitz*, ch.2.

30. Koestler, 'A Guide to Political Neuroses,' in *The Trail of the Dinosaur*, p.218.

31. Arendt, 'Organized Guilt and Personal Responsibility,' *Essays in Understanding*, p.125.

32. See Bier, *Auschwitz*, pp.75–78.

33. Giordano, *Die zweite Schuld*, p.266.

34. See Schneider, 'Deutschland erwacht,' *Konkret*, no.10, p.31. On the 'collective innocence' of German society with regard to the persecution and genocide of the Jews, see the studies assembled by Wollenberg, *'Niemand war dabei und keinen hat's gewusst.'*

35. The publication of Anne Frank's *Diary* (1967) in the fifties aroused strong if shortlived feelings.

36. See Kloke, *Israel und die deutsche Linke*, pp.106–108.

37. Jeffrey Herf, 'The *Holocaust* Reception in West Germany: Right, Center and Left,' in Rabinbach and Zipes, *Germans and Jews since the Holocaust*, pp.208–233.

38. Michael Schneider, *Die abgetriebene Revolution*, p.28.

39. For a more general approach to this theme, cf. Sichrovsky, *Naître coupable*.

40. See Diner, 'Den Westen verstehen,' *Kursbuch* 104, pp.143–153. The positions adopted by leftist pacifists are represented in a collection assembled by Bredthauer, Heinrich, and Naumann, *Krieg für Frieden?* On the interpretation of events in the Persian Gulf, in the light of the German past, see especially Michael Schneider, 'Der arabische Frankenstein,' in Bredthauer, Heinrich, and Nauman, *Krieg für Frieden?*, pp.106–119. The positions adopted by leftist intellectuals who supported the war are assembled in another collection: Klaus Bittermann, ed., *Liebesgrüsse aus Bagdad*. Henryk Broder and Wolf Biermann accused German pacifists of wanting to 'complete' the work begun by Hitler by supporting Saddam Hussein.

41. See Benjamin, *Illuminations*, p.255. See also Bülow, *L'Allemagne*, p.153, and Pohrt, 'Das Elend,' pp.76–77.

42. See Funke, 'Bergen-Belsen,' pp.20–34.

43. See Vidal-Naquet, *Assassins*.

44. Nolte, 'The Past That Will Not Pass,' in the collection *Forever in the Shadow of Hitler?*, pp.21–22.

45. See Wehler, *Entsorgung*, ch.4, part 8.

46. Nolte, 'Between Myth and Revisionism? The Third Reich and the Perspective of the 1980s,' in Koch, *Aspects*, pp.17–38. See Wehler's critique, *Entsorgung*.

47. Nolte, *Der europäische*, p.15.

48. Ibid., p.554. For an accurate and rigorous critique of Nolte's theses, see Evans, *In Hitler's Shadow*.

49. Hillgruber, *Zweierlei Untergang*, pp.24–25.

50. According to Bernard D. Weinryb, the number of victims of pogroms carried out by Denikin's army was approximately 60,000–70,000 Jews (between 180,000 and 200,000 according to Soviet sources). See Weinryb, 'Antisemitism in Soviet Russia,' in Kochan, *Jews in Soviet Russia*, p.310.

51. Levi, *Drowned and Saved*, p.96. See the illuminating observations of Combe, 'S. K. Evstigneev, roi d'Ozerlag,' *Ozerlag 1937–1964*, pp.226–227.

52. Regarding the evolution of Hitler's anti-Semitism, see Friedländer, *L'anti-sémitisme allemand*, ch.4.

53. Mommsen, 'The New Historical Consciousness and the Relativizing of National Socialism,' in Knowlton and Cates, *Forever in the Shadow?*, p.120.

54. Quoted by Fritz Stern, *Politics of Cultural Despair*, pp.86–87.

55. Klaus Hildebrand, 'The Age of Tyrants: History and Politics: The Administrators of the Enlightenment, the Risk of Scholarship, and the Preservation of a Worldview. A Reply to Jürgen Habermas,' in Knowlton and Cates, *Forever in the Shadow?*, p.51.

56. Joachim Fest, 'Encumbered Remembrance,' *ibid.*, pp.63–71.

57. Eberhard Jäckel, 'The Impoverished Practice of Insinuation,' *ibid.*, p.76.

58. See Claussen, 'Vergangenheit mit Zukunft: Über die Entsehung einer neuen deutschen Ideologie,' *Die neue deutsche Ideologie*, p.12.

59. The fact that this speech, in spite of its contents, could have been interpreted in this way shows once again that Germany is far from having 'freed' itself from its past. Regarding the Jenninger affair, see the record assembled by Priani, *Il fascino.*

60. *Le Monde*, 9 February 1990.

61. Rousso, *Le syndrome*, p.9.

62. See Friedländer, 'Some Germans Struggle with Memory,' in Hartman, *Bitburg*, p.27.

63. See Pierre Nora, 'Entre mémoire,' *Les lieux de mémoire* 1, p.xix.

64. See Paola Di Cori, 'L'oblio,' *Movimento* 13, no.3, p.300.

65. See Yerushalmi's contribution to the collective work *Usages de l'oubli.*

66. Meier, op.cit., p.279.

67. Cited by Baier, *Les Allemands*, pp.116–117.

68. Schneider, *Die abgetriebene Revolution*, p.128.

69. Grass, 'Ecrire après Auschwitz,' p.44.

70. See Habermas, 'A Kind of Settlement of Damages: The Apologetic Tendencies in German History Writing,' in Knowlton and Cates, *Forever in the Shadow?*,

pp.34–44, and 'Conscience historique,' *Ecrits politiques*. Christian Meier has described Habermas's procedure as substituting the Constitution (*Verfassung*) for the nation (*Heimat*); see Meier, *40 Jahre nach Auschwitz*, p.87.

71. See Jaspers, '*Die Schuldfrage.*'

72. Arendt, 'Organized Guilt and Universal Responsibility,' *Essays in Understanding*, p.125.

73. See Alain Brossat, 'La réunification ou la fin,' *Critique communiste*, nos.102–103, p.15.

74. Baier very pertinently recalls the case of Peter-Jürgen Boock, an ex-militant 'dissociate' of the RAF, who had taken part in no terrorist action and was three times imprisoned for life; whereas, in 1964, General Wolff, Himmler's chief of staff, implicated in the murder of 300,000 people, received a fifteen-year sentence, of which only five years were served (*Allemand*, p.95).

75. See Ermacora, *Frankfürter Rundschau*.

76. Article in the *Frankfurter Allgemeine Zeitung*, quoted by Wolfgang Schneider, *Vernichtungspolitik*, p.32.

77. Ibid.

78. Joachim Fest, 'Encumbered Remembrance,' in Knowlton and Cates, *Forever in the Shadow?*, p.66.

79. Jean Améry, *Jenseits von Schuld und Sühne*, p.127.

80. Henryk M. Broder, 'Die unheilbare Liebe deutscher Intellektueller zu toten und todkranken Juden,' in the collection *Eingriffe*, pp.67–73.

81. Alain Auffray, 'Syberberg,' *Libération*.

82. Arendt and Jaspers,*Correspondence*, p.53. The significance of this letter has been pointed out by Jean-Michel Chaumont in his essay 'La mémoire d'Auschwitz,' *Fondation Auschwitz*, no.5. 25–26, p.34.

83. See Michael Schneider, *Die abgetriebene Revolution*, p.219.

84. See Adorno, 'Eduquer après Auschwitz,' *Modèles critiques: Interventions, critiques*, p.218.

# Bibliography

Abensour, Miguel. 'Hannah Arendt et le sionisme en question,' *Passé, Présent* 3 (1984).

———, ed. *Ontologie et politique: actes du Colloque Hannah Arendt.* Paris: Editions Tierce, 1989.

Acherson, Neal. *Au sujet de Shoah.* Paris: Belin, 1990.

Adler, H. G. 'The Judeo German Symbiosis,' *Die Juden in Deutschland von der Aufklärung bis zum Nationalsozialismus.* München: Piper, 1987.

Adorno, Theodor W. 'Eduquer après Auschwitz,' *Modèles critiques: Interventions, critiques.* Paris: Payot, 1984.

———. 'Erziehung nach Auschwitz,' *Erziehung zur Mündigkeit.* Frankfurt: Suhrkamp, 1975.

———. *Minima Moralia: Reflections from a Damaged Life.* London: New Left, 1974.

———, and Max Horkheimer. 'Eléments de l'antisémitisme,' *Dialectique de la raison.* Paris: Gallimard, 1974.

Aly, Götz, and Susanne Heim. *Vordenker der Vernichtung. Auschwitz und die deutschen Pläne für eine neue europäische Ordnung.* Hamburg: Hoffmann & Campe, 1991.

Améry, Jean. 'Zwang und Unmöglichkeit, Jude zu sein,' *Jenseits von Schuld und Sühne.* Stuttgart: Klett Cotta, 1976.

Arendt, Hannah. *Auschwitz et Jérusalem.* Paris: Deux Temps Tierce, 1991.

———. *Eichmann in Jerusalem: A Report on the Banality of Evil.* New York: Penguin, 1992.

———. *Essays in Understanding 1930–1954,* ed. Jerome Kohn. New York: Harcourt Brace, 1994.

———. *The Jew as Pariah: Jewish Identity and Politics in the Modern Age.* New York: Grove, 1978.

———. *Men in Dark Times.* New York: Harcourt, Brace & World, 1968.

———. *On Revolution.* New York: Viking, 1993.

———. *The Origins of Totalitarianism.* New York: Harcourt Brace Jovanovich, 1973.

———. *Penser l'évènement.* Paris: Belin, 1989.

# Bibliography

——. *Rahel Varnhagen: The Life of a Jewish Woman.* New York: Harcourt Brace Jovanovich, 1974.

——. 'Reflections in Little Rock,' in *Dissent*, 6/1, winter 1959.

——. *Sur l'antisémitisme.* Paris: Seuil, 1984.

——. *La tradition cachée: Le Juif comme paria.* Paris: Bourgois, 1987.

——, and Karl Jaspers. *Correspondence 1926–1969.* New York: Harcourt Brace Jovanovich, 1992.

Aronson, Ronald. *The Dialectics of Disaster: A Preface to Hope.* London: Verso, 1983.

Aschheim, Steven. *Brothers and Strangers: The East European Jew in Germany and German Jewish Consciousness (1800–1923).* Madison: Univ. of Wisconsin Press, 1982.

Auffrey, Alain. 'Syberberg, un mauvais film d'Allemagne,' *Libération* (28 November 1990).

Ayçoberry, Pierre. *La question nazie: Les interprétations du national-socialisme 1922–1975.* Paris: Seuil, 1979.

Azuelos, Daniel. 'Judéité et germanité: l'impossible symbiose? (Lion Feuchtwanger, Arnold Zweig et Jakob Wassermann),' *Pardès*, no.5 (1987).

*Babylon: Baiträge zur jüdischen Gegenwart.* Frankfurt: Verlag Neue Kritik, nos.1– 9 (1986–91).

Badia, G., and C. Weill. *Rosa Luxemburg aujourd'hui.* Paris: Presses universitaires de Vincennes, 1986.

Baeck, Leo. 'The German Jews,' *Leo Baeck Institute Year Book 2* (1957).

Baier, Lothar. *Un Allemand né de la dernière guerre.* Paris: Calmann-Lévy, 1989.

——. *Les Allemands maîtres du temps: Essai sur un peuple pressé.* Paris: Découverte, 1991.

Baioni, Giuliano. *Kafka e l'ebraismo.* Torino: Einaudi, 1983.

Barnow, Dagmar. *Visible Spaces: Hannah Arendt and the German-Jewish Experience.* Baltimore: Johns Hopkins Univ. Press, 1990.

Bédarida, François, ed. *La politique nazie d'extermination.* Paris: Albin Michel, 1989.

Beetham, David, ed. *Marxism in Face of Fascism: Writings by Marxists on Fascism from the Inter-War Period.* Manchester: Manchester Univ. Press, 1983.

Bein, Alex. 'The Jewish Parasite. Notes on the Semantics of the Jewish Problem, with Special Reference to Germany,' *Leo Baeck Institute Year Book 9* (1964).

——. *Theodor Herzl: A Biography.* Philadelphia: Jewish Publication Society, 1940.

Beller, Steven. *Vienna and the Jews, 1867–1938: A Cultural History.* Cambridge: Cambridge Univ. Press, 1989.

————. *Herzl*. New York: Grove, 1991.

Benjamin, Walter. 'A Berlin Chronicle,' in *One Way Street and Other Writings*. New York: Verso, 1985.

————. *Berliner Kindheit um 1900*. Frankfurt: Suhrkamp, 1975.

————. *Deutsche Menschen: Eine Volge von Briefen*. Frankfurt: Suhrkamp, 1983.

————. *Illuminations*, translated by Harry Zohn. New York: Schocken, 1968.

————. 'Juden in der deutsche Kultur,' *Gesammelte Schriften* 2:2. Frankfurt: Suhrkamp, 1977.

————. *Moscow Diary*. Cambridge: Harvard Univ. Press, 1986.

————, and Gershom Scholem. *The Correspondence of Walter Benjamin and Gershom Scholem, 1932–1940*. New York: Schocken, 1989.

Bensussan, Gérard. 'Rosa ou l'impossible recoin,' *Questions juives*. Paris: Osiris, 1988.

Benz, Wolfgang. *Zwischen Hitler und Adenauer: Studien zur deutschen Nachkriegsgesellschaft*. Frankfurt: Fischer, 1991.

Berding, Helmut. *Moderner Antisemitismus in Deutschland*. Frankfurt: Suhrkamp, 1988.

Berlin, Isaïah. *Trois essais sur la condition juive*. Paris: Calmann-Lévy, 1973.

Bernand, Carmen, and Serge Gruzinski. *Histoire du Nouveau Monde*. Paris: Fayard, 1990.

Bernstein, Eduard. 'Wie ich al Jude in der Diaspora aufwuchs,' *Der Jude* 11 (1917–18).

Bettauer, Hugo. *Der Stadt ohne Juden*. Wien: Goriette-Verlag, 1922. *The City Without Jews*, translated by Salomea Neumark Brainin. New York: Bloch, 1926.

Bier, Jean-Paul. *Auschwitz et les nouvelles littératures allemandes*. Bruxelles: Université de Bruxelles, 1979.

Bitterman, Klaus, ed. *Liebesgrüsse aus Bagdad*. Berlin: Tiamat, 1991.

Blasius, Dirk, and Dan Diner, eds. *Zerbrochene Geschichte: Leben und Selbstverständnis der Juden in Deutschland*. Frankfurt: Fischer, 1991.

Bloch, Ernst. *The Principle of Hope*, 3 vols. Cambridge: MIT Press, 1986.

Bloom, Alexander. *Prodigal Sons: The New York Intellectuals and Their World*. New York: Oxford Univ. Press, 1986.

Blumenfeld, Kurt. *Erlebte Judenfrage*. Stuttgart: Deutsche Verlag-Anstalt, 1962.

Bock, Gisela. 'Geschichte, Frauengeschichte, Geschlechtgeschichte,' *Geschichte und Gesellschaft* 14/3, no.188.

————. *Zwangsterilisation im Nationalsozialismus. Studien zur Rassenpolitik und Frauenpolitik*. Opladen: Westdeutscher Verlag, 1986.

Böhlich, Walter, ed. *Der Berliner antisemitismusstreit*: Frankfurt: Insel, 1988.

Bolkosky, Sidney. *The Distorted Image: German Jewish Perceptions of Germans and Germany 1918–1935*. New York: Elsevier, 1975.

# Bibliography

Borries, Achim von, ed. *Selbstzeugnisse des deutschen Judentums 1861–1945.* Frankfurt: Fischer Verlag, 1988.

Botstein, Leon. *Judentum und Modernität.* Wien: Böhlau Verlag, 1991.

Boureau, Alain. *Histories d'un historien: Kantorowicz.* Paris: Gallimard, 1990.

Bourel, Dominique. 'Les Juifs et l'Occident ou la métaphore impossible,' *Esprit,* no.5 (1979).

Bourel, Dominique. 'Un soupir de Rosenzweig,' *Franz Rosenzweig: Les Cahiers de la Nuit Surveillée,* no.1 (Paris: 1982).

Bourel, Dominique, and Jacques Le Rider, eds. *De Sils-Maria à Jérusalem: Nietzsche et le judaïsme: Les intellectuels juifs et Nietzsche.* Paris: Cerf, 1991.

Bracher, Karl D. *The German Dictatorship: The Origins, Structure and Effects of National Socialism.* New York: Praeger, 1970.

Brakelmann, Günter, and Martin Rosowski, eds. *Antisemitismus.* Göttingen: Vandenhoeck, 1989.

Bredthauer, K. D., A. Heinrich, and K. Naumann. *Krieg für Frieden? Startschüsse für eine neue Weltordnung.* Berlin: Elefanten, 1991.

Brecht, Bertolt. *Work Journals, 1938–1955.* London: Methuen, 1992.

Broder, Henryk, and Michel R. Lang, eds. *Fremd im eigenen Land: Juden in der Bundesrepublik.* Frankfurt: Fischer, 1987.

Brodersen, Momme. *Spinne im eigenen Netz: Walter Benjamin Leben und Werk.* Bühl-Moos: Elster Verlag, 1990.

Bronsen, David. *Joseph Roth: Eine Biographie.* Köln: Kiepenheuer & Witsch, 1974.

———, ed. *Jews and Germans from 1866 to 1933: The Problematic Symbiosis.* Heidelberg: Carl Winter, 1979.

Brossat, Alain. 'La réunification allemande ou la fin de l'histoire,' *Critique communiste,* nos.102–103 (1991).

Brossat, A., S. Combe, J. Y. Potel, and J. C. Szurek. *A l'Èst la mémoire retrouvée.* Paris: Découverte, 1990.

Broszat, Martin. "Hitler und die Genesis der "Endlösung," ' *Vierteljahrshefte für Zeitgeschichte* 4 (1977).

———. *Der Staat Hitlers: Grundlegung und Verfassung seiner inneren Entwicklung.* München: DTV, 1969.

Broué, Pierre. *Trotsky.* Paris: Fayard, 1988.

Brumlik, Mischa, ed. *Jüdisches Leben in Deutschland seit 1945.* Frankfurt: Athenäum, 1986.

Buber, Martin. 'Das Ende der deutsch-jüdischen Symbiose,' *Der Jude und sein Judentum: Gesammelte Aufsätze und Reden.* Köln: Joseph Melzer Verlag, 1963.

———. *Fragments autobiographiques.* Paris: Stock, 1985.

———. *On Judaism.* New York: Schocken, 1967.

# Bibliography

Buglar, Peter. *Walther Rathenau: Seine Zeit, Sein Werk, Seine Persönlichkeit.* Brême: Schünemann Universitätatsverlag, 1970.

Bülow, Katharina von. *L'Allemagne entre père et fils.* Paris: Grasset, 1988.

Bunzl, John. *Juden im Orient: Jüdische Gemeinschaften in der islamischen Welt und orientalische Juden in Israel.* Wien: Junius Verlag, 1989.

Bunzi, John. *Der lange Arm der Erinnerung, Jüdisches Bewusstsein heute.* Wien: Böhlau, 1987.

Burrin, Phillippe. 'Hitler dans le IIIe Reich: Maître ou serviteur? Martin Broszat et l'interprétation fonctionaliste du régime nazi,' *Vingtieme siècle,* no.16 (1987).

―――. *Hitler et les Juifs: Genèse d'un génocide.* Paris: Seuil, 1989.

Cacciari, Massimo. *Walther Rathenau e il suo ambiente.* Bari: De Donato, 1979.

Canetti, Elias. *The Human Province.* New York: Seabury, 1978.

Carmely, Klara Pommeranz. *Das Identitätsproblem jüdischer Autoren im deutschen Sprachraum: Von der Jahrhundertwende bis zu Hitler.* Königstein: Scriptor, 1981.

Caullery, Maurice. *Le parasitisme et la symbiose.* Paris: Paris, 1950.

Chaliand, Gérard, and Yves Ternon. *Le génocide des Arménians.* Bruxelles: Complexe, 1980.

Chamisso, Adalbert von, *Peter Schlemihl.* Paris: José Corti, 1989.

Chaumont, Jean-Michel. 'La mémoire d'Auschwitz dans l'Allemagne réunifiée: pour une inscription constitutionnelle,' *Bulletin trimestrial de la Fondation Auschwitz,* nos.25−26 (1990).

Chouraqui, A. *Theodor Herzl.* Paris: Seuil, 1960.

Claussen, Detlev. *Grenzen der Aufklärung: Zur gesellschaftlichen Geschichte des modernen Antisemitismus.* Frankfurt: Fischer, 1987.

―――. *Jüdisches Leben in Deutschland seit 1945.* Frankfurt: Athenäum, 1988.

―――, ed. *Die neue deutsche Ideologie: Einsprüche gegen die Entsorgung der Vergangenheit.* Darmstadt: Luchterhand, 1988.

Cohen, Hermann. 'Deutschum und Judentum,' in C. Schulte, ed., *Deutschum und Judentum.* Stuttgart: Reclam, 1993.

Cohen, Laurent. *Variations autour de K.: Pour une lecture juive de Franz Kafka.* Paris: Intertextes, 1991.

Cohen-Solal, Annie. *Sartre.* Paris: Gallimard, 1989.

Colloque de l'EHESS. *L'Allemagne nazie et le génocide juif.* Paris: EHESS, Gallimard, Seuil, 1985.

Combe, Sonia. 'Des commémorations pour surmonter le passé nazi,' in A. Brossat, S. Combe, J. Y. Potel, and J. C. Szurek, eds. *A l'Èst la mémoire retrouvée.* Paris: Découverte, 1990.

―――. 'Mémoire collective et histoire officielle: Le passé nazi en RDA,' *Esprit,* no.10 (1987).

# Bibliography

―――. 'S. K. Evstigneev, roi d'Ozerlag,' *Ozerlag 1937–1964.* Paris: Autrement, 1991.

Cuau, Bernard, et al. *Au sujet de Shoah.* Paris: Belin, 1990.

Cziffra, Geza von. *Der heilige Trinker. Erinnerungen an Joseph Roth.* Frankfurt, Berlin: Ullstein, 1989.

Dawidowicz, Lucy. *The Holocaust and the Historians.* Cambridge: Harvard Univ. Press, 1981.

―――. *The War against the Jews.* New York: Holt, Rinehart & Winston, 1975.

Dal Lago, Alessandro, ' "Politeia": cittadinanza ed esilio nell'opera di Hannah Arendt,' *Il Mulino* 33, no.293.

de Felice, Renzo. *Storia degli ebrai italiani sotto il fascismo.* Torino: Einaudi, 1988.

Della Loggia, Ernesto Galli. 'L'olocausto e gli olocausti,' *Il Molino,* no.321 (1989).

Della Pergola, Sergio. *La transformazione demografica della diaspora ebraica.* Torino: Loescher, 1983.

Deutscher, Isaac. *The Non-Jewish Jew and Other Essays.* New York: Oxford Univ. Press, 1968.

*Devant l'histoire: Les documents de la controverse sur la singularité de l'extermination des Juifs par le régime nazi.* Paris: Cerf, 1988.

Di Cori, Paola. 'L'oblio, la storia e la politica,' *Movimento operaio e socialista* 13, no.3 (1990).

Diner, Dan. 'Den Westen verstehen. Der Golfkrieg als deutschen Lehstück,' *Kursbuch* 104 (June 1991).

―――, ed. *Ist der Nationalsozialismus Geschichte? Zu Historisierung und Historikerstreit.* Frankfurt: Fischer, 1987.

―――, ed. *Zivilisationsbruch: Denken nach Auschwitz.* Frankfurt: Fischer, 1988.

Dohm, Christian Wilhelm. *De la réforme politique des Juifs,* Paris: Stock, 1984.

Dupeux. Louis. ' "Révolution conservatrice" et hitlérisme. Essai sur la natur de l'hitlerérisme,' *Revue d'Allemagne 16,* no.3 (1984).

―――, ed. *La 'Révolution conservatrice' dans l'Allemagne de Weimar.* Paris: Kimé, 1992.

*Eingriffe: Jahrbuch für gessellschaftkritische Umtriebe,* Berlin: Tiamat, 1988.

Elias, Norbert. 'Notes sur les Juifs en tant que participant à une relation établis-marginaux,' *Norbert Elias par lui-même.* Paris: Fayard, 1990.

Ellbogen, Ismar, and Eleanore Sterling. *Die Geschichte der Juden in Deutschland.* Frankfurt: Athenäum, 1988.

Engelmann, Bernt. *Deutschland ohne Juden.* Köln: Pahl-Rugenstein, 1988.

Ermacora, Felix. *Frankfürter Rundschau* (7 August 1991).

Ettinger, Elzbieta. *Rosa Luxemburg: Une vie.* Paris: Belfond, 1990.

Evans, Richard J. *In Hitler's Shadow.* New York: Pantheon, 1989.

# Bibliography

Field, Geoffrey G. *Evangelist of Race: The Germanic Vision of Houston Stewart Chamberlain*. New York: Columbia Univ. Press, 1981.

Finkielkraut, Alain. *L'avenir d'une négation: Réflexions sur la question du génocide*. Paris: Seuil, 1982.

Fleming, Gerlad. *Hitler et la solution finale*. Paris: Julliard, 1988.

Frank, Anne. *The Diary of a Young Girl*. Garden City: Doubleday, 1967.

Frei, Norbert. 'L'Holocauste dans l'historiographie allemande: Un point aveugle dans la conscience historique?' *Vingtième siècle* 34 (1992).

Friedländer, Saul. *L'antisémitisme allemand: Histoire d'une psychose collective*. Paris: Seuil, 1971.

———. *Reflets du nazisme*. Paris: Seuil, 1982.

Frölich, P. *Rosa Luxemburg*. Paris: Harmattan, 1991.

Funke, Hajo. 'Bergen-Belsen, Bitburg, Hambach: Bericht über eine negative Katharsis,' in H. Funke, ed., *Von der Gnade der Geschenkten Nation*. Berlin: Rotbuch Verlag, 1988.

Gay, Peter. *Ein gottloser Jude*. Frankfurt: Fischer, 1988.

———. *Freud, Jews and Other Germans*. New York: Oxford Univ. Press, 1978.

———. *Weimar Culture: The Outsider as Insider*. New York: Harper & Row, 1968.

Gilman, Sander L. *Jewish Self-Hatred: Antisemitism and the Hidden Language of the Jews*. Baltimore: Johns Hopkins Univ. Press, 1986.

Giordano, Ralf. *Die zweite Schuld oder von der Last Deutscher zu sein*. München: Knaur, 1990.

Goldmann, Nahum. *Autobiographie*. Paris: Paris, 1971.

Goldsmith, Emanuel S. *Modern Yiddish Culture. The Story of the Yiddish Language Movement*. New York: Shapolsky, 1987.

Goldstein, Moritz. *Berliner Jahre: Erinnerungen 1880–1933*. München: Verlag Dokumentation, 1977.

Gordon, Milton M. *Assimilation in American Life. The Role of Race, Religion and National Origins*. New York: Oxford Univ. Press, 1964.

Grab, Walter, ed. *Gegenseitige Einflüsse deutscher und jüdischer Kultur: Von der Epoche der Aufklärung bis zur Weimarer Republik*. Tel Aviv: Instituts für deutsche Geschichte, 1982.

———, ed. *Jüdische Integration und Identität in Deutschland und Oesterreich 1848–1918*. Tel Aviv: Instituts für Deutsche Geschichte, 1984.

———, and Julius H. Schoeps, eds. *Juden in der Weimarer Republik*. Stuttgart: Burg Verlag, 1986.

Gramsci, Antonio. *Quaderni del carcere*, 6 vols. Torino: Einaudi, 1975.

Grass, Günter. 'Ecrire après Auschwitz,' *Propos d'un sans-patrie*. Paris: Seuil, 1990.

Graupe, Heinz Mosche. *Die Enstehung des modernen Judentums: Geistgeschichte des deutschen Juden 1650–1942*. Hamburg: Helmut Buske Verlag, 1977.

# Bibliography

Green, Nancy. 'Socialist anti-Semitism, Defence of a Bourgeoise Jew and Discovery of the Jewish Proletariat: Changing Attitudes of French Socialists before 1914,' *International Review of Social History* 3 (1985).

Grosser, Alfred. *Le crime et la mémoire*. Paris: Flammarion, 1990.

Grözinger, E., H. D. Zimmermann, and S. Moses, eds. *Kafka und das Judentum*. Frankfurt: Athenäum, 1987.

Grözinger, Karl Emil, ed. *Judentum im deutschen Sprachraum*. Frankfurt: Suhrkamp, 1991.

Grunfeld, Frederic. *Prophets without Honor: A Background to Freud, Kafka, Einstein and Their World*. New York: McGraw-Hill, 1979.

Haase, Norbert. *Deutsche Deserteure*. Berlin: Rotbuch Verlag, 1987.

Habermas, Jürgen. 'Conscience historique et identité post-traditionnelle: L'orientation à L'Ouest de la RFA,' *Ecrits politiques*. Paris: Cerf, 1990.

——. *Philosophical Political Profiles*. Cambridge: MIT Press, 1985.

Halevi, Ilan. *Question juive: La tribu, la loi, l'espace*. Paris: Minuit, 1981.

Harrison, James Pinckney. *The Endless War*. New York: Free Press, 1982.

Hartman, Geoffrey, ed. *Bitburg in Moral and Political Perspective*. Bloomington: Indiana Univ. Press, 1986.

Hartmann, Karl-Heinz. 'Das Dritte Reich in def DDR Literatur: Stationen erzählter Vergangenheit,' in Hans Wagner, ed., *Gegenwartsliteratur und Dritte Reich: Deutsche Autoren in der Auseinandersetzung mit der Vegangenheit*. Stuttgart: Reclam, 1977.

Hayoun, Maurice-Ruben. *Le judaïsme moderne*. Paris: Presses universitaires de France, 1989.

Heilburt, Anthony. *Kultur ohne Heimat: Deutsche Emigranten in den USA nach 1930*. Hamburg: Rowohlt, 1991.

Hein, Christoph. *Horns Ende*. Darmstadt: Luchterhand, 1985.

Heine, Heinrich. *Sämtliche Schriften*, 6 vols. to date: vol.1 (1968), vol.4 (1971). München: Hanser Verlag.

Herf, Jeffrey. *Reactionary Modernism: Technology, Culture and Politics in Weimar and the Third Reich*. New York: Cambridge Univ. Press, 1984.

Hermand, Jost. *Der alte Traum vom neuen Reich: Völkische Utopien und Nationalsozialismus*. Frankfurt: Athenäum, 1988.

——, and Gert Mattelklott, eds., *Jüdische Intelligenz in Deutschland*. Berlin: Argument Verlag, 1988.

Herz, Deborah. *Jewish High Society in Old Regime Berlin*. New Haven: Yale Univ. Press, 1988.

Herzig, Arno. 'Zur Problematik deutsch-jüdische Geschicht-schreibung,' *Menora: Jahrbuch für deutsch-jüdische Geschichte*, 1990.

# Bibliography

Herzl, Theodor. *Diaries*. New York: Dial, 1956.

------. *The Jewish State*. London: H. Pordes, 1972.

Hess, Moses. *Rome and Jerusalem: A Study in Jewish Nationalism*. New York: Block, 1918.

------. 'Über das Geldwesen,' in *Sozialistische Aufsätz (1841–1847)*. Berlin: Welt Verlag, 1921.

Higham, John. *Strangers in the Land: Patterns of American Nativism 1860–1925*. New York: Atheneum, 1985.

Hilberg, Raul. *The Destruction of the European Jews*, 3 vols. New York: Holmes & Meier, 1985.

Hildebrand, Klaus. *Das Dritte Reich*. München: Oldenbourg, 1979.

Hillgruber, Andreas. *Zweierlei Untergang: Die Zerschlagung des Deutschen Reiches und das Ende des europäischen Judentums*. Berlin: Siedler, 1986.

Hirsch, Rudolf, and Rosemarie Schuder. *Gelbe Fleck: Wurzeln und Wirkungen des Judenhasse in der deutschen Geschichte*. Berlin: Rütten & Loening, 1987.

*L'Histoire escamotée: Les tentatives de liquidation du passé nazi en Allemagne*. Paris: Découverte, 1988.

Horch, Hans Otto, ed. *Judentum, Antisemitismus und europäische Kultur*. Tübingen: Francke Verlag, 1988.

Horkheimer, Max. 'Esprit juif et esprit allemand,' *Esprit*, numéro spécial sur les Juifs et l'Allemagne 5 (1979).

Ilsar, Yehiel. 'Zum Problem der Symbiose: Prolegomena zur deutsch-jüdischen Symbiose,' *Bulletin des Leo Baeck Instituts* 14, no.51 (1975).

Jankelévitch, Vladimir. *L'imprescriptible*. Paris: Seuil, 1986.

Jaspers, Karl. 'Die Schuldfrage.' *Hoffnung und Sorge. Schriften zur deutschen Politik 1945–1965*. München: Piper, 1965.

Jay, Martin. *The Dialectical Imagination: A History of the Frankfurt School and the Institute of Social Research, 1932–1950*. Boston: Little, Brown, 1973.

------. 'Hannah Arendt: Opposing Views,' *Partisan Review* 45, no.23 (1978).

------. *Permanent Exiles: Essays on the Intellectual Migration from Germany to America*. New York: Columbia Univ. Press, 1986.

Johnston, William M. *L'esprit viennois: Une histoire culturelle et sociale 1848–1938*. Paris: Presses universitaires de France, 1991.

Junger, Ernst. 'Über Nationalismus und Judenfrage,' *Süddeutsche Monatshefte* 27 (1929/1930).

Kafka, Franz. *Letters to Friends, Family, and Editors*. New York: Schocken, 1977.

------. *Letters to Milena*. New York: Schocken, 1990.

Kampmann, Wanda. *Juden und Deutsche: Die Geschichte der Juden in Deutschland*. Frankfurt: Fischer, 1979.

# Bibliography

Kantorowicz, Ernst. *Frederich the Second*. New York: Ungar, 1967.

———. *Mourir pour la patrie et d'autres textes*. Paris: Presses universitaires de France, 1984.

Katz, Jacob. *Out of the Ghetto*. Cambridge: Harvard Univ. Press, 1974.

———. *Wagner et la question juive*. Paris: Hachette, 1986.

Kautsky, Karl. *Rasse und Judentum*. Stuttgart: Dietz Verlag, 1921.

Kaznelson, Sigmund, ed. *Juden im deutschen Kulturbereich. Ein Sammelwerk*. Berlin: Jüdischer Verlag, 1959.

*Kennzeichen 'J': Bilder, Dokumente, Berichte zur Geschichte der Verbrechen des Hitlerfaschismus an den deutschen Juden 1933–1945*. Berlin: Deutscher Verlag des Wissenschaften, 1966.

Kenrik, D., and G. Puxon. *Destins gitans: des origines à la 'solution finale.'* Paris: Calmann-Lévy, 1974.

Kershaw, Ian. *The Nazi Dictatorship: Problems and Perspectives of Interpretation*. London: Edward Arnold, 1985.

———. 'The Nazi State: An Exceptional State?' *New Left Review*, no.176 (1988).

Kessler, Count Harry. *Walther Rathenau: His Life and Work*. London: Gerald Howe, 1929.

Klemperer, Victor. 'Lingua Tertii Imperii' (presented by Sonia Combe), *Les Temps modernes*, no.521 (1989).

———. *LTI, Notizbuch eines Philologen*. Leipzig: Reclam, 1977.

Kloke, Martin W. *Israel und die deutsche Linke: Zur Geschichte eines schwierigen Verhältnis*. Frankfurt: Mag & Herchen, 1990.

Knowlton, James, and Truett Cates. *Forever in the Shadow of Hitler? Original Documents of the Historikerstreit, The Controversy Concerning the Singularity of the Holocaust*. Atlantic Highlands NJ: Humanities, 1993.

Knütter, Hans-Helmut. *Die Juden und die deutsche Linke in der Weimarer Republik*. Düsseldorf: Francke Verlag, 1977.

Koch, H. W. *Aspects of the Third Reich*. London: Macmillan, 1985.

Koch, Thilo, ed. *Porträts zur deutsch-jüdischen Geistesgeschichte*. Köln: Schlanberg, 1961.

Kochan, Lionel, ed. *The Jews in Soviet Russia*. London: Oxford Univ. Press, 1978.

Kocka, Jürgen. 'German History before Hitler: The Debate about the German *Sonderweg*,' *Journal of Contemporary History* 23 (1988).

Koestler, Arthur. *The Trail of the Dinosaurs and Other Essays*. New York: Macmillan, 1955.

Kogan, Eugen, Hermann Langbein, and Adalbert Rückerl. *Les chambres à gaz secret d'Etat*. Paris: Minuit, 1984.

Kohn, Hans. *Martin Buber*. Köln: Joseph Melzer Verlag, 1979.

# Bibliography

Kühnl, Reinhard, ed. *Streit ums Geschichtsbild: Die 'Historiker-Debatte' Dokumentation, Darstellung und Kritik.* Köln: Pahl-Rugenstein, 1987.

Kwiet, Konrad. 'Historians of the German Democratic Republic on Antisemitism and Persecution,' *Leo Baeck Institute Year Book* 21 (1976).

Lanzmann, Claude. *Shoah.* Paris: Fayard, 1985.

Laqueur, Walter. *Weimar: A Cultural History 1918–1933.* London: Weidenfeld & Nicolson, 1974.

――――. *A History of Zionism.* New York: Schocken, 1976.

――――. *The Terrible Secret: Suppression of the Truth about Hitler's 'Final Solution.'* Boston: Little, Brown, 1980.

Lazare, Bernard. *Antisemitism: Its History and Causes.* Lincoln: Univ. of Nebraska Press, 1995.

――――. *Le fumier de Job.* Strassburg: Circé, 1990.

*Leo Baeck Institute Year Book* 1–25 (1957–91).

Le Clézio, J. M. G. *Le rêve mexicain ou la pensée interrompue.* Paris: Gallimard, 1988.

Le Rider, Jacques. *Le cas Otto Weininger: Racines de l'antiféminisme et de l'antisémitisme.* Paris: Presses universitaires de France, 1982.

――――. *Modernité viennoise et crises de l'identité.* Paris: Presses universitaires de France, 1990.

Leschnitzer, Adolf. *Saul und David: Die Problematik der deutsch-jüdischen Lebensgemeinschaft.* Heidelberg: Verlag Lambert Schneider, 1954.

Lessing, Theodor. *La haine de soi: Le refus d'être juif.* Paris: Berg International, 1990 [*Der judische Selbsthass.* Judischer Verlag, Berlin, 1930].

Levi, Primo. *The Drowned and the Saved.* New York: Summit, 1988.

Lewy, Gunter. *America in Vietnam.* New York: Oxford Univ. Press, 1978.

――――. *The Reawakening.* New York: Macmillan, 1987.

――――. *Survival in Auschwitz.* New York: Summit, 1986.

Libaridian, Gérard. 'Répression finale: le génocide 1915–1917,' *Les temps modernes,* nos.504–505–506 (1988).

Liebeschutz, Hans. 'Treitschke and Mommsen on Jewry and Judaism,' *Leo Baeck Institute Year Book* 7 (1962).

Loewenberg, Peter. 'Antisemitismus und jüdischer Selbsthass,' *Geschichte und Gesellschaft* 4 (1979).

Löwenthal, Leo. 'Judentum und Deutscher Geist,' *Schriften 4. Judaica.* Frankfurt: Suhrkamp, 1984.

Löwy, Michael. *Redemption and Utopia.* Berkeley: Univ. of California Press, 1992.

Löwy, Michael, and Robert Sayre. *Révolte et mélancolie: Le romantisme à contre-courant de la modernité.* Paris: Payot, 1992.

# Bibliography

Lübbe, Herman. 'Der Nationalsozialismus im Deutschen Nachkriegsbewusstsein,' *Historische Zeitschrift*, no.236 (1983).

Luxemburg, Rosa. *J'étais, je suis, je serai. Correspondance 1914–1919.* Paris: Maspero, 1977.

Magris, Claudio. *Lontano da dove: Joseph Roth e la tradizione ebraico-orientale.* Torino: Einaudi, 1971.

———. *Il mito asburgico nella letteratura austriaca moderna.* Torino: Einaudi, 1963.

Mandel, Ernest. 'The Role of the Individual in History: The Case of World War Two,' *New Left Review*, no.157 (1986).

Mann, Heinrich. *Der Hass: Deutsche Zeitgeschichte: Essays.* Frankfurt: Fischer, 1987.

Marcuse, Herbert. *Eros and Civilization: a Philosophical Inquiry into Freud.* New York: Vintage, 1962.

Marienstras, Richard. *Etre un peuple en diaspora.* Paris: Maspero, 1975.

Marrus, Michael R. *The Holocaust in History.* Hanover NH: Univ. Press of New England, 1987.

———. *Les Juifs de France à l'époque de l'affaire Dreyfus.* Bruxelles: Complexe, 1985.

———. *The Politics of Assimilation.* New York: Oxford Univ. Press, 1971.

Martin, Marcel. *Charles Chaplin.* Paris: Seghers, 1972.

Marx, Karl. 'On the Jewish Question,' in *Early Writings*, translated by Rodney Livingstone and Gregor Benton. New York: Vintage, 1975.

Mason, Tim. 'Banalisation du nazisme? La controverse actuelle sur les interprétations du national-socialisme,' *Le Débat*, 21 (1982).

———. 'The Primacy of Politics: Politics and Economics in National Socialist Germany,' in S. J. Woolf, ed., *The Nature of Fascism*. London: Weidenfeld & Nicolson, 1968.

Massing, Paul W. *Vorgeschichte des politischen Antisemitismus.* Frankfurt: Syndikat/EVA, 1986.

Mayer, Hans. *Ein Deutscher auf Widerruf: Erinnerungen,* 2 vols. Frankfurt: Suhrkamp, 1988.

Mayer, Arno J. *Why Did the Heavens Not Darken? The 'Final Solution' in History.* New York: Pantheon, 1988.

Medvedev, Roy. *Let History Judge.* New York: Columbia Univ. Press, 1989.

Meier, Christian. *40 Jahre nach Auschwitz: Deutsche Geschichtserinnerung heute.* München: Deutsche Kunstverlag, 1987.

Meinecke, Friedrich. *Die deutsche Katastrophe: Betrachtungen und Erinnerungen.* Wiesbaden: E. Brockhaus, 1946.

Meixner, Horst. 'Berliner Salons als Ort deutsch-jüdischer symbiose,' in Walter

# Bibliography

Grab, ed., *Gegenseitige Einflüsse deutscher und jüdischer Kultur.* Tel Aviv: Univ. of Tel Aviv, 1982.

Mendelssohn, Moses. *Jérusalem.* Paris: Aujourd'hui, 1982.

Mitscherlich, Alexander and Margarete. *Le deuil impossible: Les fondements du comportement collectif.* Paris: Payot, 1972.

Momigliano, Arnaldo. 'The Jews of Italy,' *New York Review of Books* (October 1985).

Mommsen, Hans. 'The Realization of the Unthinkable: The "Final Solution" of the Jewish Question in the Third Reich,' in Gerhard Hirschfeld, ed., *The Policies of Genocide: Jews and Soviet Prisoners of War in Nazi Germany.* London: Allen & Unwin, 1986.

Moses, Stéphane. *L'Ange de l'histoire: Rosenzweig, Benjamin, Scholem.* Paris: Seuil, 1992.

———. *Système et révélation: La philosophie de Franz Rosenzweig.* Paris: Seuil, 1982.

———, ed. *Kafka und das Judentum.* Frankfurt: Athenäum, 1987.

———, and Albrecht Schöne, eds. *Juden in der deutschen Literatur.* Frankfurt: Suhrkamp, 1986.

Mosse, George L. *The Crisis of German Ideology: The Cultural Origins of the Third Reich.* New York: Grosset & Dunlap, 1984.

———. *German Jews beyond Judaism.* Bloomington: Indiana Univ. Press, 1985.

———. *Germans and Jews.* New York: Howard Fertig, 1970.

———. *Nationalism and Sexuality: Respectability and Abnormal Sexuality in Modern Europe.* New York: Howard & Fertig, 1985.

Mosse, Werner. *Jews in the German Economy: The German-Jewish Economic Elite, 1820–1935.* Oxford: Clarendon, 1987.

Mosse, Werner, and Arnold Paucker, eds. *Juden in Wilhelminischen Deutschland 1890–1914.* Tübingen: J. C. Mohr, 1976.

Müller-Funk, Wolfgang. *Joseph Roth.* München: C. H. Beck, 1989.

Musil, Robert. *The Man without Qualities.* London: Secker & Warburg, 1953.

Nettl, J. P. *Rosa Luxemburg.* New York: Oxford Univ. Press, 1966.

Neumann, Franz. *Behemoth: The Structure and Practice of National Socialism, 1933–1944.* New York: Harper & Row, 1966.

Niewyk, Donald. *The Jews in Weimar Germany.* Manchester: Manchester Univ. Press, 1980.

Nolte, Ernst, *Der europäische Bürgerkrieg 1917–1945: Nationalsozialismus und Bolchewismus.* Frankfurt: Ullstein, 1987.

———, Andreas Hillgruber, and Joachim Fest, et al. *Forever in the Shadow of Hitler? Original Documents of the Historikerstreit.* Atlantic Highlands NJ: Humanities, 1983.

# Bibliography

Nora, Pierre. 'Entre mémoire et histoire,' *Les lieux de mémoire* 1. Paris: Gallimard, 1984.

Novak, George. *America's Revolutionary Heritage*. New York: Pathfinder, 1976.

Olender, Maurice, ed. *Pour Léon Poliakov. Le racisme: mythe et sciences*. Bruxelles: Éditions Complexe, 1981.

Oppenheimer, Franz. 'Stammesbewusstsein und Volksbewusstsein,' *Die Welt* 7 (18 February 1910).

Ostow, Robin. *Jüdisches Leben in der DDR*. Frankfurt: Athenäum Verlag, 1988.

Pais, Robert. 'Walther Rathenau's Jewish Quandary,' *Leo Baeck Institute Yearbook* 13 (1968).

Palmier, Jean-Michel. *Weimar en exil*, 2 vols. Paris: Payot, 1988.

Panizza, Oskar. *Der Korsettenfritz*. München: Matthes & Seitz, 1981.

*Pardès*. 'Judéité et germanité' 5 (1987).

Pätzold, Kurt. *Faschismus, Rassenwahn, Judenverfolgung*. Berlin (East): Deutscher Verlag der Wissenschaften, 1975.

Pawel, Ernst. *The Nightmare of Reason. A Life of Franz Kafka*. New York: Farrar, Strauss & Giroux, 1984.

Paxton, Robert, and Michael R. Marrus. *Vichy France and the Jews*. New York: Basic, 1981.

Péguy, Charles. *Notre jeunesse*. Paris: Gallimard, 1988.

Plant, Richard. *The Pink Triangle. The Nazi War Against Homosexuals*. New York: Henry Holt, 1986.

Plard, Henri. 'Hannah Arendt et Rahel Levin: illusions et pièges de l'assimilation,' *Les Cahiers du Grif, Hannah Arendt*. Paris: Tierce, 1986.

Pohrt, Wolfgang. 'Das Elend des Lagerkommandanten: Kohl in Bergen-Belsen,' *Zeitgeist, Geisterzeit: Kommentare und Essays*. Berlin: Tiamat, 1988.

Poliakov, Léon. *Le bréviaire de la haine. Le IIIe Reich et les Juifs*. Bruxelles: Complexe, 1986.

———. *Histoire de l'antisémitisme*, 4 vols. Paris: Calmann-Lévy, 1981.

Politzer, Heinz. 'From Mendelssohn to Kafka: The Jewish Man of Letters in Germany,' *Commentary* (April 1974).

Pommeranz Carmely, Clara. *Das Identitätsproblem jüdischer Autoren im deutschen Sprachraum: Von der Jahrhundertwende bis zu Hitler*. Königstein: Scriptor, 1981.

Ponchaud, François. *Cambodge année zéro*. Paris: Julliard, 1977.

Poppel, Stephen. *Zionism in Germany 1897–1933. The Shaping of a Jewish Identity*. Philadelphia: Jewish Publication Society, 1977.

Postone, Moische. 'Anti-Semitism and National Socialism,' *New German Critique*, 19 (1980).

# Bibliography

Priani, Mario. *Il fascino del nazismo: Il caso Jenniger: una polemica sulla storia.* Bologna: Mulino, 1989.

Puttnies, Hans, and Gary Smith, eds. *Benjaminiana.* Giessen: Anabas Verlag, 1991.

Rabinbach, Anson. 'The Jewish Question in the German Question,' *New German Critique,* 44 (1988).

Rabinbach, Anson, and Jack Zipes, eds. *Germans and Jews since the Holocaust: The Changing Situation in West Germany.* New York: Holmes & Mayer, 1986.

Raphael, Freddy. *Judaïsme et capitalisme: Essai sur la controverse entre Max Weber et Werner Sombart.* Paris: Presses Univs. de France, 1982.

Raphaël, Freddy. 'L'étranger et le paria dans l'oeuvre de Max Weber et de Georg Simmel,' *Archives des sciences sociales des religions* 61 / 1 (1986).

Rathenau, Walther. *Briefe.* Dresden: Carl Reissner, 1928.

————. *Gesammelte Schriften.* Berlin: Fischer Verlag, 1929.

————. *Hauptwerke und Gespräche.* München: Lambert Schneider, 1977.

————. *Schriften.* Berlin: Berlin Verlag, 1965.

Raulet, Gérard, and Josef Fürnkäs, eds. *Weimar: Le tournant esthétique.* Paris: Anthropos, 1988.

Raulff, U., ed. *Ein Mann vieler Eigenschaften: Walther Rathenau und die Kultur der Moderne.* Berlin: Wagenbach, 1991.

Reichmann, Eva G. *Grösse und Verhängnis deutsch-jüdischen Existenz: Zeugnisse einer tragischen Begegnung.* Heidelberg: Schneider, 1974.

Reif, A. *Hannah Arendt, Materialen zu ihren Werk.* Wien: Europaverlag, 1979.

Reinharz, Jehuda. *Fatherland or Promised Land: The Dilemma of the German Jew 1893–1914.* Ann Arbor: Univ. of Michigan Press, 1975.

————, and Walter Schatzberg, eds. *The Jewish Response to German Culture: From the Enlightenment to the Second World War.* Hanover NH: Univ. Press of New England, 1985.

Richarz, Monika, ed. *Bürger auf Widerruf: Lebenszeugnisse deutscher Juden 1780–1945.* München: C. H. Beck, 1989.

Robert, Marthe. *D'Oedipe à Moïse: Freud et la conscience juive.* Paris: Agora / Plon, 1991.

Robertson, Ritchie. 'The Problem of "Jewish Self-Hatred" in Herzl, Kraus and Kafka,' *Oxford German Studies,* no.16 (1985).

Robin, Régine. *L'amour du yiddish. Écriture juive et sentiment de la langue.* Paris: Sorbier, 1984.

————. *Kafka.* Paris: Balland, 1989.

Robinson, David. *Chaplin, His Life and Art.* London: Collins, 1985.

Rodinson, Maxime. *Peuple juif ou problème juif?* Paris: Maspero, 1981.

# Bibliography

Rosenthal, Ludwig. *Heinrich Heine als Jude*. München: Hanser Verlag, 1973.

Rosenzweig, Franz. 'Le caractère national juif,' *Franz Rosenzweig, Les Cahiers de la nuit surveillée*. Paris, 1982.

———. *The Star of Redemption*. New York: Holt, Rinehart & Winston, 1971.

Roth, Joseph. *Der Antichrist*. Amsterdam: Albert de Lange, 1934.

———. *Berliner Saisonbericht: Reportagen und journalistische Arbeiten 1920–1939*. Köln: Kiepenheuer & Witsch, 1984.

———. *Briefe 1911–1939*. Köln: Kiepenheuer & Witsch, 1970.

———. *The Emperor's Tomb*. London: Hogarth, 1987.

———. *Erzählungen*. Köln: Kiepenheuer & Witsch, 1973.

———. *Flight without End*. New York: Penguin, 1987.

———. *Hotel Savoy*. London: Chatto & Windus, 1986.

———. *Job: The Story of A Simple Man*. New York: Overlook, 1985.

———. *Juden auf Wanderschaft*, in *Werke 2*. Köln: Kiepenheuer & Witsch, 1989.

———. *The Legend of the Holy Drinker*. New York: Overlook, 1990.

———. *The Radetzky March*. New York: Overlook, 1983.

———. *The Silent Prophet*. New York: Overlook, 1980.

———. *Werke*. Köln: Kiepenheuer & Witsch, 1989.

Rovan, Joseph. *Konrad Adenauer*. Paris: Beauchesne, 1987.

Rousso, Henry. *Le syndrome de Vichy de 1944 à nos jours*. Paris: Seuil, 1990.

Rozenblit, Marsha L. *The Jews of Vienna 1867–1914: Assimilation and Identity*. Albany: State Univ. of New York Press, 1983.

Rürup, Reinhard. *Emanzipation und Antisemitismus*. Göttingen: Vandenhoeck & Ruprecht, 1975.

Santini, Lea Ritter. 'La passione de capire: Hannah Arendt e il pensare letteratura,' Introduction to Hannah Arendt, *Il futuro alle spalle*. Bologna: Il Mulino, 1981.

Schatzberg, Walter, ed. *The Jewish Response to German Culture: From the Enlightenment to the Second World War*. Hanover NH: Univ. Press of New England, 1985.

Scheidle, Hartmut. 'Joseph Roth Flucht aus der Geschichte,' in *Text und Kritik*, 1974.

Schneider, Michael. *Die abgetriebene Revolution: Von der Staatsfirma in die DM-Kolonie*. Berlin: Elefanten, 1990.

Schneider, Wolfgang. 'Deutschland erwacht,' *Konkret*, no.10 (1991).

———, ed. *Vernichtungspolitik: Eine Debatte über den Zusammenhang von Sozialpolitik und Genozid im nationalsozialistischen Deutschland*. Hamburg: Junius, 1991.

Schnitzler, Arthur. *The Road to the Open*. New York: Alfred A. Knopf, 1923.

# Bibliography

Schoeps, Julius H., ed. *Der Patriotismus deutscher Juden und der National-sozial-ismus: Frühe Schriften 1930 bis 1933: Eine historische Dokumentationk.* Berlin: Hande & Speuersche Verlag, 1970.

——, ed. *Juden in der DDR,* in Kommission bei E. J. Brill, Duisburg, 1988.

——. 'Les Juifs dans l'Allemagne d'après-guerre,' *Matériaux pour l'histoire de notre temps* 23 (1991).

Scholem, Gershom. *From Berlin to Jerusalem.* New York: Schocken, 1980.

——. *The Messianic Idea in Judaism and Other Essays on Jewish Spirituality.* New York: Schocken, 1971.

——. *On Jews and Judaism in Crisis: Selected Essays.* Ed., Werner J. Dannhauser. New York: Schocken, 1976.

Schörken, R., and D. J. Löwitsch, eds. *Das doppelte Antlitz: Zur Wirkungsge-schichte deutsch-jüdischer Künstler und Gelehrter.* Paderborn: Schöningh, 1990.

Schorske, Carl E. *Fin-de-siècle Vienna.* New York: Alfred A. Knopf, 1970.

Schultz, Hans-Jürgen, ed. *Es ist ein Weinen in der Wel: Hommage für deutsche Juden.* Stuttgart: Quell, 1990.

Schultz, Hans-Jurgen. *Mein Judentum.* Stuttgart: Kreuz-Verlag, 1978.

Schulze, Winfried. *Deutsche Geschichtswissenschaft nach 1945.* München: Olden-bourg, 1989.

Schweickert, Uwe. 'Der rote Joseph: Politik und Feuilleton beim frühen Joseph Roth (1919–1926),' in *Text und Kritik* special issue, 1974.

Shmueli, Efraim. 'The "Pariah People" and Its "Charismatic Leadership": A Re-valuation of Max Weber, *Ancient Judaism.*' *Proceedings of the American Acad-emy for Jewish Research* 36 (1968).

Sichrovsky, Peter. *Naître coupable, naître victime.* Paris: Maren Sell, 1987.

Simmel, George. 'Exkursus über den Fremden,' *Soziologie.* München: Verlag von Duncker und Humbolt, 1922.

Sombart, Werner. *Les Juifs et la vie économique.* Paris: Payot, 1923.

Sorkin, David. *The Transformation of German Jewry 1780–1840.* New York: Ox-ford Univ. Press, 1987.

Sorlin, Pierre. *L'antisémitisme allemand.* Paris: Flammarion, 1969.

Sperber, Manès. *The Burned Bramble.* New York: Holmes & Meier, 1988.

Stern, Fritz. 'Le poids de la réussite: réflexions sur les Juifs allemands,' in *Rêves et illusions.*

——. *L'or et le fer. Bismarck et son banquier Bleichröder.* Paris: Fayard, 1990.

——. *The Politics of Cultural Despair: A Study in the Rise of the Germanic Ideol-ogy.* Berkeley: Univ. of California Press, 1961.

——. 'Walter Rathenau. Une âme divisée dans un pays divisé,' *Commentaire* 51 (1990).

# Bibliography

Stern, J. P. *Hitler: the Führer and the People*. Berkeley: Univ. of California Press, 1975.

Stora-Sandor, Judith. *L'humour juif dans la littérature de Job à Woody Allen*. Paris: Presses universitaires de France, 1984.

Strauss, H. A., and C. Hoffmann, eds. *Juden und Judentum in der Literatur*. München: DTV, 1985.

Strelke, Joseph Peter. 'L'attitude politique de Roth pendant l'exil,' *Austriaca* 30 (1990).

Stümke, Hans-Georg. *Homosexuelle in Deutschland: Eine politische Geschichte*. München: Verlag C. H. Baeck, 1989.

Susmann, Margarete. 'Vom geistigen Anteil der Juden im deutschen Raum,' *Leo Baeck Instituts Bulletin*, no.81 (1988).

Taylor, Simon. *Prelude to Genocide: Nazi Ideology and the Struggle for Power*. London: Duckworth, 1985.

Thanassekos, Y., and H. Wismann, eds. *Révision de l'histoire: Totalitarismes, crimes et genocides nazis*, Paris: Cerf, 1990.

Toller, Ernst. *I Was a German: The Autobiography of a Revolutionary*. New York: Paragon House, 1991.

*Traces*, 'Les Juifs et la culture allemande,' 6 (1983).

Traverso, Enzo. 'Homosexuels nazisme. Notes sur un crime occulté,' *Raison Présente*, no.96 (1990).

———. *The Marxists and the Jewish Question: The History of a Debate (1843–43)*. Atlantic Highlands NJ: Humanities, 1994.

———. 'Il materialismo messianico di Walter Benjamin,' *Il Ponte* 46, no.2 (1990), pp.47–70.

Trotsky, Leo. *On the Jewish Question*. New York: Pathfinder, 1970.

Tucholsky, Kurt. *Gesammelte Werke*. Reinbeck: Rowohlt, 1975.

Uhlmann, Fred. *Reunion*. New York: Farrar, Straus & Giroux, 1977.

*Usages de l'oubli*. Paris: Seuil, 1988.

Varikas, Eleni. 'Paria: Une Métaphore de l'exclusion des femmes,' *Sources, Traveaux historiques* 12 (1987).

Vidal-Naquet, Pierre. *The Assassins of Memory*. Cambridge: Harvard Univ. Press, 1993.

———. *Les Juifs, la mémoire et le présent*, 2 vols. Paris: Découverte, 1991.

Volkov, Shulamit. *Jüdisches Leben und Antisemitismus im 19. und 20. Jahrhundert*. München: C. H. Beck, 1990.

Wagner, Hans, ed. *Gegenwartsliteratur und Dritte Reich: Deutsche Autoren in der Auseinandersetzung mit der Vergangenheit*. Stuttgart: Reclam, 1977.

Wardi, Charlotte. *Le génocide dans la fiction romanesque*. Paris: Presses universitaires de France, 1988.

# Bibliography

Wassermann, Jakob. *Mein Weg als Deutscher und Jude.* Berlin: Fischer, 1921.

Weber, Max. *Ancient Judaism.* New York: Free Press, 1952.

——. *Economy and Society: An Outline of Interpretive Sociology.* New York: Bedminster, 1968.

——. *The Protestant Ethic and the Spirit of Capitalism.* London: Unwin University Books, 1967.

——. *Le savant et la politique.* Paris: Plon, 1959.

Wehler, Hans-Ulrich. *Entsorgung der deutschen Vergangenheit? Ein polemischer Essay zum 'Historikerstreit.'* München: C. H. Beck Verlag, 1988.

Weinrich, Max. *History of the Yiddish Language.* Chicago: Univ. of Chicago Press, 1980.

Weltsch, Robert. *Die deutsche Judenfrage: Ein kritischer Rückblick.* Königstein: Jüdischer Verlag, 1981.

Wertheimer, Jack. *Unwelcome Strangers: East European Jews in Imperial Germany.* New York: Oxford Univ. Press, 1987.

Westermann, Klaus. *Joseph Roth, Journalist: Eine Karriere.* Bonn: Bouvier, 1987.

Wilde, Harry, ed. *Walther Rathenau in Selbstzeugnissen und Bilddokumenten.* Hamburg: Rowohlt, 1971.

Wilson, N. *Bernard Lazare.* Paris: Albin Michel, 1985.

Wisse, Ruth R. 'Lo *Schlemihl* come eroe moderno,' *Communità* 172.

Wissman, Heinz. *Walter Benjamin et Paris.* Paris: Cerf, 1986.

Wistrich, Robert S. *The Jews of Vienna in the Age of Franz Joseph.* New York: Oxford Univ. Press, 1989.

——. *Socialism and the Jews: The Dilemmas of Assimilation in Germany and Austria-Hungary.* East Brunswick NJ: Associated Univ. Presses, 1982.

Witte, Bernd. *Walter Benjamin: Une biographie.* Paris: Cerf, 1986.

Wolf, Christa. 'Erfahrungmuster: Diskussion zur *Kindheitmuster*' (1975). *Die Dimension des Autors: Essays und Aufsätze: Reden und Gespräche 1959–1985.* Darmstadt: Luchterhand, 1987.

——. *Patterns of Childhood.* New York: Farrar, Straus & Giroux, 1984.

Wolffsohn, Michael. *Ewige Schuld? 40 Jahre deutsch-jüdisch-israelische Beziehungen.* München: Piper, 1988.

Wollenberg, Jörg, ed. *'Niemand war dabei und keinen hat's gewusst': Die deutsche Öffentlichkeit und die Judenverfolgung 1933–1945.* München: Piper, 1989.

Woolf, S. J., ed. *The Nature of Fascism.* London: Weidenfeld & Nicolson, 1968.

Wyman, David S. *The Abandonment of the Jews: America and the Holocaust, 1941–1945.* New York: Pantheon, 1984.

Young-Bruehl, Elisabeth. *Hannah Arendt: For Love of the World.* New Haven: Yale Univ. Press, 1984.

# Bibliography

Zimer, Pinchas. 'Judentum und Deutschum, Bemerkungen zur Begegnung einer monotheistischen Religion mit einer idealistischer Kultur,' *Revue d'Allemagne* 13, no.3 (1981).

Ziper, Jack. 'Die kulturelle Operationen von Deutschen und Juden in Spiegel der neueren deutschen Literatur,' *Babylon, Baiträge zur jüdischen Gegenwart* 8 (1991).

Zipes, Jack, ed. *The Operated Jew: Two Tales of Anti-Semitism*. New York: Routledge, 1991.

Zweig, Arnold. *Bilanz der deutschen Judenheit*. Köln: Joseph Melzer Verlag, 1961.

———. *Caliban oder Politik und Leidenschaft*. Potsdam: Gustav Kiepenheuer, 1929.

Zweig, Stefan. *The World of Yesterday*. Lincoln: Univ. of Nebraska Press, 1964.

# Index

acculturation, 9–13; and Jewish salons, 10; and reinterpretation of Judaism, 11; and Weimar Republic, 12. *See also* assimilation; emancipation

Adenauer, Konrad, 140

Adler, Max, 28

Adler, Victor, 28, 33

Adorno, Theodor W., 4, 33, 38, 111, 161

Aleichem, Schalom, 50

Allen, Woody, 83

Aly, Götz, 126, 127

American Jews, and symbiosis, 5

Améry, Jean, 34, 39, 159

amnesia. *See* collective amnesia

*Ancient Judaism* (Weber), 36, 43–44

*Antichrist, Der* (Roth), 73

anticommunism, and German identity, 140, 158

anti-Fascism, as Soviet ideology, 136–40

anti-Semitism: as abstraction, 144; Christian, 110, 112, 119; in Eastern Europe, 5; economic interpretation of, 125–28; and fascism, 132–33; in France, 5, 132–33; and German-Jewish culture, 37; of Hitler, 110, 114, 115, 117; and Lazare, 48; and Marxism, 124–26; Nazi, and modernity, 128–29; Nolte's thesis as, 152; racist, 110; response to German Jews to, 22–25, 28–30, 89, 91; rise of, in modern Germany, 18–22; role of, in intentionalist approach to Shoah, 117; and *völkisch* ideology, 129–30; in Weimar Republic, 12. *See also* Auschwitz; genocide; Shoah

*antisémitisme, son histoire et ses causes, L'* (Lazare), 45–46

archaism *vs.* modernity, and Nazi anti-Semitism, 128–33

Arendt, Hannah, xxii–xxiii, 5, 10, 34, 35, 38, 132; on blacks in U.S., 171 n.51; on German renunciation of anti-Semitism, 160; on Jew as pariah, 45, 48–59; on moral confusion of Germans, 143; on responsibility for Hitler's rise, 157; on *schlemihls/schnorrers*, 53–55; vs. Herzl, 56; and Zionism, 55–57

Armenian genocide, 106, 107, 108

assimilation: fables of, 39–40; in France, 5; in Germany, xx, 3, 9–22; and Jewish identity crisis, 25–29; and Jewish monologue, 40; rejection of, as reaction to anti-Semitism, 28–30; role of *Zentralverein* in, 11; Roth's view of, 68–71; self-hatred as result of, 17–18; significance of, 12–13; as threat to German culture, 20–21; and Weimar Republic, 12, 14, 32–33. *See also* acculturation; emancipation; parvenus, Jews as

atheism/atheists, and Judeo-German culture, 33–34

Auerbach, Bertold, 11

*Aufklärung*, 37, 40, 50, 98; and anti-Semitism, 10; Auschwitz as outcome of, 129; perception of Germany as home of, 103; and toleration, 12

Auschwitz, 8, 103; denial of uniqueness of, 147–48, 151–52; impossibility of understanding, 112–13; Jewish question after, 135–36; and memory, 135–61; and pogroms, 108; relativizing of, 146–52, 154–55; uniqueness of, 105, 133, 152; Vietnam War compared to, 108. *See also* anti-Semitism; genocide; Shoah

Austerlitz, Friedrich, 28

# Index

Austria: forgetfulness in, 140; Jewish demographics in, 15; Jewish domination of cultural life in, 21, 28; Jewish support for Habsburgs in, 12; pogroms in, 118

Avenarius, Ferdinand, 26

Bader-Meinhof Gruppe, 144

Baeck, Leo, 34, 37; on Judeo-German symbiosis, 8; as political parvenu, 86–87; response of, to World War I, 24

Bahr, Herman, 25

Baier, Lothar, 142

Bamberger, Ludwig, 22

Bartel, Adolf, 31

Bary, Anton de, 3

Bauer, Otto, 28, 33, 124

Baum, Herbert, 137

Beer, Michael, 43

*Behemoth* (Neumann), 115, 125

Benjamin, Walter, xix, 3, 4, 34, 35, 36, 38, 52, 98; intellectual influence of, 4–5; on Jewish adoption of German lifestyle, 15–16; on Jewish identity, 27; and Roth, 74, 75; theory of language, 74

Berding, Helmut, 10

Berlin, Isaïah, 35

Bernstein, Eduard, xxiii, 22–23, 60

Bettauer, Hugo, xxi

Bettelheim, Bruno, 38

Bierman, Wolf, 159

biological racism, 105, 110, 131

Birnbaum, Nathan, 29, 34, 90

Bismark, Otto von, 17, 84–85

Bitburg, Reagan visit to, 146, 152

Blanqui, Louis Auguste, 98

Bleichröder, Gerson, as economic parvenu, 17, 34, 84–85

Bloch, Ernst, 4, 34, 38, 51, 52, 72, 137

Bloch, Josef, xxiii, 34

Blücher, Hans, 131

Blumenfeld, Kurt, 24, 34

Böll, Heinrich, 143

bolshevism, nazism as response to, 147–48, 149, 150, 152

Boreau, Alain, 88

Bourel, Dominique, xxiii

bourgeoisification of German Jews, 16–17

Bracher, Karl, 114

Brandt, Willy, 144, 145–46

Braudel, Fernand, 112

Brecht, Bertold, 35, 52, 137

Broch, Hermann, 77

Brod, Max, xxii, 27

Broder, Henryk M., 160

Broszat, Martin, 115, 119

Bruck, Arthur Möller Van der, 19, 151

Buber, Martin, xix, xxiii, 25, 28, 34, 36; on Jewish identity, 29, 30; on Judeo-German symbiosis, 8

Caftan Jews, 18

Cambodia, Khmer Rouge massacre in, 106, 107

Canetti, Elias, 34, 38

Caullery, Maurice, 4

Celan, Paul, 38

Central Association of German Citizens of the Israelite Faith, 11

Chagall, Marc, 111

Chamberlin, Houston Stewart, racist views of, 18, 19, 21, 29, 94, 130, 151

Chamisso, Adalbert von, 54

Chaplin, Charlie, 50, 53, 170 n.23

Claussen, Detlev, 128–29

Clézio, J. M. G., 110

Cohen, Hermann, 11, 24–25, 34, 83, 167 n.74

collective amnesia: German reunification as example of, 155–59; and sham memory, 159–61. *See also* memory, and Auschwitz

collective memory, 141–42, 142

conversions, of Jews, 10, 13, 14

Court Jews, 13, 17

Cravat Jews, 18

cultural Zionism, 29

*Destruction of the European Jews, The* (Hilberg), 120–21

Deutscher, Isaac, 112–13

# Index

*Deutschland ohne Deutsche* (Heyck), 31

Diederichs, Eugen, 19

Dinter, Artur, 31

Döblin, Alfred, 4, 34, 53, 68

Dohm, Wilhelm von, 9, 10, 17, 83

Domba, Abraham, 113

*Drei Reden über das Judentum* (Buber), 29

Dreyfus, Alfred, 48, 89, 92

Dreyfus Affair, 48, 89

Dühring, Eugen, 91

Dutschke, Rudi, 127

Eastern Europe: anti-Semitism in, 5; assimilation in, 5; rejection of Jews from, and Jewish self-hatred, 18

East Germany (GDR), 136–40; attitude to Shoah in, 181 n.9; collective memory in, 141; purge of former Nazis in, 136–37; suppression of Jewish question in, 137–40

economic interpretations of Shoah, 123–28

*Economy and Society* (Weber), 43–44

Einstein, Albert, 52

Eisler, Hans, 137

Eisner, Kurt, 30

Elias, Norbert, 34, 38

emancipation, Jewish: in France, xx; and French Revolution, 12; in Germany, xx, 3, 7, 9–10, 12, 14–15, 41, 128; in Italy, 41. *See also* assimilation; Judeo-German symbiosis

*Emperor's Tomb, The* (Roth), 78–79

endogamy: of German Jews, 14, 15, 165 n.37; as pariah trait, 44

Engels, Friedrich, 35

Ensslin, Gudrun, 144

era of forgetfulness, 140–46

*Fackel, Die*, 18

fascism, 127–28; and anti-Semitism, 132–33

Federal Republic of Germany (FRG): collective memory in, 141; era of forgetfulness in, 135, 140–43; Jewish question in, 135–36; reappointment of Nazis in, 136;

theory of totalitarianism in, 140, 158; *Wiedergutmachung* by, 141

femininity, and Judeity, 59

Fest, Joachim, 151, 152, 159

Feuchtwanger, Lion, 34

Feuerbach, Ludwig, 14

final solution. *See* Auschwitz; genocide; Shoah

foreigners, Jews as, 45. *See also* pariah Judaism

*Foundations of the Nineteenth Century, The* (Chamberlin), 21

*Fragebogen, Der* (Salomon), 143

France: anti-Semitism in, 132–33, 181 n.81; assimilation in, 5; emancipation in, 41

Frei, Bruno, 65

Freud, Sigmund, 4, 13, 34, 36, 155; on German/Jewish identity, 168 n.105; marginality of, in Germany, 4; on *schnorrer*, 171 n.41

Freytag, Gustav, 20

Friedländer, Salomo, 40

Fritsch, Theodor, 31

Fromm, Erich, 38

Fuchs, Eugen, 22

*fumier de Job, Le* (Lazare), 46

functionalist vs. intentionalist interpretation, of Shoah, 113–23

Galinski, Heinz, 160

Gans, Eduard, 11, 35

Gay, Peter, 33, 38

Geiger, Ludwig, 22

*Gemeinschaft*, 130, 131

genocide: of Armenians, 105, 106, 107, 108; of Aztecs, Incas, and Mayas, 106, 107, 110; and Cambodian massacre, 106, 107; of Gypsies, in Germany, 105; of Native Americans, 106–87; origin of term, 104; in Soviet Russia, 106, 107, 149–50; uniqueness of Shoah as, 106–10. *See also* anti-Semitism; Auschwitz; Shoah

Germanity, ix–x; and Judeity, 22–25, 130, 136; and Zionism, 23

German-Jewish dialogue, 10

# Index

German reunification, and collective amnesia, 155–61

*Gesellschaft*, 130

Goebbels, Joseph, 130

Goethe, Johann Wolfgang von, xix, 43

Goldmann, Lucien, 38

Goldstein, Moritz, 26, 35

Gottfarstein, Joseph, 65

Graetz, Heinrich, 618

Gramsci, Antonio, 41, 127

Grass, Günter, 112, 156

Grégoire, Abbé, 5

Grosz, George, 35

Grunfeld, Fredric, 35

Guérin, Daniel, 124

Gulf War, and reappraisal of Auschwitz, 145

Gypsies, genocide of, 105–6, 108–9, 177 n.13

Habermas, Jürgen, 147, 156

handicapped persons, massacre of, 110

Harden, Maximilian, 34, 87

*Haskalah*, 83

*Hass, Der* (H. Mann), 6

Heartfield, John, 35

Hegel, Friedrich G., 35

Heidegger, Martin, 131

Heim, Susanne, 126, 127

Heimann, Eduard, 36

*heimatlosigkeit*, and Roth's Judeity, 65–80

Hein, Christoph, 139

Heine, Heinrich, xix, 4, 14, 34, 38, 50; on Jew as pariah, 43; and Judeo-German dialogue, 9

"Herr Wendriner," 85–86

Herz, Henriette, 10

Herzl, Theodor, xxi, xxiii, 24, 34, 47; vs. Arendt, 56; pan-Germanism of, 88–93

Hess, Moses, 13

Heyck, Hans, 31

Heym, Stefan, 137

hidden tradition, 46; and pariah Judaism, 48–53

Hilberg, Raul, 111, 120–21, 122

Hildebrand, Klaus, 151, 152

Hilferding, Rudolf, 28

Hillgruber, Andreas, 114, 148–49, 152

Hirsch, Samson-Raphael, 33

*Historikerstreit. See* quarrel of historians

historiography: and Judeo-German dialogue, 7; and memory, 153–54

Hitler, Adolf, 9, 76, 103, 140; anti-Semitism of, 110, 113, 114, 115, 150; in functionalist interpretation of Shoah, 115–17; in intentionalist interpretation of Shoah, 113–14, 179 n.32; policy toward handicapped / mentally ill, 110; responsibility for rise of, 157–58

holocaust, 104–5. *See also* Auschwitz; genocide; Shoah

*Holocaust* (film), 144–45

homosexuals, German repression of, 109

Horkheimer, Max, 4, 33, 38, 124

Husserl, Edmund, 4

Huxley, Aldous, 73

intentionalist *vs.* functionalist approach, to Shoah, 113–23

Israel, state of, 104, 145

Italy: anti-Semitic legislation in, 181 n.81; assimilation of Jews in, 41

Jabotinski, Vladimir, 29

Jäckel, Eberhard, 152

Jacob, Benno, 32

Jaspers, Karl, 35, 143, 157, 160

Jay, Martin, 58

Jellinek, Adolf, 87

Jesenska, Milena, 4, 27

Jewish Agency, 136

Jewish monologue, 40

Jewish orthodoxy, and Judeo-German culture, 33

Jewish question: in Adenauer era, 140–43; in East Germany, 136–40; in Germany after Auschwitz, 135–61; Nazi approach to, 120–21, 122, 128; normalization of, and quarrel of historians, 146–53; in post-Adenauer Germany, 144–46; re-

# Index

pression of, by workers' movement, 125, 137–38

Jewish salons of Berlin, 10, 33

*Jewish State, The*, 89, 90, 92–93

*Jews and Economic Life, The* (Sombart), 21–22

*Job* (Roth), 71

Jogiches, Leo, 60–61, 63

journalism, Jewish presence in, 15

Judaism, as "religion of reason," 11

*Judaism in Music* (Wagner), 21

Judaization, myth of, 20–21. *See also* anti-Semitism

Judeity, ix–x, 3, 5; and anti-Semitism, 37; assimilation as escape from, 12–13, 17–18; conversion as escape from, 10, 13; and femininity, 59–63; and Germanity, 22–25, 130, 136; as *heimatlosigkeit*, and Joseph Roth, 65–80

*Juden auf Wanderschaft* (Roth), 68–69, 70

Judeo-Christian dialogue, 36, 160

Judeo-German symbiosis: after Auschwitz, 136; as explosion of Jewish creativity, 36; and German intellectuals, 36; H. Mann on, 6–7; Jewish affirmations of, 7–8; as Jewish illusion, 9, 33–39; myth of, xx, 3–41; Nuremberg Laws as end of, 39; philosophical foundation of, 24–25; problematic nature of, 4–5; Rosenzweig on, 41; Scholem on, 6; in Weimar Republic, 12; present-day idealization of, 160, 161

Jüdische Gemeinde: East German, 137–38; West German, 136

Jünger, Ernst, 32

Kafka, Franz, xix, xxii, xxiii, 4, 28, 50; and assimilation, 27–28, 34, 68, 82; cultural paradox of, 4–5; and *Yiddishkeit*, 98

Kantorowicz, Ernst, 34, 137; as intellectual parvenu, 87–88, 98

Katz, Jacob, 13, 15, 38

Kautsky, Karl, 20, 62

*Kindheitsmuster* (Wolf), 139

Kirchner, Peter, 138

Kisch, Egon Erwin, 33, 65

Koestler, Arthur, 77, 143

Kogon, Eugen, 143

Kohl, Helmut, 146, 161

Kracauer, Siegfried, 4, 38, 73

Kraus, Karl, xxii, 4, 33; and Jewish self-hatred, 18

*Kristallnacht*, 37, 88, 118, 138, 156, 160

Lagarde, Paul de, 19, 151

Landauer, Gustav, xxi, xxiii, 23, 30, 34

Lang, Fritz, 4

Langbehn, Julius, 19, 130, 151

Lanzmann, Claude, 105, 111

Lazare, Bernard, 5, 50; on Jews as pariahs, 43, 45–48, 57

Lazarus, Moritz, 22

Lemkin, Raphaël, 104

Lessing, Gotthold Ephraim, 12

Lessing, Theodor, 17–18, 49

Levi, Hermann, 18

Levi, Paul, 30

Levi, Primo, 104, 135, 149–50

Leviné, Eugen, 30

Levin-Varnhagen, Rahel, 10, 34, 48, 50; Arendt on, 48, 51–52, 60

Lieb, Fritz, 36

Liebermann, Max, 37

Lissauer, Ernst, 26

Lowenberg, Jakob, 26, 32

Löwenthal, Leo, 38

Löwith, Karl, 34

Löwy, Michael, 111

Lübbe, Hermann, 142

Lueger, Karl, 21, 28, 150

Lukács, Georg, 4, 33

Luxemburg, Rosa, 5, 30, 50, 59–64; Arendt on, 60, 61–62, 64; relationship to Judeity, 63–64; relationship with Jogiches, 60–61; and women's emancipation, 61–63

Magris, Claudio, 78, 80

Mahler, Gustav, 4

Mann, Heinrich, 53; on German-Jewish relations, 6–7

# Index

Mann, Thomas, xix, 36, 52

Mannheim, Karl, 4, 33

*Man without Qualities, The* (Musil), 81, 94

Marcuse, Herbert, 33, 38, 128

Marr, Wilhelm, 151

Marx, Karl, 4, 33, 35, 36; on Judaism, 13–14; marginality of, in Germany, 4

Marxist interpretations of Shoah, 123–28

Mason, Tim, 127

*Mass Ornament, The* (Kracauer), 73

Mayer, Arno J., 121–22

Mayer, Hans, 15

Meinecke, Friedrich, 113

memory, and Auschwitz, 112, 113; absence of Jewish memory, 154; contradictory responses to, 144–46; in East Germany, 136–40; end of forgetfulness, 152–53; era of forgetfulness, 140–43; and German reunification, 155–59; in 1945 Germany, 135–36; and quarrel of historians, 146–52; and sham memory, 159–61

Mendelssohn, Moses, 9, 83–84

Mennicke, Carl, 36

mentally ill persons, massacre of, 110

Merker, Paul, 138

Mitscherlich, Alexander, 142

Mitscherlich, Margarete, 142

modernity: and Nazi anti-Semitism, 128–29; Roth's attack on, 72–74

Momigliano, Arnaldo, 41

Mommsen, Hans, 115–16, 150

Mommsen, Theodor, 20

Momper, Walter, 155

"Monsieur Fischel," 81

Mosse, George L., 38

Mühsam, Erich, 34

Müller-Funk, Wolfgang, 71

Musil, Robert, 81, 94

*Nathan the Wise* (Lessing), 12, 35, 49

National Socialism, 37, 113, 114, 115; and archaism/modernity, 128–33; and Jewish question, 120–21, 122, 128, 154; and logic of nonacceptance, 128–29; place of anti-Semitism in, 118; and worker's movement, 123–24

nazism. *See* National Socialism

negative dialectic, stages of, 9–12

negative identity, and anti-Semitism, 19

Nettl, John Paul, 60

Neumann, Franz, 115, 125

Neumann, Max, 34

Neusüss, Christel, 62

Niemöller, Martin, 143

Nietzsche, Friedrich Wilhelm, 36

Nolte, Ernst, revisionism of, 147–48, 149, 150–51, 152, 158

nonacceptance of Jews, logic of, 128–29

non-Jewish Jew, 13

Nora, Pierre, 155

Nordau, Max, xxiii, 34

Nuremberg Laws, 7, 9, 39, 118

*On Revolution* (Arendt), 57

*operierte Jud, Der* (Panizza), 39–40

Oppenheimer, Franz, 23

*Origins of Totalitarianism* (Arendt), 59

Ossietzsky, Karl von, 35

Panizza, Oskar, 39–40

parasites, Jews as, 4

parasitism, defined, 4

pariah Judaism/tradition; Arendt on, 43, 48–59; and German-Jewish intelligentsia, xxii–xxiii, 4–5, 36–37; Lazare on, 43, 45–48, 57; pariah qualities/traits, 44–45, 51; and Rosa Luxemburg, 64; and *schlemihls*, 53–55; and shame, 51–52; and socialism, 58; Weber on, 43–45, 57. *See also* parvenus, Jews as

parvenus, Jews as; Arendt on, 50; characteristics of, 84; economic parvenus, 84–86; and German-Jewish intellectuals, xxii–xxiii, 87; and Herzl's Zionism, 88–93; Lazare on, 47; literary archetypes of, 81–84; political parvenus, 86–87; and Rathenau, 93–98; tragic fate of, 98–99. *See also* pariah Judaism/tradition

Pätzold, Kurt, 125

Péguy, Charles, 48–49

*Peter Schlemihls wundersame Geschichte* (Chamiso), 54

# Index

Pinsker, Leo, 87
polycracy, in Nazi Germany, 115
Prague, Jewish cultural influence in, xx

quarrel of historians, and Auschwitz, 146–53, 154–55; Fest, 151, 152; Hildebrand, 151–52; Hillgruber, 148–49, 152; Jäckel, 152; Nolte, 147–48, 149, 150–51, 152, 158

racist biology, 105, 110
Radwanski, Tadeus, 63
Rathenau, Walther, xxi, 34; as parvenu, 93–98
reactionary modernism, 131
Reagan, Ronald, Bitburg visit of, 146
*Reawakening, The* (Levi), 135
Regler, Gustav, 79
Reinhart, Max, 4
Reisser, Gabriel, 11
reparations: Jewish attitude toward, 182 n.23; and non-Jewish victims, 182 n.24; post-war German policy of, 141
responsibility, for Shoah, 157–58
Rohling, August, 19
Röhm, Ernst, 109
Rosenberg, Alfred, 19, 110, 151
Rosenberg, Arthur, 124
Rosenstock, Eugen, 36
Rosenzweig, Franz, 15, 25, 32, 34, 36; on Judeo-German symbiosis, 41
Rote Armee Faktion (RAF), 144, 158
Roth, Joseph, viii, xix, xxi, xxiii, 4, 28, 34, 65–80; and assimilation, 68–71; dual cultural allegiance of, 67–71; flight from history of, 76–80; and modernity, 72–74; rootlessness of, 65–67; and Russian Revolution, 74–76; and Zionism, 71
Roth, Karl-Heinz, 126
Rottem, Simha, 113
Rousso, Henry, 154

Salomon, Ernst von, 143
Schipper, Isaac, 104
*schlemihl:* derivation of word, 54–55; as

hero of *Yiddishkeit*, 55; pacifism of, 87; pariah as, 53–55
Schleyer, Hans-Martin, 158
Schmitt, Carl, 19, 39
Schneider, Michael, 156
Schnitzler, Arthur, 17, 34, 82
*schnorrer*, 53, 54, 55; Freud on, 171 n.41. See also *schlemihl*
Schoeps, Hans-Joachim, 34, 86, 87
Scholem, Gershom, xxiii, 3, 27, 34, 38; on German-Jewish dialogue, 6; on rise of Nazi Germany, 123; on turn-of-century Jewish cultural/psychological climate, 16
Schönberg, Arnold, 4, 34
Schönerer, Georg von, 19, 28, 150
Schorske, Carl E., 89
Schumacher, Kurt, 141
Schwaner, Wilhelm, 96
Seghers, Anna, 137
self-hatred, Jewish, 17–18; and parvenus, 82, 84; and Roth, 70
shame, and pariahs, 51–52
sham memory, and Auschwitz, 159
Shoah; anonymous nature of, 117; and biological racism, 105, 110; compared to other genocides/massacres, 106–9; functionalist vs. intentionalist interpretation of, 113–23; German forgetfulness of, 140–43; and Marxism, 123–28; modernity of, 108; as nonevent for postwar Germans, 142; and pogroms, 108; qualitative uniqueness of, 105; responsibility for, 157–58. See also anti-Semitism; Auschwitz; genocide
*Shoah* (film), 105, 113
Simmel, Georg, 33; on Jews as foreigners, 45
Singer, Isaac Bashevis, 6, 54, 111
social Darwinism, 4, 129, 130
socialism, and pariahs, 58
*Soll und Haben* (Freytag), 20
Sombart, Werner, 21, 25–26, 95, 130
Speer, Albert, 131
Spengler, Oswald, 19, 72, 151

# Index

Sperber, Mänes, 34, 38, 58, 68

Srebnik, Simon, 113

*Stadt ohne Juden, Der* (Bettauer), xxi

Stalin, Josef, 106

Stalinism, 107, 158, 159

Stepel, Wilhelm, 19

Stern, Fritz, 84–85

Stier, Walter, 116

Stöcker, 19

Strauss, Ludwig, 27

Stürmer, Michael, 152

*Sünde wider das Blut, Die* (Dinter), 31

Susmann, Margarete, 7

Syberberg, Hans-Jürgen, 160

symbiosis: defined, 3–4. *See also* Judeo-German symbiosis

Thalheimer, August, 124, 127

Thälmann, Ernst, 137

*Theses on the Philosophy of History* (Benjamin), 35, 38, 111

Tillich, Paul, 36

Toller, Ernst, 30, 32, 34, 74

totalitarianism, theory of, in FRG, 140

Treitschke, Heinrich von, 20, 22, 130, 151

*Trial, The* (Kafka), 82

Trotsky, Leon, 5, 58, 123, 124; and fascism, 127–28

Tucholsky, Kurt, 4, 33, 85–86

Turner, Frederick Jackson, 106

*Über die bürgerliche Verbesserung der Juden* (Dohm), 9–10

Uhlman, Fred, 81

Ulbricht, Walter, 137

Vesper, Bernward, 145

Vietnam War, and Auschwitz, 108, 177 n.12

Vishniac, Roman, 111

*völkisch:* ideology, and anti-Semitism, 129–31, 161; Zionism, 29–30

Volkov, Shulamit, 19

Wagner, Richard, 20–21, 64

Wannsee Conference, 120, 122

Wasserman, Jakob, 28, 34

Weber, Max, 5, 13, 36, 130; on Jews as pariahs, 43–45, 51, 57

*Weg ins Frei, Der* (Schnitzler), 82

Wehler, Hans Ulrich, 147

Weimar Republic: anti-Semitism in, 12, 30–32; and assimilation, 12, 32–33; constitution of, 132; Eastern European Jews in, 18; and Judeo-German culture, 32–33; number of Jews in, 14; repression of homosexuals in, 109

Weininger, Otto, 34, 60

Weizmann, Chaim, 147

Weizsäcker, Viktor von, 36

Werfel, Franz, 77

*Why Did the Heavens Not Darken* (Mayer), 121–22

*Wiedergutmachung. See* reparations

Wiesel, Elie, 112

Wissenschaft des Judentums, 8, 11

Wittgenstein, Ludwig, 39

Wittig, Joseph, 36

Wolf, Christa, 139

Women, as pariahs, 59–60. *See also* Luxemburg, Rosa

workers' movement: Nazi destruction of, 124, 132; repression of Jewish question by, 125, 137–40; response of, to Hitler's rise, 123–24, 137, 157

World Jewish Congress, 136

World War I, response of German Jews to, 24–25

Yerushalmi, Yosef Hayim, 155

*Yiddishkeit,* xxiii, 30; destruction of, 111; golden age of, 5–6; *schlemihl* as hero of, 55

Zatkin, Clara, 62

Zentralverein deutscher Staatsbürger jüdischen Glaubens, 11, 22, 24, 32, 123

Zhitlowsky, Chaim, 92

Zionism/Zionists: Arendt's relationship with, 55; cultural Zionism, 29, 34; and Germany, 23, 24; and Judeo-German

# Index

culture, 25–26, 34; Lazare on, 47; and Nazis, 118; and pan-Germanism, 88–93; and Roth, 71; *völkisch* Zionism, 29–30; in Weimar Republic, 32

Zollschan, Ignaz, 29

Zunz, Leopold, 11

Zweig, Arnold, 7, 34, 83, 137

Zweig, Stefan, 28, 34, 77

*Zwei Quellen, Die* (Lowenberg), 32

Zygielbojm, Samuel, 125